Wilkinson, Marguerite
Bigelow, 1883-1928.

New voices

NEW VOICES

THE MACMILLAN COMPANY
NEW YORK · BOSTON · CHICAGO · DALLAS
ATLANTA · SAN FRANCISCO

MACMILLAN & CO., LIMITED
LONDON · BOMBAY · CALCUTTA
MELBOURNE

THE MACMILLAN CO. OF CANADA, LTD.
TORONTO

NEW VOICES

AN INTRODUCTION TO CONTEMPORARY POETRY

BY

MARGUERITE WILKINSON

New York
THE MACMILLAN COMPANY
1920

Set up and electrotyped. Published June, 1919

TO THE MEMORY OF

J. SCOTT CLARK, A. M., LITT. D.

PROFESSOR OF THE ENGLISH LANGUAGE
AT NORTHWESTERN UNIVERSITY, 1892–1911,
THIS WORK OF A PUPIL

Quæcumque sunt vera,
Proba, justa, mera,
Omnia hæc dona
Præbes nobis bona,
Alma Mater cara,
Benedicta, clara,
Celsa in honore
Nostro et amore.

University Hymn by J. SCOTT CLARK.

ACKNOWLEDGMENTS

The thanks of the author are due to the following publishers and editors for their kind permission to reprint the following selections for which they hold copyright:

To The Macmillan Company for "Penetralia" and "The Winds," from "Poems," by Madison Cawein; for "Spring Sows Her Seeds," from "The Drums in Our Street," by Mary Carolyn Davies; for "Breakfast," "The Father," "The Messages," and "The Old Bed," from "Battle and other Poems," by Wilfrid Wilson Gibson; for "Up A Hill and A Hill" and "Moon Folly," from "Myself and I," by Fannie Stearns Davis Gifford; for "Broadway," from "Poems and Ballads," by Hermann Hagedorn; for "Transformations" and "The Wind Blew Words," from "Moments of Vision," by Thomas Hardy; for "The Bull," from "Poems," by Ralph Hodgson; for "The Santa Fé Trail," "Aladdin and the Jinn" and "The Leaden-Eyed," from "The Congo and other Poems," by Vachel Lindsay; for "The Broncho That Would not be Broken," from "The Chinese Nightingale and Other Poems," by Vachel Lindsay; for "Patterns" and "The Bombardment," from "Men, Women and Ghosts," by Amy Lowell; for "Old Age," from "Collected Poems," by Percy Mackaye; for "Ships," from "The Story of the Round House," by John Masefield; for "Cargoes" and "A Consecration," from "Salt Water Ballads and Poems," by John Masefield; for one sonnet from "Lollingdon Downs," by John Masefield; for "Isaiah Beethoven," "Lucinda Matlock" and "Anne Rutledge," from "The Spoon River Anthology," by Edgar Lee Masters; for "Draw the Sword, O Republic" and "My Light with Yours," from "Toward the Gulf," by Edgar Lee Masters; for "Mystery" and "Interlude," from "The New Day," by Scudder Middleton; for "Love Song" and "Mountain Song," from "You and I," by Harriet Monroe; for "The Child's Heritage," from "The Quest," by John G. Neihardt; for "Flammonde," from "The Man against the Sky," by Edwin Arlington Robinson; for "Deirdre," from "Songs from the Clay," by James Stephens; for "In the Poppy Field," from "The Hill of Vision," by James Stephens; for "On the Day when the

Lotus Bloomed," from "Gitanjali," by Rabindranath Tagore; for two narratives from "Fruit-Gathering," by Rabindranath Tagore; for "Leaves" and "The Answer," from "Rivers to the Sea," by Sara Teasdale; for "Peace," "I Would Live in Your Love" and "The Lamp," from "Love Songs," by Sara Teasdale; for "The Flight," from "The Flight and other Poems," by George Edward Woodberry; for "The Song of Wandering Aengus," from "Poems," by William Butler Yeats; for the lyric beginning "The Wind Blows out of the Gates of Day," from "The Land of Heart's Desire," by William Butler Yeats:

To Messrs. Houghton Mifflin Company for "After Two Years," by Richard Aldington, from "Some Imagist Poets, 1916"; for "Dawn," by Richard Aldington from "Some Imagist Poets, 1917"; for "Her Words," from "The Shoes that Danced and other Poems," by Anna Hempstead Branch; for "An Unbeliever," from "The Heart of the Road," by Anna Hempstead Branch; for two poems, each called "Song," from "Poems," by Florence Earle Coates; for "Sea Gods," by H. D., from "Some Imagist Poets, 1916"; for "Windmills," by John Gould Fletcher, from "Arizona Poems," in "Some Imagist Poets, 1916"; for one strophe from "Lincoln," by John Gould Fletcher in "Some Imagist Poets, 1917" and for one strophe from "Irradiations," by John Gould Fletcher; for "Pandora's Song," from "The Firebringer," by William Vaughn Moody; for "Love Is a Terrible Thing," from "The Sister of the Wind," by Grace Fallow Norton; for "The House and the Road" and "The Cedars," from "The Singing Leaves," by Josephine Preston Peabody; for "Frost in Spring" and "Patrins," from "The Door of Dreams," by Jessie B. Rittenhouse; for "Scum O' The Earth," from the volume of the same name by Robert Haven Schauffler; for "Vistas" and "Certain American Poets," from "A Lonely Flute," by Odell Shepard:

To Messrs Henry Holt & Company for "The Cuckoo" and "The Virgin's Slumber Song," from "My Ireland," by Francis Carlin; for "Comrade Jesus," from "Portraits and Protests," by Sarah N. Cleghorn; for "An Old Woman of the Roads" and "The Furrow and the Hearth," from "Wild Earth and other Poems," by Padraic Colum; for "Miss Loo" and "The Listeners," from "The Listeners," by Walter de la Mare; for "Jim Jay" and "Silver," from "Peacock Pie," by Walter de la Mare; for "The Sound of the Trees," "The Gum Gatherer," "An Old Man's Winter Night," "The Cow in Apple

Time" and "Brown's Descent," from "Mountain Interval," by Robert Frost; for "Fog," "Monotone" and "Child," from "Chicago Poems," by Carl Sandburg; for "Loam," "Cool Tombs" and "Monosyllabic," from "Cornhuskers," by Carl Sandburg; for "A Cyprian Woman: Greek Folk Song" and "Remembrance: Greek Folk Song," from "The Factories and other Poems," by Margaret Widdemer; for "The Dark Cavalier," from "The Old Road to Paradise and other Poems," by Margaret Widdemer:

To The Century Company for "Merchants from Cathay," from the volume of the same name by William Rose Benét; for "After Sunset," from *The Century Magazine*, by Grace Hazard Conkling; for "Seal Lullaby" and Road-Song of the Bandar-Log," from "The Jungle Book," by Rudyard Kipling; for "Cherry Way," from "The Night Court and other Verse," by Ruth Comfort Mitchell; for "Said the Sun," from "War and Laughter," by James Oppenheim; for "The Runner in the Skies," from "Songs for the New Age," by James Oppenheim; for "Daybreak," from *The Century Magazine*, by Louis Untermeyer; for "How Much of Godhood" and "Caliban in the Coal Mines," from "Challenge," by Louis Untermeyer:

To Messrs Charles Scribner's Sons for "Path Flower," from the volume of the same name by Olive Tilford Dargan; for "At Night" and "Maternity," from "Poems," by Alice Meynell; for "I Have a Rendezvous with Death," from "Poems," by Alan Seeger; for "Richard Cory," from "The Children of the Night," by Edwin Arlington Robinson; for "Miniver Cheevy," from "The Town Down the River," by Edwin Arlington Robinson; for several sentences from "The Enjoyment of Poetry," by Max Eastman:

To The John Lane Company for two sonnets called "The Dead" from "The Collected Poems" of Rupert Brooke; for "Lepanto" from "Poems," by G. K. Chesterton; for "Da Leetla Boy" from "Carmina," by Thomas Augustine Daly; for "The Iron Music" and "The Old Houses of Flanders," from "On Heaven and Poems Written on Active Service," by Ford Madox Hueffer; for "I Sat among the Green Leaves," from "The Lamp of Poor Souls," by Majorie L. C. Pickthall:

To Mr. Alfred Knopf for "Coming to Port" and " Invocation," from "Colors of Life," by Max Eastman; for "The Fox" and "Said a Blade of Grass," from "The Madman," by Kahlil Gibran; for "Assault Heroic," from "Fairies and Fusiliers," by Robert Graves; for "Homage," by Helen Hoyt, from "Others: An Anthology of the New Verse"; for "Little Things," from "Asphalt and Other Poems," by Orrick Johns; for "Idealists" and "Old Manuscript," from "Mushrooms," by Alfred Kreymborg; for lyrics by William H. Davies:

To Messrs Harper & Brothers for "Paper Roses" and "Roses in the Subway," from "Poems," by Dana Burnet; for "The Ballad of The Cross," by Theodosia Garrison; for "The Path of the Stars," by Thomas E. Jones, Jr., from *Harper's Magazine;* for "The Birth" from "Dreams and Dust," by Don Marquis; for "Sacrifice," from "Flower O' the Grass," by Ada Foster Murray:

To Mr. Mitchell Kennerley for a selection from "The New World," by Witter Bynner; for two sonnets from "Sonnets of a Portrait Painter," by Arthur Davison Ficke; for "The Jew to Jesus," from the volume of the same name by Florence Kiper Frank; for "Renascence," from the volume of the same name by Edna St. Vincent Millay; for "Psalm," by Jessie E. Sampter, from "The Lyric Year":

To Messrs. Doubleday Page & Company for "The Dying Patriot," from "The Collected Poems of James Elroy Flecker; for "The Man with the Hoe," from "The Man with the Hoe and Other Poems," copyright, 1899 by Edwin Markham; for "Lincoln," from "Lincoln and Other Poems," copyright, 1901, by Edwin Markham; for "The Fugitives," from "The Far Country," by Florence Wilkinson; for "The Flower Factory," from "The Ride Home," by Florence Wilkinson:

To Messrs. George H. Doran Company for "A Lynmouth Widow," from "In Deep Places," by Amelia Josephine Burr; for "My Mirror," from "Candles that Burn," by Aline Kilmer; for "Trees," "Martin," and "Rouge Bouquet," from the memorial edition of "Joyce Kilmer: Poems, Essays and Letters," edited by Robert Cortes Halliday:

To Messrs. E. P. Dutton & Company for "Around the Sun," from "The Retinue and Other Poems," by Katharine Lee Bates, copyright, 1918; for "The Common Street," from "A Chant of Love for England and Other Poems," by Helen Gray Cone; for "The Kiss" and "Absolution," from "The Old Huntsman and Other Poems," by Siegfried Sassoon:

To Messrs. Frederick A. Stokes Company for "Grieve not for

Beauty," from "Grenstone Poems," by Witter Bynner; for "Nearer" and "Out of Trenches: The Barn, Twilight," copyright, 1918, by Robert Nichols; for "Forty Singing Seamen," from the volume of the same name by Alfred Noyes:

To The Four Seas Company for "Dawn" and "After Two Years," from "Images," by Richard Aldington; for "The Morning Song of Senlin" and two lyrics from "Variations," all from "The Charnel Rose and Other Poems," by Conrad Aiken:

To Mr. Thomas B. Mosher for "Love Came Back at Fall O' Dew" and "A Christmas Folk Song," from "A Wayside Lute," by Lizette Woodworth Reese; and for "Frost To-night," from "The Flower from the Ashes," by Edith M. Thomas:

To Mr. Ralph Fletcher Seymour for "What Dim Arcadian Pastures" and "Two Voices," from "The Spinning Woman of the Sky," by Alice Corbin, and for "The Most Sacred Mountain" from "Profiles from China," by Eunice Tietjens:

To Mr. B. W. Huebsch for "So Beautiful You are Indeed," from "Songs to Save a Soul," by Irene Rutherford McLeod; for "Clay Hills," from "Growing Pains," by Jean Starr Untermeyer:

To Stewart & Kidd Company for "The Strong Woman," from "The Man Sings," by Roscoe Gilmore Stott, published by Stewart & Kidd Company:

To Mr. A. M. Robertson for "The Black Vulture," from "The House of Orchids," by George Sterling; for "The Last Days," from "Beyond the Breakers," by George Sterling:

To Mr. David McKay for "Perennial May," from "Songs of Wedlock," by Thomas Augustine Daly; for "Da Leetla Boy," from "Canzoni," by Thomas Augustine Daly:

To The Yale University Press for "The Falconer of God," from the volume of the same name by William Rose Benét:

To The Manas Press for "Cinquains," from "Verse," by Adelaide Crapsey:

To Mr. James Terry White for "Canticle," from "City Pastorals," by William Griffith:

To Mr. William Stanley Braithwaite for "Spring," by John Gould Fletcher; and for "Good Company," by Karle Wilson Baker, both poems originally published in *The Poetry Review* and now included in The Golden Treasury of Magazine Verse:

To Messrs. Duffield & Company for "The Vigil of Joseph," from "The Frozen Grail," by Elsa Barker; for "June" and "Desire in Spring," from "Songs of The Fields," by Francis Ledwidge:

To The Page Company for "Lord of My Heart's Elation," from "The Green Book of the Bards," by Bliss Carman, copyright, 1903:

To Messrs. Boni & Liveright for "Calling-One's-Own," from "The Path on the Rainbow," edited by George Cronyn:

To Messrs. Small, Maynard & Company for "An April Morning," from "April Airs," by Bliss Carman, copyright, 1916, reprinted by permission of the publishers, Small, Maynard & Company, Inc.:

To Messrs. Dodd, Mead and Company for "Symbols" from "Poems: 1908-1914," by John Drinkwater:

To Mr. Richard G. Badger for "Grandmither," from "April Twilights," by Willa Sibert Cather:

To the Woodberry Society for one sonnet from "Ideal Passion," by George Edward Woodberry:

To Mr. John Hall Wheelock for "Nirvana," from "The Beloved Adventure," published by Sherman, French & Company:

To Mr. Egmont Arens for a selection from "Night," by James Oppenheim:

To the Little Book Publishing Company for "A Woman," from "Streets and Faces," by Scudder Middleton:

To the Oxford University Press, Toronto, Canada, for "I Sat Among the Green Leaves," from "The Lamp of Poor Souls," by Marjorie L. C. Pickthall:

To the Editors of *Poetry, A Magazine of Verse* for "Tampico," by Grace Hazard Conkling; for "Sunrise on Rydal Water," by John Drinkwater; for "Indian Summer," by William Ellery Leonard; for "Maternity," by Alice Meynell; for "In the Mohave," by

Patrick Orr; for "A Day for Wandering," by Clinton Scollard; for "Who Loves the Rain," by Frances Shaw; for "The Bacchante to Her Babe," by Eunice Tietjens; for "The Bird and the Tree," and "Santa Barbara Beach," by Ridgely Torrence; for "Down Fifth Avenue," by John Curtis Underwood; for "On the Great Plateau," by Edith Wyatt:

To *The Yale Review* for "Ash Wednesday," by John Erskine; and for "Earth," by John Hall Wheelock:

To *The North American Review* for "Motherhood," by Agnes Lee:

To *The Independent* for "Phantasm of War: The Cornucopia of Red and Green Comfits," by Amy Lowell:

To *The Touchstone* for "The Time Clock," by Charles Hanson Towne:

To *The Outlook* for "Night's Mardi Gras," by Edward J. Wheeler:

To *The Nation* for "Standards," by Charles Wharton Stork:

To *Much Ado* of St. Louis for "Rain, Rain," by Zoë Akins:

To *The Los Angeles Graphic* for "White Iris," by Pauline B. Barrington:

To *The New York Sun* for "God You have been Too Good to Me," by Charles Wharton Stork:

To *The New York Times* for "Epitaph," by Louis Driscoll:

To Mr. Samuel Roth for his sonnet:

The brief quotations from Clement Wood's poetry are taken from "Glad of Earth," published by Laurence J. Gomme:

The brief quotations from the work of Ezra Pound are to be found in "Lustra" (Knoff) and in "Provenca" (Small, Maynard) and in the files of *Poetry A Magazine of Verse.*

The thanks of the author are due, also, to the following publishers in Great Britain and Ireland for the privilege of reprinting the following selections published by them:

To Messrs. Macmillan & Company, Ltd., London, for "Transformations" and "The Wind Blew Words," from "Moments of Vision," by Thomas Hardy; for "Seal Lullaby" and "Road-Song of the Bandar-Log," from "The Jungle Book," by Rudyard Kipling; for

"Deirdre," from "Songs from the Clay," by James Stephens; for two narratives from "Fruit-Gathering," by Rabindranath Tagore; and for "On the Day when the Lotus Bloomed," from "Gitanjali," by Rabindranath Tagore; for "The Song of Wandering Aengus," from "Poems," by William Butler Yeats, and for the lyric beginning "The Wind Blows out of the Gates of Day," from "The Land of Heart's Desire," by William Butler Yeats:

To Messrs. Constable & Company, Ltd., for "Jim Jay " and "Silver," from "Peacock Pie," by Walter de la Mare, and for "Listeners" and "Miss Loo," from "The Listeners," by Walter de la Mare; for "I Have a Rendezvous with Death," from "Poems," by Alan Seeger; for "Windmills" and brief quotations from poems by John Gould Fletcher, for "Sea Gods," by H. D., and for "Dawn" and "After Two Years," by Richard Aldington, from "Some Imagist Poets, 1916" and "Some Imagist Poets, 1917":

To Mr. Elkin Mathews for "Cargoes" from "Ballads" and "A Consecration," from "Salt Water Ballads" for "The End of the World," from "Chambers of Imagery, Second Series," by Gordon Bottomley; for "Breakfast," "The Father," "The Messages" and "The Old Bed," from "Battle and Other Poems," by Wilfrid Wilson Gibson:

To Mr. William Heinemann for "The Kiss" and "Absolution," from "The Old Huntsman and Other Poems," by Siegfried Sassoon; for "Assault Heroic" from "Fairies and Fusiliers," by Robert Graves; for "Ships," by John Masefield, and for one sonnet from "Lollingdon Downs and Sonnets," by John Masefield:

To Messrs. Maunsel & Company, Ltd., Dublin, for "In the Poppy Field," from "The Hill of Vision," by James Stephens; for "The Old Woman," from "Irishry," by Joseph Campbell; for "The Furrow and the Hearth" and "An Old Woman of the Roads," from "Wild Earth and Other Poems," by Padraic Colum:

To John Lane, The Bodley Head, London, for "The Iron Music" and "The Old Houses of Flanders," from "On Heaven and Poems Written on Active Service," by Ford Madox Hueffer; for "I Sat Among the Green Leaves," from "The Lamp of Poor Souls," by Marjorie L. C. Pickthall:

To Messrs. Chatto & Windus for "So Beautiful You are Indeed," from "Songs to Save a Soul," by Irene Rutherford McLeod, and for "Nearer" and "Out of Trenches: The Barn, Twilight," by Robert Nichols:

To Messrs. J. M. Dent & Sons for "The Common Street," from "A Chant of Love for England and Other Poems," by Helen Gray Cone; for "Path Flower," from the volume of the same name by Olive Tilford Dargan:

To Messrs. Sidgwick and Jackson for two sonnets, "The Dead," by Rupert Brooke, and for "Symbols" and "Sunrise on Rydal Water," by John Drinkwater:

To Messrs. Hodder & Stoughton for "Trees," "Martin," and "Rouge Bouquet," by Joyce Kilmer:

To Mr. A. C. Fifield for "Days Too Short," "The Rain" and "Nature's Friend," by William H. Davies:

To Mr. Grant Richards for "The Runner in the Skies," from "Songs for the New Age," by James Oppenheim:

To Messrs. Burns and Oates for "At Night" and "Maternity," by Alice Meynell, and for "Lepanto," by G. K. Chesterton:

To Messrs William Blackwood & Sons, Edinburgh, London, for "Forty Singing Seamen," by Alfred Noyes:

To Messrs. Herbert Jenkins, Ltd., for "Desire in Spring" and "June," from "Songs of the Fields," by Francis Ledwidge:

To Mr. A. T. Stevens and The Flying Fame for "The Bull," by Ralph Hodgson:

To Mr. Martin Secker for "The Dying Patriot," from "The Golden Journey to Samarkand" by James Elroy Flecker:

To *The British Review* for "The Song of the Full Catch," by Constance Lindsay Skinner:

The thanks of the authors are due, also, to the distinguished poets who contributed to the chapter on "How Poems are Made," William Rose Benét, Padraic Colum, Sara Teasdale, Harriet Monroe and Edwin Markham:

And thanks are due, also, to Mary Fanton Roberts, Editor of *The Touchstone*, for permission to reprint portions of articles that appeared for the first time in her magazine.

CONTENTS

NEW VOICES

NEW VOICES

THE READER'S APPROACH TO CONTEMPORARY POETRY

LONG ago, in Jerusalem, was a pool called Bethesda. In our Bibles we find a quaint folk story of the life-giving power of this pool. From time to time an angel "troubled the waters," and then the sick and the infirm who went down first into the pool were healed of their infirmities.

Poetry is like the Pool of Bethesda. Until they have been plunged into eddies of rhythmical and imaginative beauty, many human intellects are, to a certain extent, sick and infirm. And sometimes the waters of the pool seem to be still, so that we are not aware of the divine life laboring in the spirit of the race to create waves and ripples of sound and sense by which we may be refreshed and strengthened. Then, after such periods of rest, comes the inspiration of the genius or of the group of strong singers, and the waters are "troubled." Those who go first into this life-giving movement are regenerated and rejuvenated by sharing the greatest joy of their own generation and its dynamic life. But others, fearing that they will be accused of bad taste if they take an interest in work that may not "live," stand aside, awaiting the decisive judgment of critics and scholars. For such men and women, afraid of their own taste, the waters are never troubled; and, as a result of their procrastination, their intellectual hauteur, they miss the invigorating gladness of hearing the greatest singers of their own period.

Ten years ago, in this country, the waters were still. Many educated persons supposed that poetry had died an unnatural death with the passing of Tennyson. In spite of the fact that our intellectual leaders allowed themselves to feel a restrained enthusiasm for the work of William Vaughn Moody, Bliss Carman, and a few others, most of us were not greatly interested in contemporary poetry. Indigent and neglected persons, who lived on top of the top story, still wrote it. A few old fashioned people of blessed memory kept scrap-books, although they were a little bit ashamed of the laudable habit. But no influential organizations and specialized magazines were working for the advancement of poetry as an art. Publishers said that poetry could not be sold. We were told that the age of poetry was gone never to return and that, so far as this country was concerned, poetry would always be a dead art.

But these were the words of false prophets, as time has proved. John Masefield, England's greatest living poet of the people, visiting this country early in 1918, said that poetry as an art seemed to be very much alive among us. "America is making ready for the coming of a great poet," he said. "In England, in the days before Chaucer, many people were reading and writing verse. Then he came. The same intense interest in poetry was shown again just before the coming of Shakespeare. And now, in this country, you are all writing poems or enjoying them. You are making ready for a master. A great poetic revival is in progress."

Unprejudiced persons who have watched the trend of literary events for the past ten years and who share the æsthetic and intellectual impulses of our times, can hardly fail to agree with Mr. Masefield. To-day men and women from all classes, men and women of many temperaments, are reading poetry and talking about it. In many cases they have even lost that furtive and fortunate self-consciousness which used to save the tyro from the indiscretion of sharing his own perfervid effusions with his friends. Poets have persuaded the public that they are competent to talk about their own craft and to read their own poems. Publishers welcome new poets. Many poets have been discovered and have made substantial reputations in the past decade. Of these the most notable are John Masefield and Rupert

Brooke in England, Robert Frost, Vachel Lindsay, Amy Lowell, Edgar Lee Masters and Sara Teasdale in the United States. Rabindranath Tagore, well known in India for his poetry in the Bengali language, was not known at all as a poet of the English tongue until the first of his English poems to appear in print were published in *Poetry, A Magazine of Verse*, soon after the founding of that famous little magazine.

We all know that nothing grows where nothing has been planted. This is only another way of saying that great changes in the thought and emotion of a great people are not fortuitous. There have been three good and sufficient reasons for the strong and steady growth of popular interest in poetry in the past ten years.

In the first place we American people are coming into our own æsthetic self-hood and consciousness. For several generations we were occupied with the conquest of the continent and the development of our material resources. This made necessary an extraordinary progress in the use of the practical intellect, but gave us little leisure for the enjoyment of beauty. For a long time after the colonial period our people were drilled for efficiency in practical life. We worshipped utility and morals. Most of us supposed that the arts were "handmaids" to ethics or philosophy or reform. But in the past decade we have outgrown the "handmaid" theory of art. We have come to believe that Art is a real princess, to be loved for the sake of her beauty and served for the sake of life and mankind. We have rejoiced, as never before, in music. We have begun to dream dreams of "the city beautiful" and of a distinctive national architecture. We have re-discovered the dance. We have re-discovered folklore and fairyland. We have begun to express ourselves, our peculiar national consciousness, our times, our life, in patterns of beauty.

Another reason for the growth of interest in poetry is to be found in the fact that a number of unselfish men and women have been working for poetry as for a cause. Critics, editors and professors, convinced of the importance of poetry as the word of the people and the echo of the gods, have given themselves up to the work of winning attention and sympathy for poets.

The first of these altruistic pioneers was Jessie B. Rittenhouse, who began working for poetry in Boston in 1900. When her "Younger American Poets" was published in 1904, Elsa Barker, a poet friend, wrote and congratulated her on being "all alone in a great green field." And from that time to this Miss Rittenhouse has been working with unabated enthusiasm as an interpreter of the contemporary poet. She has written numerous tolerant and discriminating reviews, given many lectures before women's clubs and in universities, and has made excellent anthologies. "The Little Book of Modern American Verse" is a small and choice anthology from which no friend of contemporary poetry is willing to be separated for very long at a time. Miss Rittenhouse is generally considered conservative in taste, but it should be stated that she has been among the first to welcome the greatest of modern innovators, the most important poets who are bringing into American poetry a new spirit and new forms. Many young poets have cause to be grateful for her recognition.

Another faithful worker for the cause of poetry is Edward J. Wheeler, for many years editor of *Current Opinion*, a magazine that has done much to introduce the work of new poets to the public. And in 1909 Mr. Wheeler and Miss Rittenhouse, aided and abetted by a number of poets in and near New York, founded *The Poetry Society of America*, the leading organization of poets and patrons of poetry in this country. To this society, which has grown very rapidly, nearly all poets of established reputation belong, and many young singers from all the states in the Union. The meetings are held once a month, during the winter season, in the beautiful old National Arts Club in Gramercy Park, New York. At these meetings poems submitted by members are read and polemically discussed. The society is known from coast to coast and the monthly bulletins furnish news of poets and poetry to all parts of the country. Smaller societies organized in universities and as departments of women's clubs are now

Cut 0

affiliated with the parent organization and are working together for the advancement of poetry as an art.

Still another pioneer who has helped to lead people out of the wilderness and into the old wonderland is William Stanley Braithwaite of *The Boston Transcript,* known from coast to coast as a compiler of anthologies. Every year Mr. Braithwaite selects from the magazines the poems which he considers "poems of distinction" and classifies them, including in his annual anthology those he likes best. The first anthology was published in 1913, as the natural result of the making of an annual summary of poetic achievement for *The Boston Transcript.* But Mr. Braithwaite had been working in the good cause of poetry long before that.

None of the workers for poetry in this country, however, has done more than Harriet Monroe, poet, critic, editor. She has done a thing unprecedented. She has given poets a place of their own where theories of craftsmanship may be discussed and where poems created in the new spirit and the new form of new times may be presented to an ever-increasing public. *Poetry, A Magazine of Verse,* was the first of our "poetry magazines" and it was founded in 1912. To insure its continuance and to make it independent of advertisers, Miss Monroe collected an endowment fund which enabled her to carry the magazine safely and creditably through the first few years of its life. "Creditably" is not a strong enough adverb. It would be rather better to say "triumphantly." For Miss Monroe has achieved a genuine success and reigns in Chicago as "the autocrat of all the poetries." She "discovered" Sir Rabindranath Tagore. She made Vachel Lindsay famous. She was chief sponsor for Carl Sandburg. She contributed largely to the success of Edgar Lee Masters, who was "discovered" by William Marion Reedy, one of our ablest critics. As an editor, Miss Monroe has shown a rarely catholic taste. She has accepted and published free verse rhapsodies, polyphonic prose, classical sonnets and substantial blank verse. And few indeed are the poets of distinction in any school, in England or in this country, who have not been contributors to *Poetry, A Magazine of Verse.* For this reason the little room in Cass Street, Chicago, where the magazine is edited, has already possessed itself of an atmosphere of romance.

Naturally enough Miss Monroe's experiment was imitated. Other "poetry magazines" were founded. Few, unfortunately, survive. Of these only one is widely known. That is *Contemporary Verse,* published in Philadelphia and ably edited by Charles Wharton Stork. Mr. Stork is a conservative and less hospitable to poetic experiment than Miss Monroe. Therefore the poetry which appears in his magazine has won the praise of good conservative critics like William Dean Howells. A very large amount of good poetry is published in *Contemporary Verse* and the magazine deserves attention and interest.

More recent arrivals in the field are *The Lyric* and *Youth. The Lyric* is the organ of *The Lyric Society,* an organization that works for the advancement of poetry and tries to make American poets better known to the American public. Samuel Roth is Editor of *The Lyric. Youth* has been founded and is edited by a group of young poets at Harvard University, assisted by corresponding editors in other parts of the world. *Youth* aims to be international in scope and interest.

These editors and authors, faithful workers for the advancement of poetry, could have done little or nothing to interest readers, however, if poetry written by contemporary poets had been poor. By clever advertising a market man may secure purchasers for a stock of green peaches. But no amount of advertising will lure purchasers again when they have been disappointed. And this brings us to a consideration of the third reason for the revival of interest in poetry, and it is by far the most important reason,—the fact that American poets are giving us more good poetry to-day than has ever been produced by American poets in any other period of our history. True, we have no Poe, no Whitman, no Lanier, no Emerson. We have no single colossal genius that we all recognize. But we have many strong, fine talents. And in this book I shall hope to

CHARLES WHARTON STORK

enable the reader to approach their work with confidence, understanding and sympathy. I should like to believe that this book will enable readers to find in poetry a new solace, recreation and inspiration, just the things which they might expect to find in music, or in a beautiful friendship.

Unfortunately the approach to poetry is not always made easy for the reader. Every day in the year more false things than true are said about it. Poets are frequently misunderstood and misrepresented by creditable persons who are quite unconscious of their own polite mendacity. Superstitions flourish like weeds in a field or wild vines in a jungle. A dense clutter of nonsense, spurious scholarship, pedantry and fatuity must be cut away in the beautiful grove so that men and women may see the big trees. And because this thicket chokes the way many people who might otherwise come to know the full sweetness and power of poetry are held back from the enjoyment of it.

The most common of these superstitions is the belief that poetry "just comes" to any one at any time, to society queen or labor leader, and that anyone to whom it "just comes" can write it. We may know that children can learn to make music only by long hours of practice. We may realize that the painter must know how to use paint and brush and canvas before he can achieve a masterpiece. But it is commonly supposed that very little emotional or intellectual labor is involved in the making of a poem and that no discipline is required for the maker. Poetry is sometimes thought to be a painless twilight sleep out of which beauty is accidentally born.

But perhaps in all the universe there are no accidents. Perhaps the chain of cause and effect is linked together in little things and in great things always. And perhaps that which seems to be accidental is really the result or fruition of causes that were the result of other causes. However that may be, biographies of great poets tell us of their labor and of their much practicing. The best poets of to-day labor as did their peers in days gone by. Robert Frost, to be sure, writes rapidly and seldom revises his successful poems. But for years he wrote poems that served only as practice work and were never offered to the world. Witter Bynner worked for seven or eight years on "The New World" before he gave it to the public, and it was revised seventeen or eighteen times. Vachel Lindsay writes his social or choral poetry very slowly and is grateful for the criticism of his friends. He has rewritten some of his poems as many as forty or fifty times. The poet is truly what Lord Dunsany calls him, "an artificer in ideas" and "the chief of workers."

Moreover he is an artificer in rhythms and rhymes and in the qualities and associations of words, a student of sound as combined with sense. The idea, the mood, which is the raw material of a poem, may "just come" to any person at any time. A poem may be born of a bit of color, a scent, a vague whim or impression. But this raw material of poetry belongs to all men and women and, if it were the sum total of poetry, all poets would be as great as Shakespeare. But in order that this raw material may be made, or in order that it may grow into poems—perfect and unalterable works of beauty—the artist-poet must cleanse it of all that is irrelevant and superfluous, must give it its own luster and completeness. In such measure as he is a true artist the poems will be strong, compelling, and even apparently artless, to many generations of readers. The poet pays the price of the reader's satisfaction. And the paying of that price is his privilege and joy. That is why only a few of us, those who give themselves up to their great task with devotion, can learn to make great poems. And I once heard Edwin Markham say that poems which "just come" to the ordinary person out of the circumambient ether should usually be returned whence they came!

But nearly all of us, all, surely, who are capable of warm, quick sympathy and who love beauty, can learn to understand and *feel* poetry. Sympathy is the one personal quality without which no one can go far in the love and understanding of the arts, and with which anyone can go very far indeed. The inflexible soul will never be touched by the beauty of any masterpiece. Without the capacity for sharing other people's moods, their love, joy, irony, rancor, sorrow and enthusiasm, their acrid dislikes and their reasons for laughter, their pleasure in color, texture, form, scent and movement, none of us can get much from poetry. For without this capacity none of us can get much out of life. And poetry is simply the sharing of life in patterns of rhythmical words. But no person capable of sympathy and the love of beauty need be frightened away from poetry by the abracadabra of critics. For poetry is not, after all, an intricate puzzle game for sophisticated intellects. It is, like music, like sculpture, a natural, joyous, life-sharing art, concerned with feelings that we all share and appealing to sympathies engendered and fostered by the imagination.

Poetry is everybody's wonderland. It is for the business man, tired or rested, and for his wife. It is for rich employers (for the fortification of their souls!) and for poor employees (for the comfort of their hearts!). It is only required of us that we desire to perceive and enjoy and understand what is beautiful.

But many persons erroneously suppose that they have found beauty when they have taken pleasure in what is merely pretty, and this is unfortunate, for it makes it necessary to differentiate between what is pretty and what is beautiful. Yet one might spend a whole day or many days at this labor, giving concrete illustrations, and still fail to show the lover of prettiness why he is not a lover of beauty. But the lover of beauty would know without explanation. Therefore it is necessary to say here only this—that to the lover of prettiness love is a little frosted cake, joy a luscious bonbon, sorrow a dose of bitter medicine. Prettiness is ephemeral. But beauty is powerful and memorable. Prettiness is external to us and has no more effect upon our lives than a pebble thrown into a stream has upon the swirl of waters. But beauty changes us. The current of our lives runs swifter and clearer for it, perhaps, or deeper, or with a richer music. Prettiness is pleasant and negligible, a light coquette. But beauty is strong, profound, austere, a great maternal force. And those who desire what is pretty will seek out the lightest of literature. But those who desire beauty will find poetry.

If he really wishes to seek beauty in poetry, the greatest difficulty for the new reader of contemporary verse will be found in the fact that it is not "just like" the poetry to which he has been accustomed. Many persons like the poetry of Tennyson and Longfellow, or of Swinburne and Keats, chiefly because they have been accustomed to it. *A particular kind* of poetry *means poetry* to them. They have taken it habitually and for granted as they have taken coffee for breakfast. And the best contemporary poetry is no more like the poetry of Tennyson and Longfellow than the fragrance of nectar is like the fragrance of the matutinal coffee. The strange flavor of it is alarming at the first taste, and timorous persons, afraid of the new beauty, run away without taking enough of a taste to know what it really is like.

To reassure such persons it is only necessary to say that what was good and beautiful in the work of Tennyson is as good and beautiful to-day as it ever was, but that it is not necessary, or desirable, for all poetry to be like Tennyson's in spirit and manner. They may have coffee for breakfast—and nectar also! And no modern poet worthy of the name would have it otherwise. For the best poetry of our times has grown out of the life of our times,which life, in turn, grew out of the life that preceded it. And the love of the elder singers is the best preparation for the love of the younger choir, although the new choristers do not sing the same songs in just the same way. If contemporary poets were content to go on imitating their great predecessors, they would be frustrating all the natural processes of growth in life and art. They would be untrue to all great traditions, (to which ultra-conservatives would hold them too inflexibly). They would be making a plant of dead wax to mimic a living tree, instead of giving us a living, branching, blossoming reality, the inevitable result of life and growth. The poets of to-day are true to the memory of their great predecessors, not when they imitate them in thought and feeling and manner, halting beside the past that is gone and making graven images of it; but when, living fully in their own times, as well as in the past and in the future, they make their craftsmanship conform to the living spirit which is the significance of their work, carrying on the noble traditions of our thought and speech, and producing works remarkable for a new dignity, originality and power. If they lived to-day, the old masters would be the first to applaud such work.

The reader, then, must expect a new kind of beauty in the technique and in the spirit of contemporary verse. In spite of all that ultra-conservatives may say and in spite of all that ultra-radicals may seem to demonstrate, there is a new poetry. It is not the poetry of those whose imaginations itch because they are bitten with a desire to describe trivial, petty, disagreeable experiences, moods and ideas in lines of uneven length, without rhyme, rhythm or design. Nor is it the poetry of those unimportant imitators of preceding periods whose lyrics are dull-colored, too mellifluous, and sticky with sentimentality. It is, rather, the poetry of the great main body of the poets, of the English Georgians, John Masefield, Wilfrid Wilson Gibson, Walter de la Mare, Gordon Bottomley, Ralph Hodgson, Rupert Brooke and Siegfried Sassoon. It is the poetry of Irishmen like James Stephens, Padraic Colum and William Butler Yeats. It is the poetry of Americans like Robert Frost, Vachel Lindsay, Amy Lowell, Arthur Davison Ficke, Witter Bynner, Sara Teasdale, Edwin Arlington Robinson, and Grace Hazard Conkling.

In reading the work of these poets, who have held the interest of the laity and won both the praise and the censure of critics—sometimes equally valuable—the thoughtful person will notice that a few ideals of craftsmanship seem to belong to all of them, differentiating their work from the work of the minor Victorians and their followers. For the reader's convenience it may be well to set down here, briefly, these ideals of poetry and of craftsmanship, which will be discussed at greater length in the pages that are to follow.

Because poetry is an art, the contemporary poet believes that a poem must have a design or pattern worked out in thought and words. It must not be a mere haphazard collection of thoughts and words. But the design may be worked out in any one of many ways and the designer must feel free to choose his own way.

He believes, also, that rhythms must bear direct and constant relation to the meanings and emotions with which they are combined. They must not be used arbitrarily, for mere correctness is not the ideal. They must be used flexibly and fluently, as the perfectly fitting accompaniment of the sense of the poem.

He believes that poetry differs from prose partly in being more concise. All ornament, therefore, must be structural, not super-added and superficial. Irrelevant words, phrases, sentences, must be cut out relentlessly no matter how good they may seem in and of themselves. And there must be no long-winded explanatory moralizing. Images and symbols that suggest meanings are to be preferred, as a rule, to crude statement. Everything said in a poem must contribute to its poignancy and power.

The diction of the best contemporary poetry is the diction of the best contemporary speech, although narrative and dramatic poetry must be true, of course, to the characters presented. All literary affectations, high-flown verbiage and conventional formulæ are to be avoided.

The contemporary poet demands absolute freedom in his choice of themes. He knows that his choice will be determined by the quality of his own personality. Anything which fires his spirit and engages his enthusiasm seems to him to be a fit subject for a poem. Anything which bores him seems to be a poor subject for him, no matter how many others have found it inspiring. He will write about a guttering candle, or about the Pleiades, at his pleasure.

All good modern poetry is written to be read aloud. No one has ever read a good poem until he has read it aloud, with his own voice, for the pleasure of his own ears!

Most of the poetry discussed and reprinted in this book has been published since the year nineteen-hundred. In cases where poems appeared before that time and have been used as examples, it has been because they seemed to me to be strictly in accord with the spirit of the poetry of to-day and representative in an especially valuable way of qualities difficult to describe. Many good poets there are who are not represented. I am sorry that I could not mention all. But perhaps some readers of this book will go on voyages of discovery and find these others with the added pleasure of surprise.

For the rest—all critics disagree. I can say only that I have tried to treat all kinds of beauty with respect and to tell the truth as I understand it, without fear or favor, for the sake of poetry, for the sake of my readers.

Let the reader who would learn to understand and enjoy contemporary poetry say something like this to himself: "Life has its limitations. I must be what I am, one person with one person's experience. But if I will, I can have, through poetry, a share in the lives and adventures of others. I can travel on roads that my feet have never touched, visit in houses that I have never entered, share hopes and dreams and conquests that have never been mine. Poetry can be. for me, the fishing trip that I was never able to take, the great city that I have not seen, the great personalities that I have not met and fathomed, the banquets to which I have not been invited, the prizes that I did not win, the achievement that was a little beyond my reach. It can even be the love that I have not known. Through poetry I shall share the life of my own times, of all times, I shall know the soul of all men and my own soul." If he approaches poetry in this way, simply, naturally, expectantly, the technique of contemporary poets—their way of weaving beauty with words—will trouble him very little. Sooner or later he will wander through the anthologies into Wonderland.

But he must beware of the mild sheep in wolves' clothing who bleat at the moon that there is no contemporary poetry worth reading, who cry out against anything new in life or art, whose faith is in what is static, not in what is dynamic. They would have To-day slumber beside Yesterday and then lead To-morrow to repose beside them both. Once they were many. Now they are very, very few. But Walter de la Mare has described the fate of such reactionary persons in a quaint little fable which I quote.

JIM JAY

Do diddle di do,
  Poor Jim Jay
Got stuck fast
  In Yesterday.
Squinting he was
  On cross-legs bent,
Never heeding
  The wind was spent.
Round veered the weathercock,
  The sun drew in—
And stuck was Jim
  Like a rusty pin . . .
We pulled and we pulled
  From seven till twelve,
Jim, too frightened
  To help himself.
But all in vain.
  The clock struck one,
And there was Jim
  A little bit gone.
At half-past five
  You scarce could see
A glimpse of his flapping
  Handkerchee.
And when came noon,
  And we climbed sky-high,
Jim was a speck
  Slip-slipping by.
Come to-morrow,
  The neighbors say,
He'll be past crying for;
  Poor Jim Jay.

PART I

THE TECHNIQUE OF CONTEMPORARY POETRY

AMY LOWELL

HARRIET MONROE

THE PATTERN OF A POEM

Not long ago a geologist made a collection of claystones found near a great river. They were marvellously designed in whorls and loops and medallions of clay that had once been plastic, not to the hands of man, but to the living fingers of water, heat, cold, pressure, and to the unnamed forces that began and have carried on the evolution of our earth. "They were lying there," said the geologist, "loose in a clay bank." And he added, "Is it not wonderful?"

It is indeed wonderful. Why should a handful of clay, here and there in the great bank, gradually take to itself this form of beauty? Why should the great bank of clay show no such strongly marked and easily perceived design? Why does Nature give such perfect and perceptible designs to claystones, quartz crystals and butterflies, while she lets the small hillocks ramble at will across the surface of the land? Why does she spread the forests about in uneven patches upon the hills, cut jagged gashes chaotically through the august sides of mountains, and make no regular plan for the windings of rivers? In small things Nature seems to perfect her designs and to work them out in strict symmetry. What is the law for great things?

Great things, also, have a pattern or design. All mountains are clearly manifest to us as mountains. We can see that a river is a river, though rivers have many ways of winding. It is just possible that great things have a symmetry which we, potent to the extent of five and a half feet, or so, of flesh and blood, eyes the size of a robin's egg and brains that could be carried in salt sacks, are not well able to perceive. Perhaps Nature's larger designs are too large to seem symmetrical to us, who see them only in part. The far away worlds in space may be arranged in sequence, in a gigantic and balanced composition of which we know very, very little. This much is certain—in all the large things that we do know we find order and design as an expression of the primal genius, even though we do not find a symmetry as strict as the symmetry of design in little things. And in every design variety pulls against symmetry as love pulls against law, the dynamic against the static, life against death.

Symmetry and variety, then, in the natural world, pull against each other and create order, design. When symmetry is sacrificed to variety there is bad design—failure. When a tree grows with all of its branches on one side, that tree is in peril; a great wind after a heavy rain may blow it down. And again, when variety is sacrificed to symmetry we have bad design—failure. When no alien pollen is brought to fertilize the flower, the seed of a plant deteriorates. Self-fertilization causes the plant's strength to dwindle. But, always, when the forces that make for symmetry are pulling hard against the forces that make for variety, so that a tension is created and an equilibrium maintained between them, we have the design at its very best in the world where Dame Nature is artist.

Now all of our human arts, to a certain degree, are subject to the same laws that govern nature. We human beings, little artists, possessed of some small share of the primal genius, have risen through many ranks of being and consciousness into that humanity of which we are inordinately proud. And when we are proud, it is often because we alone, of all living creatures, can consciously create patterns for our own pleasure. In all that we make for use, beauty and enduring life, we use patterns, good and bad. And in all patterns we find that the law of symmetry and the law of variety must be remembered. The penalty of forgetting either law is failure. Let us see how this applies to poetry, and especially to the poetry of our own period.

First of all we must realize that in all times when poems have been well made poets have made patterns for them; and these patterns have been of many kinds. The Psalms in our Bibles, those sublime lyrics of worship, were made in accordance with the Hebrew idea of design, a parallelism, or balancing of words and phrases, emotions and ideas, one against another. Take, for example, the first two verses of Psalm XXIX:

> Give unto the Lord, O ye mighty, give unto the Lord
> glory and strength.
> Give unto the Lord the glory due unto his name;
> worship the Lord in the beauty of Holiness.

This parallelism was the Hebrew way of providing for symmetry in the design of a poem. Variety was subtly secured in symbol, cadence and diction. The Japanese, who think that we have too many words in our poems, have exalted symbolism and made it the basic principle in the designs of their little poems in thirty-one or in seventeen syllables.

But a very large part of the world's poetry has found its symmetry of design in rhythm, and in most English poetry (by which I mean most poetry written in the English tongue) poets have added rhyme as a secondary symmetry, marking and defining rhythm. The variety of most of our poetry has been secured by the use of images and symbols, appropriate changes of cadence, extra syllables interpolated in a line that would otherwise be typical, to swing it momentarily from a too rigid symmetry, that the reader may enjoy the return. Variety has also been secured by the use of contrasted phrases or meanings, by vowel echoes and in countless little ways that the cunning of craftsmen has provided for the pleasure of readers. But just because the poetry of our tongue has usually found its symmetry in rhythm and its variety in other ways, we must be the more careful to remember that not all poetry has been made in this way in all places and times. And he would be rash indeed who would maintain that the best poetry must always be of one kind, must always meet the requirements of one race, one language and one artistic credo. When our poets, after studying the craftsmanship of other lands and times, try to introduce into our literature new ways of designing, it should be our joy to read, understand, evaluate and encourage their attempts.

One more fact should be noted before we discuss in detail the kinds of patterns that are being made by poets of to-day. That is the matter of the effect of the length of the poem upon the design. Just as in nature the pattern seems to be more clearly defined and more symmetrical in small things than in large, so, in the poetry that has lived, short poems seem to be more strictly symmetrical than long poems; long poems seem to be more varied in design than short poems. A short poem is like a claystone in the river bank. A long poem is like the river.

We can make only one generalization with reference to the designs of contemporary poetry. And that is that the present tendency is toward a great freedom and variety in composition. This is a healthy thing, in the main, and a sign of power. In the Elizabethan period the same thing was true. The sonnet and other foreign forms had been introduced into English poetry and all good poets were experimenting with them. They were inventing forms and devices of their own. They were playing with rhythms and rhymes and symbols for the sheer joy of it, in the true craftsman's way. They were not trying to achieve a correct formality. They were, rather, audacious and joyful in their search for ways of making their poems vivid, fresh, colorful, strong. And they succeeded so well, and so often, that if we had no other English poetry at all but that which belongs to the Elizabethan period, our heritage would be rich beyond the power of words to tell. Therefore, when we say that the poets of today are seeking variety in their craft as the Elizabethans sought it, we say that they have a spiritual vitality like that of their great predecessors.

But unlike the best of the Elizabethan poets, many of those who call themselves poets in our day seem to have forgotten the importance of structural symmetry. In so far as that is true their achievement is poor. Their poetry, unfortunately, sometimes teeters and topples like a chair that has lost one leg. This disregard of symmetry in design is probably a reaction against the stringent symmetry, the tiresome and insistent symmetry of the work of minor poets in the periods immediately preceding our own. Just as some of the *minor* Victorians supposed that they might neatly enclose the thought of the world in a nice little yard surrounded by a fence of dogma, so the forms into which they cast their poetry often seem to us, of a later generation, to be so strictly confined that they lack life and vigor. They are smothered in form. And those who remember with pain the wearisome monotony of rhythm in certain poems duly and dully scanned, dissected and detested in the school rooms of a passing generation, have accepted with relief, if not with unqualified approval and gratitude, a certain amount of wild and unsymmetrical verse.

Another reason for our renewed love of variety in design is to be found in our renewed belief that all themes are themes for poems, when genius kindles to them. For the design of a poem must be of one quality with the theme and spirit of it. Certain things can be said best in sonnets, if a great poet feels them as he feels a sonnet. Certain other things can be said best in heroic rhythms, like the sonorous hexameter of the Iliad. Certain other things can be said best in free, rhapsodic cadences. A large, rough pattern may be essential to sincerity in a poem which uses a large, rough emotion or idea. It is for the poet to determine how the design shall conform to and give form to the meaning and emotion which he would convey. And it is only natural that a period in which poets are striving eagerly and devoutly for a realization of many new phases of human life and thought, a period in which even one man's personal experiences may be greater and broader than many men's personal experiences in mediaeval times, should be, also, a period of new forms in verse, of new crystalizations of beauty and of new ways of refracting the rays of life through the medium of personality.

The poets of to-day are showing their love of variety in many ways. Some of them keep the traditional patterns that have been used for many generations in our poetry, but use these patterns less sedately, with a freedom that satisfies the modern love of variety. Others refuse to use the typical and traditional patterns and make somewhat less symmetrical patterns of their own, keeping to rhythm, however, as the basic element in poetry, the structural symmetry of their verse. Still others seem to be trying to make poems in a way quite new in our language, using not rhythm, but imagery, symbolism or parallelism to secure symmetry, and letting their rhythms be varied almost as much as rhythms are varied in prose. These last often seem to be carrying the quest for variety a little too far afield. Nevertheless it sometimes happens that their work has great beauty and value.

Of all the poets who use the old fashioned designs, infusing new life into them, none is more interesting to study than Arthur Davison Ficke. For he has written an admirable sonnet sequence, "The Sonnets of a Portrait Painter," and wiseacres often tell us that "a sonnet is a sonnet"—which sounds reasonable enough to be the truth—and that one sonnet differs from another only in glory, or in type—classical or Shakespearian. But no one with ears sensitive to delicate variations in sound can read Mr. Ficke's sonnets without feeling that they differ subtly from sonnets of the elder singers. This differentiation is due, in part, to Mr. Ficke's own individuality and the flux of it in his poems. But it is also due, in part, to his modernity. The felicitous use of many feminine rhymes, the syllables made to move more rapidly than English syllables used to move in the lines of sonnets, the pauses that halt the lines more frequently—these are shy graces more easily felt than enumerated. The student who wishes to make comparisons should compare Mr. Ficke's sonnets with the sonnets of Longfellow, carefully noting the differences in sound which separate the one poet's work from the work of the other.

Of the poets who make rhythm contribute the structural symmetry of most of their work, but who try to make patterns of a new kind, Amy Lowell is a good example. A study of her poem, "Patterns," will richly reward the reader who is interested in this question of design.

"I walk down the garden paths,
And all the daffodils
Are blowing, and the bright blue squills.
I walk down the patterned garden paths
In my stiff brocaded gown.
With my powdered hair and jewelled fan,
I too am a rare
Pattern. As I wander down
The garden paths.

" My dress is richly figured,
And the train
Makes a pink and silver stain
On the gravel, and the thrift
Of the borders.
Just a plate of current fashion,
Tripping by in high-heeled, ribboned shoes.
Not a softness anywhere about me,
Only whalebone and brocade.
And I sink on a seat in the shade
Of a lime tree. For my passion
Wars against the stiff brocade.
The daffodils and squills
Flutter in the breeze
As they please.
And I weep;
For the lime tree is in blossom
And one small flower has dropped upon my bosom."

These are the two first strophes of the poem. And here is the last strophe:

"In Summer and in Winter I shall walk
Up and down
The patterned garden paths
In my stiff brocaded gown.
The squills and daffodils
Will give place to pillared roses, and to asters, and to snow.
I shall go
Up and down
In my gown,

Gorgeously arrayed,
Boned and stayed.
And the softness of my body will be guarded from embrace
By each button, hook and lace.
For the man who should loose me is dead,
Fighting with the Duke in Flanders,
In a pattern called war.
Christ! What are patterns for?"

This poem is designed in cadences, and in spite of its great variety, the symmetry is to be found, first of all, in the repetition, at more or less regular intervals, of the typical or pattern cadence of the poem,—"In my stiff brocaded gown." (It is the cadence that is repeated—not the words). The cadence is reiterated in lines like the following:

"Makes a pink and silver stain"
"Only whalebone and brocade"
"Underneath my stiffened gown"
"But she guesses he is near"
"With the weight of this brocade"
"By each button, hook and lace"
"Aching, melting, unafraid"

In other lines we find this cadence varied just a little bit. Perhaps an accent will be changed, perhaps a word with two short-sounding syllables will be substituted for a word with one long-sounding syllable, thus giving the line a new effect with the same time value as the typical cadence. (For there is certainly such a thing as quantity in English poetry, and the greatest poets have felt it and used their knowledge of it, although they have not argued about it overmuch.) Such slightly varied lines are like the following:

"Just a plate of current fashion"
"And the sliding of the water"
"Bewildered by my laughter"
"Underneath the fallen blossoms"
"Fighting with the Duke in Flanders"

Still other lines are simply combinations of the typical cadence with another line differing from it slightly, the two lines, taken together as one line, making a line with double the time value of the typical cadence. These still contribute to symmetry.

"I would be the pink and silver as I ran along the paths"
"It was brought to me this morning by a rider from the Duke"
"The blue and yellow flowers stood up proudly in the sun"
"Will give place to pillared roses and to asters and to snow"

And still other lines, like the frequently repeated "Up and down," seem to be part of the symmetry because they are like a part of the typical cadence, suggesting a pause and the rest of it.

But just as most of the lines of this poem seem to contribute to symmetry by reiterating the same or similar cadences, so many of them repeat only a part of the typical cadence, and then alter it, lengthen it, shorten it, or emphasize and accent it in new ways. This, evidently, gratifies Miss Lowell's love of rhythmical variety. And she has so very cunningly devised this poem that the proportion existing between typical and atypical lines is both tantalizing and pleasurable. The varied cadences never delay the current of the rhythm too long, but rather, relieve and rest us, so that, when the poem swings back into the familiar cadence, we know an instantaneous delight.

We should notice, also, that Miss Lowell has not been content with rhythm alone as the structural symmetry of her design. She has reinforced rhythm in several ways. The whole poem plays with the idea of the pattern. Brocade, a silk with a showy design, is mentioned seven times in the poem. The word "pattern," perhaps, is used too often. The word "stiff" is also reiterated, probably to give the picture of the lady its proper lineal effect. A double color design runs through the poem from end to end—the pink and silver of the woman and her gown, the blue and gold of daffodils and squills, of water and sunlight.

For all these reasons, this poem, a narrative of the eighteenth century told in the first person, is an unusual opportunity to take pleasure in design. Readers may ask themselves whether Miss Lowell could wisely have introduced as many lines, proportionately, varying from the typical, in a poem of half the length of this, or whether in a poem several times as long the reiteration of cadence and idea which gives "Patterns" its very real charm would have become tiresome.

Other fine examples of design which keeps to rhythm as the structural symmetry of poetry are Adelaide Crapsey's brilliant and beautiful little poems called "Cinquains." No one else has ever made five-line poems like them. But Miss Crapsey made quite a number of them and made them perfectly, and the fact that she is no longer living—an exquisitely original spirit lost to us—is a cause of grief to poets and readers. In these little poems the symbols, always true and adequate, bear the full weight of the meaning and the rhythms give a rare sense of growth and climax. In each case the pattern conforms beautifully to the meaning which it accompanies. Here is one of them, "The Warning."

> "Just now,
> Out of the strange
> Still dusk . . . as strange, as still . . .
> A white moth flew. Why am I grown
> So cold?"

As has already been said, many poets of to-day have attempted to make verse with a symmetry of design not dependent upon rhythm, allowing the rhythm to be the variable element in the composition. But only a few of these poets have succeeded in giving us memorable poems. One, which is seldom mentioned and which is by a poet not well known to the general public, is "Psalm" by Jessie E. Sampter. It was printed in "The Lyric Year," an anthology made as the result of a prize competition in 1912. The symmetry of design in this poem depends upon the principle of parallelism, in accordance with which the Psalms of the Bible were made. It is one of very few modern "psalms" that are psalms in any real and formal sense. The symmetry of design is further strengthened by the use of one symbol, the symbol of light, throughout the poem.

> "They have burned to Thee many tapers in many temples:
> I burn to Thee the taper of my heart."

Not very remote from this psalm in spirit and in structure are a number of poems by poets of the far East who are now writing in our language. Kahlil Gibran is writing poems and parables that have an individual music, a naïve charm and distinction and a structural symmetry based on symbol, contrast, repetition and parallelism. The poems of Sir Rabindranath Tagore need no introduction to American readers. They are like frail crystal cups filled with the clear waters of meditation. Unfortunately the fact that many of them are so strongly symbolic as to seem mystical here in the Occident has led a few readers to think of Sir Rabindranath as a "savior" or world hero or major prophet. It is probable that the future will show all what the present seems to show the best critics, that he is a Bengali gentleman and a poet of rare achievement. The following poem taken from "Gitanjali" is one of many that find their symmetry, in so far as they have symmetrical structure in our tongue, in symbol and story, not in rhythm.

> "On the day when the lotus bloomed, alas, my mind was straying, and I knew it not. My basket was empty and the flower remained unheeded.
>
> Only now and again a sadness fell upon me, and I started up from my dream and felt a sweet trace of a strange fragrance in the south wind.
>
> That vague fragrance made my heart ache with longing, and it seemed to me that it was the eager breath of the summer seeking for its completion.
>
> I knew not then that it was so near, that it was mine, and this perfect sweetness had blossomed in the depth of my own heart."

The rhythms of these verses are similar, but the stresses hardly recur regularly enough to create a *symmetry* in rhythm.

The same thing may be said of John Gould Fletcher's poem on Lincoln. The first division of it is a complete poem in itself. It tells the story of Lincoln's life in terms of the life of the pine tree. And although the rhythms are similar, the several lines of the three strophes are unified and held together rather more by symbol than by the regular recurrence of stress in the flowing of the rhythm.

"Like a gaunt, scraggly pine
Which lifts its head above the mournful sandhills;
And patiently, through dull years of bitter silence,
Untended and uncared for, starts to grow.

"Ungainly, laboring, huge,
The wind of the north has twisted and gnarled its branches;
Yet in the heat of midsummer days, when thunder-clouds ring the
horizon,
A nation of men shall rest beneath its shade.

"And it shall protect them all,
Hold everyone safe there, watching aloof in silence;
Until at last one mad stray bolt from the zenith
Shall strike it in an instant down to earth."

In this connection it is interesting to call to mind the fact that Walt Whitman's great threnody, "When Lilacs Last in the Dooryard Bloomed," would have had almost no symmetry of design if he had not tied the threads of meaning together by his frequently reiterated mention of lilac, star, and hermit thrush. And it is interesting to note, further, that lovers of Walt Whitman value his long poems most, and value them for the breadth of vision that is in them and for the towering spirit of democracy, rather than for the beauty of his craftsmanship, although even judged as a craftsman, Whitman had certain shining powers. But the only short poem of his which is well known is "O Captain, My Captain!" which has a symmetry of design based on rhythm and rhyme.

And now we are brought face to face with the question of the real importance of rhyme in the designing of poems. What does rhyme add to poetry and how should it be used? The contemporary poets have answered that question in several ways. The extreme conservatives hold that rhyme should be used in all English poems not written in blank verse. The extremists of the radical schools claim that rhyme is an old and worn-out device and that, because the number of possible rhymes is strictly limited, and because we have heard most of them many times, contemporary poetry is best written without rhymes. But the moderates, the greatest living poets, those recognized both by critics and by the public, use rhyme in a large part of their work, and this fact leads us naturally enough to believe that they consider it beautiful and valuable. The fact that they write some unrhymed poems leads us to believe that they think it not indispensable. Tennyson—a rather conservative poet—wrote one of his finest lyrics without rhyme, the famous "Tears, Idle Tears;" and many lyrics by contemporary poets are fluent enough and maintain their symmetry well enough to be memorable without it. One of these is "Deirdre," by James Stephens, which begins in this fashion:

> "Do not let any woman read this verse;
> It is for men, and after them their sons
> And their sons' sons.
>
> "The time comes when our hearts sink utterly;
> When we remember Deirdre and her tale,
> And that her lips are dust."

Such poems show what may be done without rhyme and many others show how beautiful rhyming may be. Only the extremists of conservative or radical theory have lost this traditional sanity with regard to the use of rhyme, the conservatives saying, in effect, "We have grown accustomed to it; therefore we must have it;" the radicals saying, in effect, "We have grown accustomed to it; therefore we had better do without it!"

What purpose does rhyme serve in a poem? That is the question which students of poetry must answer. First of all, we may say, it serves to define the rhythm by grouping together certain cadences and marking the pause that comes after them. Rhyme, most commonly, is used in this way, and this way of using it is generally understood. Such rhyming serves the same purpose in poetry that a picture frame serves with a picture. It contributes to the symmetry of the poetic pattern by marking the place where the rhythm stops.

Contemporary poets use rhymes of this sort very much as poets always have used them, but with a new scrupulousness with regard to sound values. They realize that the constant use of rhyme in English poetry has increased our sensitivity. Many rhymes which pleased earlier generations—such rhymes as "life," "strife," "love," "dove," and the like, have been used so frequently that they have become trite and tiresome. Many of the "rich rhymes," moreover, rhymes like "again," "pain," "home," "come," "gone," "won," are less pleasing to modern poets and to their readers than they were to our forefathers. The best contemporary poets avoid these "rich rhymes," really imperfect rhymes, whenever they would have to be placed in such close proximity as would make the imperfection conspicuous and distract the reader with the desire to mispronounce. Rhymes should be inconspicuously correct or beautiful enough for enjoyment. Contemporary poets prefer to use perfect rhymes. And because rhyming is usually a part of the structural symmetry in the designs of short poems, poets are careful to avoid flaws in the rhyming of short lyrics.

A poem which is an excellent example of good rhyming in a short lyric is Margaret Widdemer's "Greek Folk Song" from which the following lines are taken:

> "Under dusky laurel leaf,
> Scarlet leaf of rose,
> I lie prone, who have known
> All a woman knows."

In the third line of this stanza the reader will notice that a word at the end of the line rhymes with a word within the line—

"prone," "known." Clever poets can do much to create a structural symmetry by the clever use of this internal rhyming. Moreover it makes a poem easier to remember. And if such rhymes are well chosen, they bring into a poem a music that is like the reiterated sound of a bell. Of course, the use of such rhymes is beset with perils, the chief of these being the peril of apparent artificiality. But, to the clever craftsman, internal rhyming affords an opportunity for the perfecting of fine patterns.

One of the cleverest American poems in which internal rhyming is used is "The Song" from "Juanita" by Lauren E. Crane, one of the pioneer poets of California. Only two or three lines of it seem in any way artificial, in spite of the fact that the long lines in each stanza are rhymed three or four times each. "The Song" maintains, in most of its lines, a feeling of spontaneous sincerity which always belongs to good lyrics. Here is one stanza —the first:

"To-night the stars are flowing gold;
The light South wind is blowing cold,
Esta es, mi lucha?
The bright, bent moon is growing old,
Escucha!"

This poem, however, was written about fifty years ago. It is interesting to compare it with recent poetry in which internal rhyming is used. For the sake of contrast let us read a few lines from Amy Lowell's "The Cross-Roads," a poem written in what Miss Lowell calls "polyphonic prose." The rhyming in this passage is much needed as a contribution to the symmetry of the design.

"The stake has wrenched, the stake has started, the body, flesh from flesh has parted. But the bones hold tight, socket and ball, and clamping them down in the hard, black ground is the stake, wedged through ribs and spine. The bones may twist, and heave, and twine, but the stake holds them still in line. The breeze goes down, and the round stars shine, for the stake holds the fleshless bones in line."

Perhaps the rhyming also hurries these grewsome lines a little and contributes something to our sense of excitement.

Rhyme, after all, like rhythm and imagery and symbolism, is something which contributes to the strength and beauty of a poem— if it be used by a genius. That is the most and the least that can be said about it. Rhyme is almost always a contribution to symmetry of design and therefore it is usually more important and valuable in short poems than in long poems. It belongs to the free and nonchalant ballad and to brief lyrics. It is not an essential in the making of dramatic poems and long narratives. Like rhythm and imagery, rhyme can be used insincerely and inappropriately. When this has been the case the lines will jingle in vain. Posterity will never hear them. But posterity will return, again and again, to a psalm, or a poem in blank verse, nobly conceived and sincerely written. However, when rhyme is well used, it is beautiful and has genuine mnemonic value. It may enable men to remember what might otherwise be forgotten.

After all, what makes a poem live? The answer is both simple and complex. One may say, quickly and thoughtlessly, "The beauty and truth that are in it." And this will be a true answer. But this answer becomes less simply sufficient when we go on to explain that beauty and truth in a poem are the result of beauty and truth in a human spirit, combined with and expressed by such excellent craftsmanship as can present the beauty and truth to other human beings impressively and memorably. Then, when we have used that word, "memorably," we have explained the vital importance of design.

We all know how much easier it is to remember a poem that has a decided pattern in rhyme, rhythm, thought, imagery or symbol, than it is to remember a poem which flows on incoherently from one thought or emotion to the next. In spite of all that dilettantes of the "saffron schools" may tell us, poems that live, live because they are so well designed that they can hardly be forgotten. A well known American poet says that he can test the value of his own work by its mnemonic quality.

When he can remember a poem that he has written he usually finds that the poem is remembered and enjoyed by many other people. His weaker poems fade rapidly out of his own mind.

Beautiful sentiments and ideas taken alone, or grouped together without clearly defined order, may win a hearing for a poem and give it a temporary value in the generation to which it belongs. But a poem will live only because its parts are held together and unified in a symmetrical pattern and because variety is a dynamic force moving in it from line to line. Whenever this is true, little poems are as perfect as claystones found in a river bank and long poems have the sinuous beauty of streams.

PATTERNS

I walk down the garden paths,
And all the daffodils
Are blowing, and the bright blue squills.
I walk down the patterned garden paths
In my stiff, brocaded gown.
With my powdered hair and jewelled fan,
I too am a rare
Pattern. As I wander down
The garden paths.

My dress is richly figured,
And the train
Makes a pink and silver stain
On the gravel, and the thrift
Of the borders.
Just a plate of current fashion,
Tripping by in high-heeled, ribboned shoes.
Not a softness anywhere about me,
Only whalebone and brocade.
And I sink on a seat in the shade
Of a lime tree. For my passion
Wars against the stiff brocade.
The daffodils and squills
Flutter in the breeze
As they please.

And I weep;
For the lime tree is in blossom
And one small flower has dropped upon my bosom.

And the plashing of waterdrops
In the marble fountain
Comes down the garden paths.
The dripping never stops.
Underneath my stiffened gown
Is the softness of a woman bathing in a marble basin,
A basin in the midst of hedges grown
So thick, she cannot see her lover hiding,
But she guesses he is near,
And the sliding of the water
Seems the stroking of a dear
Hand upon her.
What is Summer in a fine brocaded gown!
I should like to see it lying in a heap upon the ground.
All the pink and silver crumpled up on the ground.

I would be the pink and silver as I ran along the paths,
And he would stumble after,
Bewildered by my laughter.
I should see the sun flashing from his sword hilt and the buckles on
his shoes.
I would choose
To lead him in a maze along the patterned paths,
A bright and laughing maze for my heavy-booted lover,
Till he caught me in the shade,
And the buttons of his waistcoat bruised my body as he clasped me,
Aching, melting, unafraid.
With the shadows of the leaves and the sundrops,
And the plopping of the waterdrops,
All about us in the open afternoon—
I am very like to swoon
With the weight of this brocade,
For the sun sifts through the shade.

Underneath the fallen blossom
In my bosom,
Is a letter I have hid.

It was brought to me this morning by a rider from the Duke.
"Madam, we regret to inform you that Lord Hartwell
Died in action Thursday se'nnight."
As I read it in the white, morning sunlight,
The letters squirmed like snakes.
"Any answer, Madam?" said my footman.
"No," I told him.
"See that the messenger takes some refreshment.
No, no answer."
And I walked into the garden,
Up and down the patterned paths,
In my stiff, correct brocade.
The blue and yellow flowers stood up proudly in the sun,
Each one.
I stood upright too,
Held rigid to the pattern
By the stiffness of my gown.
Up and down I walked,
Up and down.

In a month he would have been my husband.
In a month, here, underneath this lime,
We would have broke the pattern;
He for me, and I for him,
He as Colonel, I as Lady,
On this shady seat.
He had a whim
That sunlight carried blessing.
And I answered, "It shall be as you have said."
Now he is dead.

In Summer and in Winter I shall walk
Up and down
The patterned garden paths
In my stiff, brocaded gown.
The squills and daffodils
Will give place to pillared roses, and to asters, and to snow.
I shall go
Up and down,
In my gown.
Gorgeously arrayed,

Boned and stayed.
And the softness of my body will be guarded from embrace
By each button, hook, and lace.
For the man who should loose me is dead,
Fighting with the Duke in Flanders,
In a pattern called a war.
Christ! What are patterns for?

Amy Lowell

RENASCENCE *

All I could see from where I stood
Was three long mountains and a wood;
I turned and looked another way,
And saw three islands in a bay.
So with my eyes I traced the line
Of the horizon, thin and fine,
Straight around till I was come
Back to where I'd started from;
And all I saw from where I stood
Was three long mountains and a wood.
Over these things I could not see;
These were the things that bounded me;
And I could touch them with my hand,
Almost, I thought, from where I stand.
And all at once things seemed so small
My breath came short, and scarce at all.
But, sure, the sky is big, I said;
Miles and miles above my head;
So here upon my back I'll lie
And look my fill into the sky.
And so I looked, and, after all,
The sky was not so very tall.
The sky, I said, must somewhere stop,
And—sure enough!—I see the top!
The sky, I thought, is not so grand;
I 'most could touch it with my hand!
And, reaching up my hand to try,
I screamed to feel it touch the sky.

* This poem is reprinted by special permission of Mitchell Kennerley, publisher of the volume *Renascence and Other Poems* from which it is taken.

I screamed, and—lo!—Infinity
Came down and settled over me;
Forced back my scream into my chest,
Bent back my arm upon my breast,
And, pressing of the Undefined
The definition on my mind,
Held up before my eyes a glass
Through which my shrinking sight did pass
Until it seemed I must behold
Immensity made manifold;
Whispered to me a word whose sound
Deafened the air for worlds around,
And brought unmuffled to my ears
The gossiping of friendly spheres,
The creaking of the tented sky,
The ticking of Eternity.
I saw and heard, and knew at last
The How and Why of all things, past,
The present, and forevermore.
The Universe, cleft to the core,
Lay open to my throbbing sense
That, sick'ning, I would fain pluck thence
But could not,—nay! But needs must suck
At the great wound, and could not pluck
My lips away till I had drawn
All venom out.—Ah, fearful pawn!
For my omniscience paid I toll
In infinite remorse of soul.
All sin was of my sinning, all
Atoning mine, and mine the gall
Of all regret. Mine was the weight
Of every brooded wrong, the hate
That stood behind each envious thrust,
Mine every greed, mine every lust.
And all the while for every grief,
Each suffering, I craved relief
With individual desire,—
Craved all in vain! And felt fierce fire
About a thousand people crawl;
Perished with each,—then mourned for all!

A man was starving in Capri;
He moved his eyes and looked at me;
I felt his gaze, I heard his moan,
And knew his hunger as my own.
I saw at sea a great fog-bank
Between two ships that struck and sank;
A thousand screams the heavens smote;
And every scream tore through my throat.
No hurt I did not feel, no death
That was not mine; mine each last breath
That, crying, met an answering cry
From the compassion that was I.
All suffering mine, and mine its rod;
Mine, pity like the pity of God.
Ah, awful weight! Infinity
Pressed down upon the finite me!
My anguished spirit, like a bird,
Beating against my lips I heard;
Yet lay the weight so close about
There was no room for it without.
And so beneath the weight lay I
And suffered death, but could not die.

Long had I lain thus, craving death,
When quietly the earth beneath
Gave way, and inch by inch, so great
At last had grown the crushing weight,
Into the earth I sank till I
Full six feet under ground did lie,
And sank no more,—there is no weight
Can follow here, however great.
From off my breast I felt it roll,
And as it went my tortured soul
Burst forth and fled in such a gust
That all about me swirled the dust.

Deep in the earth I rested now;
Cool is its hand upon the brow
And soft its breast beneath the head
Of one who is so gladly dead.
And all at once, and over all

The pitying rain began to fall;
I lay and heard each pattering hoof
Upon my lowly, thatchèd roof,
And seemed to love the sound far more
Than ever I had done before.
For rain it hath a friendly sound
To one who's six feet under ground;
And scarce the friendly voice or face:
A grave is such a quiet place.

The rain, I said, is kind to come
And speak to me in my new home.
I would I were alive again
To kiss the fingers of the rain,
To drink into my eyes the shine
Of every slanting silver line,
To catch the freshened, fragrant breeze
From drenched and dripping apple-trees.
For soon the shower will be done,
And then the broad face of the sun
Will laugh above the rain-soaked earth
Until the world with answering mirth
Shakes joyously, and each round drop
Rolls, twinkling, from its grass-blade top.
How can I bear it; buried here,
While overhead the sky grows clear
And blue again after the storm?
O, multi-colored, multi-form,
Beloved beauty over me,
That I shall never, never see
Again! Spring-silver, autumn-gold,
That I shall nevermore behold!
Sleeping your myriad magics through,
Close-sepulchred away from you!
O God, I cried, give me new birth,
And put me back upon the earth!
Upset each cloud's gigantic gourd
And let the heavy rain, down-poured
In one big torrent, set me free,
Washing my grave away from me!

I ceased; and, through the breathless hush
That answered me, the far-off rush
Of herald wings came whispering
Like music down the vibrant string
Of my ascending prayer, and— crash!
Before the wild wind's whistling lash
The startled storm-clouds reared on high
And plunged in terror down the sky,
And the big rain in one black wave
Fell from the sky and struck my grave.
I know not how such things can be
I only know there came to me
A fragrance such as never clings
To aught save happy, living things;
A sound as of some joyous elf
Singing sweet songs to please himself,
And, through and over everything,
A sense of glad awakening.
The grass, a-tiptoe at my ear,
Whispering to me I could hear;
I felt the rain's cool finger-tips
Brushed tenderly across my lips,
Laid gently on my sealèd sight,
And all at once the heavy night
Fell from my eyes and I could see,—
A drenched and dripping apple-tree,
A last long line of silver rain,
A sky grown clear and blue again.
And as I looked a quickening gust
Of wind blew up to me and thrust
Into my face a miracle
Of orchard-breath, and with the smell,—
I know not how such things can be!—
I breathed my soul back into me.
Ah! up then from the ground sprang I
And hailed the earth with such a cry
As is not heard save from a man
Who has been dead, and lives again.
About the trees my arms I wound;
Like one gone mad I hugged the ground;

I raised my quivering arms on high;
I laughed and laughed into the sky,
Till at my throat a strangling sob
Caught fiercely, and a great heart-throb
Sent instant tears into my eyes;
O God, I cried, no dark disguise
Can e'er hereafter hide from me
Thy radiant identity!
Thou canst not move across the grass
But my quick eyes will see Thee pass,
Nor speak, however silently,
But my hushed voice will answer Thee.
I know the path that tells Thy way
Through the cool eve of every day;
God, I can push the grass apart
And lay my finger on Thy heart!

The world stands out on either side
No wider than the heart is wide;
Above the world is stretched the sky,—
No higher than the soul is high.
The heart can push the sea and land
Farther away on either hand;
The soul can split the sky in two,
And let the face of God shine through.
But East and West will pinch the heart
That can not keep them pushed apart;
And he whose soul is flat—the sky
Will cave in on him by and by.

Edna St. Vincent Millay

INDIAN SUMMER

(*After completing a book for one now dead.*)

(*O Earth-and-Autumn of the Setting Sun,*
She is not by, to know my task is done!)

In the brown grasses slanting with the wind,
Lone as a lad whose dog's no longer near,
Lone as a mother whose only child has sinned,

Lone on the loved hill . . . . and below me here
The thistle-down in tremulous atmosphere
Along red clusters of the sumach streams;
The shrivelled stalks of goldenrod are sere,
And crisp and white their flashing old racemes.
(. . . forever . . . forever . . . forever . . .)
This is the lonely season of the year,
This is the season of our lonely dreams.

(*O Earth-and-Autumn of the Setting Sun,*
She is not by, to know my task is done!)
The corn-shocks westward on the stubble plain
Show like an Indian village of dead days;
The long smoke trails behind the crawling train,
And floats atop the distant woods ablaze
With orange, crimson, purple. The low haze
Dims the scarped bluffs above the inland sea,
Whose wide and slaty waters in cold glaze
Await yon full-moon of the night-to-be,
(. . . far . . . and far . . . and far . . .)
These are the solemn horizons of man's ways,
These are the horizons of solemn thought to me.

(*O Earth-and-Autumn of the Setting Sun,*
She is not by, to know my task is done!)
And this the hill she visited, as friend;
And this the hill she lingered on, as bride—
Down in the yellow valley is the end:
They laid her . . . in no evening autumn tide . . .
Under fresh flowers of that May morn, beside
The queens and cave-women of ancient earth . . .

This is the hill . . . and over my city's towers,
Across the world from sunset, yonder in air,
Shines, through its scaffoldings, a civic dome
Of piled masonry, which shall be ours
To give, completed, to our children there . . .
And yonder far roof of my abandoned home
Shall house new laughter . . . Yet I tried . . . I tried . . .
And, ever wistful of the doom to come,
I built her many a fire for love . . . for mirth . . .

(When snows were falling on our oaks outside,
Dear, many a winter fire upon the hearth) . . .
(. . . farewell . . . farewell . . . farewell . . .)
We dare not think too long on those who died,
While still so many yet must come to birth.

William Ellery Leonard

THE DYING PATRIOT

Day breaks on England down the Kentish hills,
Singing in the silence of the meadow-footing rills,
Day of my dreams, O day!
  I saw them march from Dover, long ago,
  With a silver cross before them, singing low,
Monks of Rome from their home where the blue seas break in foam,
  Augustine with his feet of snow.

Noon strikes on England, noon on Oxford town,
—Beauty she was statue cold—there's blood upon her gown:
Noon of my dreams, O noon!
  Proud and godly kings had built her, long ago,
  With her towers and tombs and statues all arow,
With her fair and floral air and the love that lingers there,
  And the streets where the great men go.

Evening on the olden, the golden sea of Wales,
When the first star shivers and the last wave pales:
O evening dreams!
  There's a house that Britons walked in, long ago,
  Where now the springs of ocean fall and flow,
And the dead robed in red and sea-lilies overhead
  Sway when the long winds blow.

Sleep not, my country: though night is here, afar
Your children of the morning are clamorous for war:
Fire in the night, O dreams!
  Though she send you as she sent you, long ago,
  South to desert, east to ocean, west to snow,
West of these out to seas colder than the Hebrides I must go
Where the fleet of stars is anchored, and the young Star-captains glow.

James Elroy Flecker.

CINQUAINS

Fate Defied

As it
Were tissue of silver
I'll wear, O fate, thy grey,
And go, mistly radiant, clad
Like the moon.

The Guarded Wound

If it
Were lighter touch
Than petal of flower resting
On grass, oh still too heavy it were,
Too heavy!

November Night

Listen . . .
With faint dry sound,
Like steps of passing ghosts,
The leaves, frost-crisp'd, break from the trees
And fall.

Adelaide Crapsey

THE CEDARS

All down the years the fragrance came,
The mingled fragrance, with a flame,
Of Cedars breathing in the sun,
The Cedar-trees of Lebanon.

O thirst of song in bitter air,
And hope, wing-hurt from iron care,
What balm of myrrh and honey, won
From far-off trees of Lebanon!

Not from these eyelids yet, have I
Ever beheld that early sky.
Why do they call me through the sun?—
Even the trees of Lebanon?

Josephine Preston Peabody

TAMPICO

Oh, cut me reeds to blow upon,
  Or gather me a star,
But leave the sultry passion-flowers
  Growing where they are.

I fear their sombre yellow deeps,
  Their whirling fringe of black,
And he who gives a passion-flower
  Always asks it back.

Grace Hazard Conkling

WHO LOVES THE RAIN

Who loves the rain,
And loves his home,
And looks on life with quiet eyes,
Him will I follow through the storm;
And at his hearth-fire keep me warm;
Nor hell nor heaven shall that soul surprise,
Who loves the rain,
And loves his home,
And looks on life with quiet eyes.

Frances Shaw

A CYPRIAN WOMAN: GREEK FOLK SONG

Under dusky laurel leaf,
  Scarlet leaf of rose,
I lie prone, who have known
  All a woman knows.

Love and grief and motherhood,
  Fame and mirth and scorn—
These are all shall befall
  Any woman born.

Jewel-laden are my hands
  Tall my stone above,
Do not weep that I sleep
  Who was wise in love.

Where I walk, a shadow gray
Through gray asphodel,
I am glad, who have had
All that life can tell.

Margaret Widdemer

33 Men of 75

PSALM

They have burned to Thee many tapers in many temples:
I burn to Thee the taper of my heart.

They have sought Thee at many altars, they have carried lights to find Thee:
I find thee in The white fire of my heart.

They have gone forth restlessly, forging many shapes, images where they seek Thee, idols of deed and thought:
Thou art the fire of my deeds; Thou art the white flame of my dreams.

O vanity! They know things and codes and customs,
They believe what they see to be true; but they know not Thee,
Thou art within the light of their eyes that see, and the core of fire.

The white fire of my heart forges the shapes of my brain;
The white fire of my heart is a sun, and my deeds and thoughts are its dark planets;
It is a far flame of Thee, a star in Thy firmament.

With pleasant warmth flicker the red fires of the hearth,
And the blue, mad flames of the marsh flare and consume themselves:
I too am an ember of Thee, a little star; my warmth and my light travel a long way.

So little, so wholly given to its human quest,
And yet of Thee, wholly of Thee, Thou Unspeakable,
All the colors of life in a burning white mist
Pure and intense as Thou, O Heart of life!

Frail is my taper, it flickers in the storm,
It is blown out in the great wind of the world:

Yet when the world is dead and the seas are a crust of salt,
When the sun is dark in heaven and the stars have changed their
courses,
Forever somewhere with Thee, on the altar of life
Shall still burn the white fire of my heart.

Jessie E. Sampter

DEIRDRE

Do not let any woman read this verse;
It is for men, and after them their sons
And their sons' sons.

The time comes when our hearts sink utterly;
When we remember Deirdre and her tale,
And that her lips are dust.

Once she did tread the earth: men took her hand;
They looked into her eyes and said their say,
And she replied to them.

More than a thousand years it is since she
Was beautiful: she trod the waving grass;
She saw the clouds.

A thousand years! The grass is still the same,
The clouds as lovely as they were that time
When Deirdre was alive.

But there has never been a woman born
Who was so beautiful, not one so beautiful
Of all the women born.

Let all men go apart and mourn together;
No man can ever love her; not a man
Can ever be her lover.

No man can bend before her: no man say—
What could one say to her? There are no words
That one could say to her!

Now she is but a story that is told
Beside the fire! No man can ever be
The friend of that poor queen.

James Stephens

AN APRIL MORNING *

Once more in misted April
The world is growing green.
Along the winding river
The plumey willows lean.

Beyond the sweeping meadows
The looming mountains rise,
Like battlements of dreamland
Against the brooding skies.

In every wooded valley
The buds are breaking through,
As though the heart of all things
No languor ever knew.

The golden-wings and bluebirds
Call to their heavenly choirs.
The pines are blued and drifted
With smoke of brushwood fires.

And in my sister's garden
Where little breezes run,
The golden daffodillies
Are blowing in the sun.

Bliss Carman

THE ANSWER

When I go back to earth
And all my joyous body
Puts off the red and white
That once had been so proud,

***From *April Airs* by Bliss Carman, copyright, 1916, reprinted by permission of the publishers, Small, Maynard & Company, Inc.**

If men should pass above
With false and feeble pity,
My dust will find a voice
To answer them aloud:

"Be still, I am content,
Take back your poor compassion!—
Joy was a flame in me
Too steady to destroy.
Lithe as a bending reed
Loving the storm that sways her—
I found more joy in sorrow
Than you could find in joy."

Sara Teasdale

WHAT DIM ARCADIAN PASTURES

What dim Arcadian pastures
Have I known
That suddenly, out of nothing,
A wind is blown,
Lifting a veil and a darkness,
Showing a purple sea—
And under your hair the faun's eyes
Look out on me?

Alice Corbin

ORGANIC RHYTHM

NOT many years ago, when we of this generation attended school, the word "rhythm" had an occult and mysterious sound. We heard very little about it. But we heard of "meter" quite frequently. "Meter" meant tiresome exercises in "scansion." "Meter" meant memorizing formidable definitions of words like "anapæst" and "amphibrach." How we hated it! "Meter" and "scansion" were good for us because they provided "mental drill," and poetry was the disastrous result of the invention of "anapaest" and "amphibrach." How we hated the poets! We resolved that when we had left school and could choose freely we would have nothing to do with poetry! Unfortunately many of us kept the resolution.

On the other hand, when we became men and women, many of us realized that such words as "anapaest" and "amphibrach" were made and defined by grammarians and critics, not by poets. We realized that this technical language could be made useful and satisfactory in its own way. Very likely the ability to analyze and dissect the metrical structure of a poem has a real importance for the well-educated man or woman. But many of us learned too late what might have brought us nearer to the joy of poetry if we had learned it sooner, that this ability to analyze and dissect metrical structures according to the rules of teachers and critics is of small importance in comparison with the ability to feel a beautiful rhythm and enjoy a fine poem. Who ever gave us a clue to the meaning of rhythm in poetry? Who shared with us a sense of the joy and beauty in the rhythms of English verse? Did anyone ever tell us, for our comfort, that many a maker of beautiful lyrics has made them with no knowledge at all of the school-book definitions of "anapæst" and "amphibrach"?

Therefore it may be a very fortunate thing that we use that prosaic little word "meter" less nowadays, and that we have more to say about rhythm. For even when poets can not define "anapæst" and "amphibrach," they are much concerned with the use of them and with their effect and meaning.

"Rhythm" is a larger, kinder, and more poetic word than "meter." It comes from a good old Greek root that means "to flow." We may think of rhythm, therefore, as we think of waves or ripples. It is the wave-like flowing of sequences of sound in poetry. And, in thinking of it in this way, we shall be thinking of something more fundamentally important than the rules of prosody as given in our rhetorics. We shall be thinking of the force that is behind and beyond those rules. We shall be returning to the source whence came the thing about which rules have been made.

In English poetry nearly always, and in almost all other poetry, rhythm has been more powerfully felt than any other element. So powerfully does a strong rhythm work upon us that many persons like to think that rhythm, in and of itself, is poetry. This is not true, of course, for any jargon can be set to the tune of a strong rhythm. And many rhythms actually have been misused in this way, stupidly by imitators, cleverly by parodists. Nevertheless, poems that have rhythmical vitality, poems that sway like wind-driven trees, leap like great geysers, roll sonorous monotones in upon consciousness at regular intervals, like the sea, or dance gaily like little white fountains, such poems will be heard and remembered when many brilliant pictures and proverbs, solemn saws and pretty sentiments, have been forgotten.

This is inevitable and natural, for we live and have our being in rhythm. A flaw in the rhythm of the breath may mean a disease of the lungs. A flaw in the rhythm of the blood may mean a disease of the heart. A break in the rhythm may mean death. And all emotions change the rhythms of the body, quickening or retarding, accentuating or interrupting. In these facts we find the reasons for the value of rhythm in poetry.

In these facts, also, we find the reason for the emotional effects of the several kinds of rhythm. The cadence or sound which is the true result of personal emotion will produce in the reader an effect of the same or similar emotion. Or, when a poet is more than personal, when he shares the ebb and flow of racial or national feeling and puts this into a poem, there will be something more than mere personal emotion in the effect of his rhythm upon his reader. Doubtless the great and typical rhythms that distinguish the poetry of the great races—English blank verse, for example, or the heroic hexameter of the Greek, are the result of the racial way of feeling things and putting them into speech. The epic measure of the Iliad gives again to all sensitive listeners a share in the emotions of the men of Homer's nation. The Irish dirges used in keening give a sense of sorrow and death to any person in any land whose sense of rhythmical values has not been destroyed by bad training; and they give also what we may call an Irish sense of sorrow and death. The poets of the Celtic revival in the United States, poets whose work is imitative and written *à la mode,* with an enthusiasm for the Celtic revival as an inspiring influence, have never been able to get into their work any of this unforgettable racial quality of rhythm. A triolet, on the other hand, is simply a rhythmical echo of pretty, whimsical, personal emotion. When we hear a good triolet read, even in a language that we do not know, we feel that touch of pretty, whimsical, personal emotion in the rhythm. We are stroked by the wings of a butterfly, chastised by thistledown; we are not shaken by thunder, whipped by the wind.

Therefore it would seem reasonable to suppose that, when a rhythm is chosen arbitrarily, selected from a chapter on prosody in a rhetoric, and forced into unwilling wedlock with a mood or meaning which might have been fruitfully happy with its own congenial cadence, the result is fundamental disharmony, bad poetry. Moreover, in the minds of great lyric singers it usually happens that emotion suggests the idea of the poem and the rhythm of it simultaneously, and that sense and sound grow together as it is made. The mood and the rhythm, growing together in the mind, have that organic unity which is likely to stir the emotion of the reader as the poet's emotion is stirred; and this is what the contemporary poet means when he speaks of "organic rhythm." It is rhythm of one kind with the mood and meaning of the poem.

Many of the best conscious craftsmen of our time are studying these matters of the emotional causes of rhythm and its emotional effect. They are trying many experiments. Most of the experiments fail, but the new endeavor to create new beauty may lead to a new kind of skill and to the production of new rhythmical masterpieces. And tolerant persons will welcome experiments even when they do not like the immediate results.

What is sometimes called "the *vers libre* movement" seems to have been valuable chiefly because it has been a way of making experiments with rhythm. Few poets have used the free rhythms creditably, not to say beautifully. And unfortunately, numerous poetasters undisciplined in the artistic use of rhythm, and ignorant of the ancient, symmetrical designs of English verse, persons who could not write a couplet or a quatrain correctly, seized the opportunity afforded by the vogue of free verse to place themselves before the public in the guise of poets. It was never anything more than a mask. They wrote in what they supposed was free verse for no better reason than that given by the lazy housewife who had beans instead of potatoes for dinner. "It's less bother. You don't have to peel 'em." Such poetasters simply cut up long lines of level prose rhythms into random lengths, and set them down on pages that would have been better off clean. Such chopped up prose lines had no poetic cadence because no poetic lift of emotion produced them, or produced a rhythm for them. Therefore they had no power to produce an emotion in the reader. At best they put before us a more or less trivial mental picture or stimulated us intellectually and superficially by their specious imaginative cleverness. At worst they were simply banal, or else they aroused in the reader by shock and sensationalism what they could not awaken in the ways natural and appropriate to poetry, a sense of perverted excitement. But, when the novelty of it had worn off, we were bored rather than amused by the shrieking, grimacing, headline quality of much that was called free verse. Such experiments failed because the motives of their makers were wrong. Such experiments were not sincerely made with the desire to create a living beauty. They were idly and easily made with the desire to write quickly.

In general it may be said that the poets who have written best in free verse have been poets skilled in the use of the regular rhythms of English verse. But even these poets have failed far more frequently than they have succeeded in the making of free verse. The reason for their failures seems to be found in the fact that their very great interest in craftsmanship for its own sake has caused them sometimes to work too intellectually. They have sometimes disregarded the fact that real emotion is the genesis of all good rhythm. When Amy Lowell and Ezra Pound fail to make good poems, in spite of their comprehensive knowledge of the art of poetry, it is quite probably because they are creating according to theory and not as result of genuine feeling. The great law never fails: the rhythm that is the result of emotion is likely to have value, be it never so primitive; the rhythm that is the result of intellectual striving will be as dead as the dry, still sand in the desert at noon.

But in spite of the fact that few good poems have been written in free verse, the art of poetry has been enriched by the greater facility which this experimenting with rhythms has made possible. No one has shown that symmetry of design may not be secured in a poem by other means than the use of rhythm, letting rhythm be varied from line to line in accordance with mood and meaning; and the ideal of a great poem written in verse freer than that of any known masterpiece and yet powerfully rhythmical and well designed, is an ideal which no poet should be willing to banish from his heart and hope. For the few good poems written in free verse are so very good that they confirm us in the faith that verse, made by a master, may be very free and very beautiful. Whenever free verse has been written in accordance with an ideal of poetic beauty, and sincerely, as the result of genuine emotion, it has a characteristic and unforgettable magic.

Constance Lindsay Skinner's poems of the life of the American Indian are written in admirable free verse. They are strongly charged with the primitive emotions of life. They are very simple, natural and direct in style. And in spite of the fact that the typical cadences are not repeated frequently enough, in most of the poems, to make a very regular pattern, we find in the cadences a very real pleasure, the kind of pleasure that we feel in simple, passionate speech. Her "Song of The Full Catch" is more symmetrical in design than most of the other poems and has a most moving rhythm. It is an unusually beautiful poem, beginning with the lines,

> "Here's good wind, here's sweet wind,
> Here's good wind and my woman calls me!"

In her "Song of Cradle-Making" the cadences are even more like the cadences of speech:

> "I will trim thy cradle with many shells, and with cedar-fringes;
> Thou shalt have goose feathers on thy blanket!
> I will bear thee in my hands along the beach,
> Singing as the sea sings,"

Sure and strong fidelity to the laws of passionate human speech is what makes these lines poetry.

Carl Sandburg is another American poet who makes his poems with what we may call the rhythms of speech. In all of his poems we hear a man talking. He rarely sings. His song is always speech. Sometimes the speech is inflated and bombastic and oratorical. But always it is vivid and interesting and always it shares life with us. In his quaint little poem, "Monosyllabic," he even says this very thing about himself.

"Let me be a monosyllabic to-day, O Lord.
Yesterday I loosed a snarl of words on a fool, on a child.
To-day, let me be monosyllabic . . . a crony of old men who wash sunlight in their fingers and enjoy slow-pacing clocks."

This is simply beautiful speech—especially beautiful in the last line—arranged in a rhythm of aspiration—or, if you like it better, of petition—prayer. In his screed addressed to "A Contemporary Bunkshooter" he is simply a man talking violently, more violently than anybody who is not a poet can talk. And in his serenely beautiful poem, "Cool Tombs," we find poetic speech again.

"Pocahontas' body, lovely as a poplar, sweet as a red haw in November or a paw-paw in May, did she wonder? does she remember? . . . in the dust, in the cool tombs?

Here the long, level, undulating rhythms of ordinary prose are broken just as they would be in intimate and eloquent conversation.

John Gould Fletcher is another American poet who has written creditable free verse. But his ideal is not an ideal of speech in poetry. He is not a poet of Mr. Sandburg's kind. He is an Imagist, and believes that poetry is the setting forth of "images" in rhythmical language in such a way as will make them stimulate emotion in the reader. His best work is excellent poetry, really felt, heartily imagined, adequately expressed in rhythm. One of the finest strophes he has written, and one quite typical of his genius, is the first in "Irradiations." It should be read aloud and with due regard for the pauses. Otherwise the beauty of it may be lost.

"Over the roof-tops race the shadows of clouds:
Like horses the shadows of clouds charge down the street.

Whirlpools of purple and gold,
Winds from the mountains of cinnabar,
Lacquered mandarin moments, palanquins swaying and balancing,

Amid the vermillion pavilions, against the jade balustrades;
Glint of the glittering wings of dragon flies in the light
Silver filaments, golden flakes settling downwards;
Rippling, quivering flutters; repulse and surrender,
The sun broidered upon the rain,
The rain rustling with the sun.

Over the roof-tops race the shadows of clouds;
Like horses the shadows of clouds charge down the street."

In this poem, obviously, the cadences are conditioned by the imagery. They move with it fluently and are of one kind with it. Organic rhythm again and free rhythm again, but a rhythm of a kind very different from that used by Miss Skinner and Mr. Sandburg. To be sure the chief cunning of this poem is to be found in the picture presented with shrewdly chosen color-words and words that show movement. "Vermillion pavilions," "jade balustrades," "golden flakes settling downward," "rippling, quivering flutters"—what a group of pictures, what a series of sound echoes! But in the rhythm of the two lines that begin and end the strophe we find another good and sufficient reason for the vitality of this free verse.

Somewhat less regularly stressed is the rhythm of "The Most Sacred Mountain" by Eunice Tietjens. This is a poem of exultation, and the rhythm of it is rhapsodic, passionate, and, for that very reason, fluent and free. The first three lines say, with absolute fidelity to emotion, what one might desire to say in a mood of exultation, what one would be likely not to say, for lack of power to feel and speak at the same time.

"Space, and the twelve clean winds of heaven,
And this sharp exultation, like a cry, after the slow six thousand feet of climbing!
This is Tai Shan, the beautiful, the most holy."

The truth of this rhythm as an expression of emotion can be felt strongly even by persons who do not like the kind of free verse which has been called "shredded prose." Where then, can we find the boundary line between verse and prose? Perhaps we can not find it. As the lines grow longer and vary more in the matter of the recurrence of stresses, the rhythms become more like prose, less like song. But it would be very difficult indeed to tell just when lines become too long and level to belong to verse. And other matters must be considered with the matter of rhythm in determining whether any bit of literature is poetry or prose. We must take into account the conciseness of the expression, the emotional or intellectual quality, the imagery and symbolism, the power of the imagination in the presentation of the theme. But if any bit of literature be good literature, we may find legitimate enjoyment in it, even if we are unable to classify it. As a craftsman's attempt at classification, however, Amy Lowell's definition seems to be the most satisfactory definition yet made. It is geometrical. Miss Lowell says that regularly stressed verse may be represented by a line sharply curved back upon itself, that prose may be represented by an undulating line running straight ahead in any one direction, and that free verse may be represented by a line with a curve less sharp than the line representing regularly stressed verse. Perhaps she would say that her own polyphonic prose is like a line undulating more regularly than the line of ordinary prose. At any rate, that would be a good description of the rhythm of her polyphonic prose. And since polyphonic prose is a new kind of organic rhythm, something should be said about it here.

In the first place, Miss Lowell introduced it into our language, and no one else who is writing English poetry has made any noteworthy attempt to use it. It is a prose with typical cadences reiterated at intervals and with many rhymes and sound echoes. Like regular verse and like the best free verse its source is in genuine emotion. But like prose it is not lyrical. It does not sing. The lines of it move forever forward. There is no backward curve, no return. It is, therefore, an admirable form for narratives. For it intensifies our sense of excitement and bears us on to the end with a greater fluency than that of ordinary prose. The reading of polyphonic prose gives a sense of rapid movement that level, unrhymed prose lacks. The quality of Miss Lowell's polyphonic prose rhythms is essentially dramatic. These lines from a superb narrative poem, "The Bronze Horses," show what polyphonic prose can be at its best:

"What is the sound? The marble city shivers to the treading of feet. Cæsar's legions marching, foot—foot—hundreds, thousands of feet. They beat the ground, rounding each step double. Coming—coming—cohort after cohort, with brazen trumpets marking the time. One—two—one—two—laurel-crowned each one of you, cactus-fibred, harsh as sand grinding the rocks of a treeless land, rough and salt as Dead Sea wind, only the fallen are left behind. Blood-red plumes, jarring to the footfalls; they have passed through the gate, they are in the walls of the mother city, of marble Rome. Back to Rome with a victor's spoils, with a victor's wreath on every head, and Judah broken is dead, dead! '*Io triumphe!*' The shout knocks and breaks upon the spears of the legionaries."

Our illustrations might be multiplied without giving an adequate sense of the pleasure to be had from reading a whole poem in polphonic prose aloud. For that is the only way to test the value of it. Free verse and polphonic prose have received more superficial attention than honest consideration; and that is unfortunate, for superficial attention is only advertisement; honest consideration may find a recipe or a cure. But if many persons would read these poems aloud and if we might have a consensus of their opinions, we might find a way of estimating the value of such rhythms. Before the value of any kind of poetry can be determined it must be set free from the print on the pages of a book.

Before we go on to a consideration of organic rhythms of a kind more regularly stressed and in more symmetrical designs, it is well to note that William Morrison Patterson of Columbia University has written a book which should go into the hands of young poetry craftsmen in company with Sidney Lanier's "Science of English Verse." It is called "The Rhythm of Prose," and in it Professor Patterson describes his tests of the time-values of rhythm. The book is written in a scientific rather than an inspirational vein, but is the more valuable for that reason. Poets can usually find inspiration. But their knowledge of rhythm can be increased by a careful presentation of facts discovered through experiment. This is a book for all who wish to make a thorough and careful study of the subject of rhythm.

The poets who have written in free verse are not the only poets who have rediscovered the ancient law of all good poetry, which is that rhythm must rise out of the emotion felt. All of the poets who have recently won the attention of critics and the interest of the most intelligent and imaginative public are poets who have shown a reverence for this law.

One of the masterpieces of modern rhythm is Gilbert K. Chesterton's "Lepanto," a superb martial ballad about the Battle of Lepanto fought between the Turks and Don John of Austria in 1571. From end to end of the poem the rhythm is a delight. Words, phrases, images flash and sparkle, riding lightly on the surface of the tune. But the rhythm stirs the very depths of the spirit, for it is very swift and strong, very large and ample, yet never monotonous, for it includes a great variety of minor cadences. Just when the length of the long lines with their powerful stresses can hardly be sustained any longer by heart and voice, the lines ebb into shorter lines with sharper rhythmical curves and with accents like arrows newly fallen and quivering with shock. These lines illustrate the power of the rhythm of the poem as well as any other lines that might be taken from it to stand alone:

"In that enormous silence, tiny and unafraid,
Comes up along a winding road the noise of the Crusade.
Strong gongs groaning as the guns boom far,
Don John of Austria is going to the war,
Stiff-flags straining in the night-blasts cold
In the gloom black-purple, in the glint old-gold,
Torchlight crimson on the copper kettle-drums,
Then the tuckets, then the trumpets, then the cannon, and he comes.

Don John laughing in the brave beard curled,
Spurning of his stirrups like the thrones of all the world,
Holding his head up for a flag of all the free.
Love-light of Spain—hurrah!
Death-light of Africa!
Don John of Austria
Is riding to the sea."

In strong contrast with the martial clangor and speed of this rhythm is the swaying and restful movement of Max Eastman's "Coming To Port," a rhythm with all the enchanting languor of movement that is in the great steamer slowing down to anchor beside a dock. One does not need to be a sapient critic to feel the oneness of this rhythm with the theme and emotion of the poem. It is wistful and quiet in sound and meaning, a slow and sensuous reverie.

"Our motion on the soft, still, misty river
Is like rest; and like the hours of doom
That rise and follow one another ever
Ghosts of sleeping battle cruisers loom
And languish quickly in the liquid gloom."

Very often in rhymed and regularly stressed poetry, as in the free verse which we have already discussed, we can trace the origin of good rhythm by taking a clue from the opening line or lines, which seem to be like natural speech. In Walter de la Mare's charmingly melodic poem, "The Listeners," it seems possible that the rhythm of the whole may have been determined by the cadence of the first line.

"'Is there anybody there?' said the Traveller,
Knocking on the moonlit door;
And his horse in the silence champed the grasses
On the forest's ferny floor:
And a bird flew up out of the turret,
Above the Traveller's head:
And he smote upon the door again a second time;
'Is there anybody there?' he said."

If this poem had been as well begun by a man without genius, it would certainly have been spoiled in the third line. It would have faltered, flattened out and become monotonous. We should have had a third line something like this—"His horse would champ the grasses." And the rest of the poem, which is a masterpiece of its kind, would have been made to go by jerks. The sense and style would have been sacrificed to regularity and a very beautiful and original rhythm would never have been heard. Let us be thankful that Mr. de la Mare wrote his poem—all of it!

Similarly Rudyard Kipling, whose rhythms are exceedingly modern in quality, although he began writing before most of our contemporary poets who are famous to-day, seems to take a cadence of speech as the rhythmical beginning of many of his poems. And it is a well known fact that his rhythms are largely responsible for the great popularity of his poetry. In that jolly "Road Song of the Bandar Log" we find the following lines:

"Here we go in a flung festoon
Half way up to the jealous moon!
Don't you envy our pranceful bands?
Don't you wish you had extra hands?
Wouldn't you like if your tail were—so—
Curved in the shape of a Cupid's bow?
Now you're angry, but—never mind,
Brother, thy tail hangs down behind!"

It may very well be that Mr. Kipling, visualizing in his own mind that "branchy row" of monkeys, began his rhythm quite spontaneously, and, in the reader's mind, irresistibly, with that natural bit of speech "Here we go." If this be true, he had only to add the good imagery of "in a flung festoon" to have a fine rhythmical tune for his poem.

Another poem, an excellent lyric which may have been made in much the same way, is Margaret Widdemer's "Remembrance: Greek Folk Song." The rhythm of the whole poem seems to have grown naturally from the first cadence. "Not unto the forest, O my lover!"

MARGARET WIDDEMER

More than any poet who uses regularly stressed rhythms, Robert Frost is influenced by the tunes of human conversation, and he is the greatest living master of the poetry that talks. Although he has written a few good lyrics, song is not his gift. But in all of his poems we find something of the warmth and depth and richness, the sudden humor, the droll whimsy, the characteristic innuendo and flexible intimacy of conversation. To read them is to share profound mirth, amazing tragedy, delicious irony made out of talk and of one substance with it. But Mr. Frost's poems are always more than speech. They are always poetry. They never become mere oratory. And most of them keep very close to blank verse as a basic rhythm, the old racial rhythm of our language. Perhaps it would be true to say that Mr. Frost uses a relaxed form of blank verse, a blank verse greatly modified by the cadences of speech.

"Something there is that doesn't love a wall," says Mr. Frost. A Post-Victorian imitator of the great Victorians would never have written such a line. He might have said something like this—

> "A wall, I think, is quite superfluous!"

thereby sacrificing nature and imagination—poetry—to a school-book rule of accent. The poem would have lacked what all poems must have—life. Consider the homely life in this passage taken from the same poem, "Mending Wall."

> "He only says, 'Good fences make good neighbors.'
> Spring is the mischief in me, and I wonder
> If I could put a notion in his head?
> Why do they make good neighbors? Isn't it
> Where there are cows? But here there are no cows.
> Before I built a wall I'd ask to know
> What I was walling in or walling out,
> And to whom I was like to give offence.
> Something there is that doesn't love a wall,
> That wants it down. I could say 'Elves' to him,
> But it's not elves exactly, and I'd rather
> He said it for himself."

When we read lines like these we do not need to be told that Mr. Frost uses blank verse as others have not used it. Here is blank verse written with respect for the plain, stubborn wills and voices of his story, the wills and voices that twist and turn and alter and exalt language by their daily use of it. It is probable that critics who have called Mr. Frost's work lumpy and uneven have simply failed to understand his idea of what poetry ought to be.

But one of the finest examples of rhythm as the accompaniment of mood and meaning, organic rhythm at its best, is "The Santa Fé Trail" by Vachel Lindsay. And in all American literature we find no greater master of rhythm than he. It is our absurd fashion to treat his poems with jocular kindness because they are popular, and because they are so full of our folk lore and our folk spirit that we fail to perceive how very good they are. It may be worth while to say that when William Butler Yeats last visited this country he went to Chicago and met Vachel Lindsay. He greeted him as the first American poet of to-day.

Certainly Vachel Lindsay can do anything he likes with rhythm. His rhythms skip and turn somersaults, rock and reel, whirl giddily, bend and sway solemnly, march slowly in great circles, shake the air looser in the heavens and give a new exhilaration and exuberance to all but the stiff-necked and stupid. No other poem shows his power as a master of poetic music better than "The Santa Fé Trail."

In it are three tunes. First there is the tune of the racing automobiles going westward on the road that runs parallel to the double-track railroad, and of their honking horns that speak the souls of their owners. This is a crashing, blaring, hurrying, discordant tune. When we hear it we forget that we are reading poetry. We see those speeding cars. We watch the United States going by. We hear the shrill and the raucus voices of the horns. Nothing could be better in the way of verisimilitude of presentation.

> "On through the ranges the prairie-dog tills,
> Scooting past the cattle on the thousand hills. . .

Ho for the tear-horn, scare-horn, dare-horn,
Ho for the gay-horn, bark-horn, bay-horn.
Ho for Kansas, land that restores us
When houses choke us and great books bore us!"

It is to that pace that the first tune runs.

The second tune is the tune of the poet's reverie as he sits "by another big Santa Fé stone," a quiet and slow rhythm although it is closely related to the first noisy and speedy rhythm.

"My goal is the mystery the beggars win.
I am caught in the web the night-winds spin.
The edge of the wheat-ridge speaks to me;
I talk with the leaves of the mulberry tree."

And the third tune is the tune of the "Rachel-Jane" singing "far away," a little lyric melody not at all like the other tunes of the poem and yet belonging to both of them.

"Sweet, sweet, sweet, sweet!
Dew and glory,
Love and truth—
Sweet, sweet, sweet, sweet!"

We shall find this rhythmical verisimilitude of presentation in all of Mr. Lindsay's best work, his social and choral poetry, and we shall look a long time for it before we find it elsewhere. It is the very strength of "The Kallyope Yell." Who that has heard the "Kallyope" on circus day does not remember its "Willy, willy, wah-hoo!" and the humorous finality of its "Szz-fizz?" Who has not heard it squeal and shriek,

"I am the Kallyope, Kallyope, Kallyope,
Tooting hope, tooting hope, tooting hope, tooting hope!"

And then there is that much bigger and more important work, "The Congo," one of the best poems ever written about the American negro, a poem full of the strength, the music, the barbaric love of color, and the wild religion of the race. The rhythmical tune of it is so much a part of the sense of it and of the emotion and picturing that one can hardly separate it from them for purposes of analysis.

> "Fat black bucks in a wine-barrel room,
> Barrel-house kings with feet unstable,
> Sagged and reeled and pounded on the table,
> Pounded on the table,
> Beat an empty barrel with the handle of a broom,
> Hard as they were able,
> Boom, boom, boom,
> With a silk umbrella and the handle of a broom,
> Boomlay, boomlay, boomlay, boom.
> *Then* I had religion, *then* I had a vision
> I could not turn from their revel in derision.
>
> *Then I saw the Congo creeping through the black,*
> *Cutting through the forest with a golden track.*"

Perhaps enough has been said about organic rhythm in contemporary poetry to show what the best living poets think about it and how they use it. They are teaching us what men forgot in the ages when poetry was a bookish art, what minstrels have always made us remember and what lyric singers dream of—the beautiful art of *hearing*. Once again our ears are being trained to hear the beauty of the Word. Poetry to-day, like the best poetry of all periods, is the result of a sincere act of creation that unites meaning and emotion with melody, as with images and symbols. Nothing is artistically worse than indignation waltzing, unless it is sorrow capering to the lilt of a tango or joy droning a dirge.

THE SANTA FÉ TRAIL—A HUMORESQUE

I asked the old negro, "What is that bird that sings so well?" He answered, "That is the Rachel-Jane." "Hasn't it another name—lark, or thrush, or the like?" "No, jus' Rachel-Jane."

I

In which a Racing Auto comes from the East.

This is the order of the music of the morning:—
First, from the far East comes but a crooning;
The crooning turns to a sunrise singing.
Hark to the calm-horn, balm-horn, psalm-horn;
Hark to the faint-horn, quaint-horn, saint-horn . . . .

To be sung delicately to an improvised tune

Hark to the pace-horn, chase-horn, race-horn!
And the holy veil of the dawn has gone,
Swiftly the brazen car comes on.
It burns in the East as the sunrise burns
I see great flashes where the far trail turns.
Its eyes are lamps like the eyes of dragons.
It drinks gasoline from big red flagons.
Butting through the delicate mists of the morning,
It comes like lightning, goes past roaring.
It will hail all the wind-mills, taunting, ringing,
Dodge the cyclones,
Count the milestones,
On through the ranges the prairie-dog tills,
Scooting past the cattle on the thousand hills . . . .

To be sung or read with great speed

Ho for the tear-horn, scare-horn, dare-horn,
Ho for the gay-horn, bark-horn, bay-horn.
Ho for Kansas, land that restores us
When houses choke us, and great books bore us!
Sunrise Kansas, harvester's Kansas,
A million men have found you before us.

To be read or sung in a rolling bass with some deliberation.

II

In which Many Autos pass Westward.

I want live things in their pride to remain.
I will not kill one grasshopper vain

In an even, deliberate, narrative manner

Though he eats a hole in my shirt like a door.
I let him out, give him one chance more.
Perhaps, while he gnaws my hat in his whim,
Grasshopper lyrics occur to him.

I am a tramp by the long trail's border,
Given to squalor, rags and disorder.
I nap and amble and yawn and look,
Write fool-thoughts in my grubby book,
Recite to the children, explore at my ease,
Work when I work, beg when I please,
Give crank drawings, that make folks stare,
To the half-grown boys in the sunset-glare;
And get me a place to sleep in the hay
At the end of a live-and-let-live day.

I find in the stubble of the new-cut weeds
A whisper and a feasting, all one needs:
The whisper of the strawberries, white and red,
Here where the new-cut weeds lie dead.
But I would not walk all alone till I die
Without some life-drunk horns going by.
Up round this apple-earth they come,
Blasting the whispers of the morning dumb:—
Cars in a plain realistic row.
And fair dreams fade
When the raw horns blow.

On each snapping pennant
A big black name—
The careering city
Whence each car came.

Like a train-caller in Union Depot

They tour from Memphis, Atlanta, Savannah,
Tallahassee and Texarkana.
They tour from St. Louis, Columbus, Manistee,
They tour from Peoria, Davenport, Kankakee.
Cars from Concord, Niagara, Boston,
Cars from Topeka, Emporia and Austin.
Cars from Chicago, Hannibal, Cairo,
Cars from Alton, Oswego, Toledo.
Cars from Buffalo, Kokomo, Delphi,

Cars from Lodi, Carmi, Loami.
Ho for Kansas, land that restores us
When houses choke us, and great books bore us!
While I watch the highroad
And look at the sky,
While I watch the clouds in amazing grandeur
Roll their legions without rain
Over the blistering Kansas plain—
While I sit by the milestone
And watch the sky,
The United States
Goes by!

Listen to the iron horns, ripping, racking.
Listen to the quack horns, slack and clacking!
Way down the road, trilling like a toad,
Here comes the dice-horn, here comes the vice-horn,
Here comes the snarl-horn, brawl-horn, lewd-horn,
Followed by the prude-horn, bleak and squeaking:—
(Some of them from Kansas, some of them from Kansas.)
Here comes the hod-horn, plod-horn, sod-horn,
Nevermore-to-roam-horn, loam-horn, home-horn,
(Some of them from Kansas, some of them from Kansas.)

To be given very harshly with a snapping explosiveness

Far away the Rachel-Jane,
Not defeated by the horns,
Sings amid a hedge of thorns;
"Love and life,
Eternal youth—
Sweet, sweet, sweet, sweet!
Dew and glory,
Love and truth,
Sweet, sweet, sweet, sweet!"

To be read or sung well-nigh in a whisper

While smoke-black freights on the double-tracked rail-
road,
Driven as though by the foul-fiend's ox-goad,
Screaming to the west coast, screaming to the east,
Carry off a harvest, bring back a feast,
Harvesting machinery and harness for the beast.

Louder and louder, faster and faster

The hand-cars whiz, and rattle on the rails;
The sunlight flashes on the tin dinner-pails.

In a rolling bass with increasing deliberation

And then, in an instant,
Ye modern men,
Behold the procession once again!

With a snapping explosiveness

Listen to the iron horns, ripping, racking!
Listen to the wise-horn, desperate-to-advise horn,
Listen to the fast-horn, kill-horn, blast-horn . . . .

To be sung or read well-nigh in a whisper

Far away the Rachel-Jane,
Not defeated by the horns,
Sings amid a hedge of thorns:—
"Love and life,
Eternal youth—
Sweet, sweet, sweet, sweet!
Dew and glory,
Love and Truth—
Sweet, sweet, sweet, sweet!"

The mufflers open on a score of cars
With wonderful thunder,
CRACK, CRACK, CRACK,

To be brawled in the beginning with a snapping explosiveness ending in languorous chant

CRACK-CRACK, CRACK-CRACK,
CRACK-CRACK-CRACK, ...
Listen to the gold-horn . . . .
Old-horn . . . .
Cold-horn . . . .
And all of the tunes, till the night comes down
On hay-stack, and ant-hill, and wind-bitten town.

To be sung to exactly the same whispered tune as the first five lines

Then far in the west, as in the beginning,
Dim in the distance, sweet in retreating,
Hark to the faint-horn, quaint-horn, saint-horn,
Hark to the calm-horn, balm-horn, psalm-horn . . . .

This section beginning sonorously, ending in a languorous whisper

They are hunting the goals that they understand:—
San Francisco and the brown sea-sand.
My goal is the mystery the beggars win.
I am caught in the web the night-winds spin.
The edge of the wheat-ridge speaks to me;
I talk with the leaves of the mulberry tree.
And now I hear, as I sit all alone
In the dusk, by another big Santa-Fé stone,

The souls of the tall corn gathering round,
And the gay little souls of the grass in the ground.
Listen to the tale the cotton-wood tells
Listen to the wind-mills singing o'er the wells.
Listen to the whistling flutes without price
Of myriad prophets out of paradise . . . .
Hearken to the wonder that the night-air carries.
Listen . . . to . . . the . . . whisper . . .
Of . . . the . . . prairie . . . fairies
Singing over the fairy plain:
"Sweet, sweet, sweet, sweet!
Love and glory, stars and rain,
Sweet, sweet, sweet, sweet!"

To the same whispered tune as the Rachel-Jane song—but very slowly

Vachel Lindsay

COMING TO PORT

Our motion on the soft still misty river
Is like rest; and like the hours of doom
That rise and follow one another ever,
Ghosts of sleeping battle cruisers loom
And languish quickly in the liquid gloom.

From watching them your eyes in tears are gleaming,
And your heart is still; and like a sound
In silence is your stillness in the streaming
Of light-whispered laughter all around,
Where happy passengers are homeward bound.

Their sunny journey is in safety ending,
But for you no journey has an end;
The tears that to your eyes their light are lending
Shine in softness to no waiting friend;
Beyond the search of any eye they tend.

There is no nest for the unresting fever
Of your passion, yearning, hungry-veined;
There is no rest nor blessedness forever
That can clasp you, quivering and pained,
Whose eyes burn forward to the unattained.

Like time, and like the river's fateful flowing,
Flowing though the ship has come to rest,
Your love is passing through the mist and going,
Going infinitely from your breast,
Surpassing time on its immortal quest.

The ship draws softly to the place of waiting,
All flush forward with a joyful aim,
And while their hands with happy hands are mating,
Lips are laughing out a happy name—
You pause, and pass among them like a flame.

Max Eastman

MONOTONE

The monotone of the rain is beautiful,
And the sudden rise and slow relapse
Of the long multitudinous rain.

The sun on the hills is beautiful,
Or a captured sunset, sea-flung,
Bannered with fire and gold.

A face I know is beautiful—
With fire and gold of sky and sea,
And the peace of long warm rain.

Carl Sandburg

THE BOMBARDMENT

Slowly, without force, the rain drops into the city. It stops a moment on the carved head of Saint John, then slides on again, slipping and trickling over his stone cloak. It splashes from the lead conduit of a gargoyle, and falls from it in turmoil on the stones in the Cathedral square. Where are the people, and why does the fretted steeple sweep about in the sky? Boom! The sound swings against the rain. Boom again! After it, only water rushing in the gutters, and the turmoil from the spout of the gargoyle. Silence. Ripples and mutters. Boom!

The room is damp, but warm. Little flashes swarm about from the firelight. The lustres of the chandelier are bright, and clusters of rubies leap in the bohemian glasses on the *étagère*. Her hands are restless, but the white masses of her hair are quite still. Boom! Will it ever cease to torture, this iteration! Boom! The vibration shatters a glass on the *étagère*. It lies there, formless and glowing, with all its crimson gleams shot out of pattern, spilled, flowing red, blood-red. A thin bell-note pricks through the silence. A door creaks. The old lady speaks: "Victor, clear away that broken glass." "Alas! Madame, the bohemian glass!" "Yes, Victor, one hundred years ago my father brought it—" Boom! The room shakes, the servitor quakes. Another goblet shivers and breaks. Boom!

It rustles at the window-pane, the smooth, streaming rain, and he is shut within its clash and murmur. Inside is his candle, his table, his ink, his pen, and his dreams. He is thinking, and the walls are pierced with beams of sunshine, slipping through young green. A fountain tosses itself up at the blue sky, and through the spattered water in the basin he can see copper carp, lazily floating among cold leaves. A wind-harp in a cedar-tree grieves and whispers, and words blow into his brain, bubbled, iridescent, shooting up like flowers of fire, higher and higher. Boom! The flame-flowers snap on their slender stems. The fountain rears up in long broken spears of dishevelled water and flattens into the earth. Boom! And there is only the room, the table, the candle, and the sliding rain. Again, Boom!—Boom!—Boom! He stuffs his fingers into his ears. He sees corpses, and cries out in fright. Boom! It is night, and they are shelling the city! Boom! Boom!

A child wakes and is afraid, and weeps in the darkness. What has made the bed shake? "Mother, where are you? I am awake." "Hush, my Darling, I am here." "But, Mother, something so queer happened, the room shook." Boom! "Oh! What is it? What is the matter?" Boom! "Where is Father? I am so afraid." Boom! The child sobs and shrieks. The house trembles and creaks. Boom!

Retorts, globes, tubes, and phials lie shattered. All his trials oozing across the floor. The life that was his choosing, lonely, urgent, goaded by a hope, all gone. A weary man in a ruined laboratory, that is his story. Boom! Gloom and ignorance, and the jig of drunken brutes.

Diseases like snakes crawling over the earth, leaving trails of slime. Wails from people burying their dead. Through the window, he can see the rocking steeple. A ball of fire falls on the lead of the roof, and the sky tears apart on a spike of flame. Up the spire, behind the lacings of stone, zigzagging in and out of the carved tracings, squirms the fire. It spouts like yellow wheat from the gargoyles, coils round the head of Saint John, and aureoles him in light. It leaps into the night and hisses against the rain. The Cathedral is a burning stain on the white, wet night.

Boom! The Cathedral is a torch, and the houses next to it begin to scorch. Boom! The bohemian glass on the *étagère* is no longer there. Boom! A stalk of flame sways against the red damask curtains. The old lady cannot walk. She watches the creeping stalk and counts. Boom!—Boom!—Boom!

The poet rushes into the street, and the rain wraps him in a sheet of silver. But it is threaded with gold and powdered with scarlet beads. The city burns. Quivering, spearing, thrusting, lapping, streaming, run the flames. Over roofs, and walls, and shops, and stalls. Smearing its gold on the sky, the fire dances, lances itself through the doors, and lisps and chuckles along the floors.

The child wakes again and screams at the yellow petalled flower flickering at the window. The little red lips of flame creep along the ceiling beams.

The old man sits among his broken experiments and looks at the burning Cathedral. Now the streets are swarming with people. They seek shelter and crowd into the cellars. They shout and call, and over all, slowly and without force, the rain drops into the city. Boom! And the steeple crashes down among the people. Boom! Boom, again! The water rushes along the gutters. The fire roars and mutters. Boom!

Amy Lowell

THE VIRGIN'S SLUMBER SONG

Shoon-a-shoon,
I sing no psalm
  Little Man
Although I am
Out of David's
  House and Clann.
Shoon-a-shoon
I sing no psalm.
(Hush-a-hoo,
  Blowing of pine;
Hush-a-hoo,
  Lowing of kine:
Hush-a-hoo,
  Though even in sleep,
His ear can hear
  The shamrock's creep.)

Moons and moons
And suns galore,
  Match their gold
On Slumber's shore,
With your glittering
  Eyes that hold,
Moons and moons
And suns galore.
(Hush-a-hoo,
  Oceans of earth;
Hush-a-hoo,
  Motions of mirth:
Hush-a-hoo,
  Though over all,
His ear can hear
  The planets fall.)

O'er and o'er
And under all,
  Every star
Is now a ball,

For Your little
  Hands that are
O'er and o'er
And under all.

(Hush-a-hoo,
  Whirring of wings;
Hush-a-hoo,
  Stirring of strings:
Hush-a-hoo,
  Though in slumber deep,
His ear can hear
  My Song of Sleep.)

Francis Carlin

SEAL LULLABY*

Oh! hush thee, my baby, the night is behind us,
  And black are the waters that sparkled so green.
The moon, o'er the combers, looks downward to find us
  At rest in the hollows that rustle between.
Where billow meets billow, there soft be thy pillow;
  Ah, weary wee flipperling, curl at thy ease!
The storm shall not wake thee, nor shark overtake thee,
  Asleep in the arms of the slow-swinging seas.

Rudyard Kipling

THE LISTENERS

"Is there anybody there?" said the Traveller,
  Knocking on the moonlit door;
And his horse in the silence champed the grasses
  Of the forest's ferny floor;
 And a bird flew up out of the turret,
  Above the Traveller's head.
And he smote upon the door again a second time;
  "Is there anybody there?" he said.
But no one descended to the Traveller;
  No head from the leaf-fringed sill

*Taken from "The Jungle Book" by permission of The Century Co.

Leaned over and looked into his grey eyes,
  Where he stood perplexed and still.
But only a host of phantom listeners
  That dwelt in the lone house then
Stood listening in the quiet of the moonlight
  To that voice from the world of men:
Stood thronging the faint moonbeams on the dark stair,
  That goes down to the empty hall,
Hearkening in an air stirred and shaken
  By the lonely Traveller's call.
And he felt in his heart their strangeness,
  Their stillness answering his cry,
While his horse moved, cropping the dark turf,
  'Neath the starred and leafy sky;
For he suddenly smote on the door, even
  Louder, and lifted his head:—
"Tell them I came, and no one answered,
  That I kept my word," he said.
Never the least stir made the listeners,
  Though every word he spake
Fell echoing through the shadowiness of the still house
  From the one man left awake:
Ay, they heard his foot upon the stirrup,
  And the sound of iron on stone,
And how the silence surged softly backward,
  When the plunging hoofs were gone.

Walter de la Mare

REMEMBRANCE: GREEK FOLK SONG

Not unto the forest—not unto the forest, O my lover!
Why do you lead me to the forest!
  Joy is where the temples are,
  Lines of dancers swinging far,
  Drums and lyres and viols in the town—
It is dark in the forest.
  And the flapping leaves will blind me
  And the clinging vines will bind me
  And the thorny rose-boughs tear my saffron gown—
And I fear the forest.

Not unto the forest—not unto the forest, O my lover!
There was one once who led me to the forest.
Hand in hand we wandered mute
Where was neither lyre nor flute
Little stars were bright above the dusk
(*There was wind in the forest*)
And the thickets of wild rose
Breathed across our lips locked close
Dizzy perfumings of spikenard and of musk . . .
I am tired of the forest!

Not unto the forest—not unto the forest, O my lover—
Take me from the silence of the forest!
I will love you by the light
And the throb of drums at night
And the echoing of laughter in my ears,
But here in the forest
I am still, remembering
A forgotten, useless thing,
And my eyelids are locked down for fear of tears . . .
There is memory in the forest.

Margaret Widdemer

THE BACCHANTE TO HER BABE

Scherzo
Come, sprite, and dance! The sun is up,
The wind runs laughing down the sky
That brims with morning like a cup.
Sprite, we must race him,
We must chase him—
You and I!
And skim across the fuzzy heather—
You and joy and I together
Whirling by!

You merry little roll of fat!—
Made warm to kiss, and smooth to pat,
And round to toy with, like a cub;
To put one's nozzle in and rub

And breath you in like breath of kine,
Like juice of vine,
That sets my morning heart a-tingling,
Dancing, jingling,
All the glad abandon mingling
Of wind and wine!

Sprite, you are love, and you are joy,
A happiness, a dream, a toy,
A god to laugh with,
Love to chaff with,
The sun come down in tangled gold,
The moon to kiss, and spring to hold.

There was a time once, long ago,
Long—oh, long since . . . I scarcely know. .
Almost I had forgot . . .
There was a time when you were not,
You merry sprite, save as a strain,
The strange dull pain
Of green buds swelling
In warm, straight dwelling
That must burst to the April rain.
A little heavy I was then,
And dull—and glad to rest. And when
The travail came
In searing flame . . .
But, sprite, that was so long ago!—
A century!—I scarcely know.
Almost I had forgot
When you were not.

So, little sprite, come dance with me!
The sun is up, the wind is free!
Come now and trip it,
Romp and skip it,
Earth is young and so are we.
Sprite, you and I will dance together
On the heather,

Glad with all the procreant earth,
With all the fruitage of the trees,
And golden pollen on the breeze,
With plants that bring the grain to birth,
With beast and bird,
Feathered and furred,
With youth and hope and life and love,
And joy thereof—
While we are part of all, we two—
For my glad burgeoning in you!

So, merry little roll of fat,
Made warm to kiss and smooth to pat
And round to toy with, like a cub,
To put one's nozzle in and rub,
My god to laugh with,
Love to chaff with,
Come and dance beneath the sky,
You and I!
Look out with those round wondering eyes,
And squirm, and gurgle—and grow wise!

Eunice Tietjens

THE MOST-SACRED MOUNTAIN

Space, and the twelve clean winds of heaven,
And this sharp exultation, like a cry, after the slow six thousand feet of climbing!
This is Tai Shan, the beautiful, the most holy.

Below my feet the foot-hills nestle, brown with flecks of green; and lower down the flat brown plain, the floor of earth, stretches away to blue infinity.
Beside me in this airy space the temple roofs cut their slow curves against the sky,
And one black bird circles above the void.

Space, and the twelve clean winds are here;
And with them broods eternity—a swift, white peace, a presence manifest.

The rhythm ceases here. Time has no place.
  This is the end that has no end.

Here when Confucius came, a half a thousand years before the Nazarene, he stepped with me, thus into timelessness.
The stone beside us waxes old, the carven stone that says: *On this spot once Confucius stood and felt the smallness of the world below.*

Eunice Tietjens

SONG OF THE FULL CATCH

Here's good wind, here's sweet wind,
Here's good wind and my woman calls me!
Straight she stands there by the pine-tree,
Faithful waits she by the cedar,
She will smile and reach her hands
When she sees my thousand salmon!
Here's good wind and my woman calls me.

Here's clear water, here's swift water,
Here's bright water and my woman waits me!
She will call me from the sea's mouth—
Sweet her pine-bed when the morning
Lights my canoe and the river ends!
Here's good wind, here's swift water,
Strong as love when my woman calls me!

Constance Lindsay Skinner

LITTLE THINGS

There's nothing very beautiful and nothing very gay
About the rush of faces in the town by day,
But a light tan cow in a pale green mead,
That is very beautiful, beautiful indeed. . .
And the soft March wind, and the low March mist
Are better than kisses in the dark street kissed. . .
The fragrance of the forest when it wakes at dawn,
The fragrance of a trim green village lawn,
The hearing of the murmur of the rain at play—
These things are beautiful, beautiful as day!

And I shan't stand waiting for love or scorn
When the feast is laid for a day new-born. . .
Oh, better let the little things I loved when little
Return when the heart finds the great things brittle;
And better is a temple made of bark and thong
Than a tall stone temple that may stand too long.

Orrick Johns

IMAGES AND SYMBOLS

Thou shalt not make to thyself any graven image.

Ex. xx. 4.

Remember now thy Creator in the days of thy youth, while the evil days come not, nor the years draw nigh, when thou shalt say, I have no pleasure in them.

While the sun, or the light, or the moon, or the stars be not darkened, nor the clouds return after the rain:

In the days when the keepers of the house shall tremble, and the strong men shall bow themselves, and the grinders cease because they are few, and those that look out of the windows be darkened.

And the doors shall be shut in the streets, when the sound of the grinding is low, and he shall rise up at the voice of a bird, and all the daughters of musick shall be brought low;

Also, when they shall be afraid of that which is high, and fears shall be in the way, and the almond tree shall flourish, and the grasshopper shall be a burden, and desire shall fail: because man goeth to his long home, and the mourners go about the streets:

Or ever the silver cord be loosed, or the golden bowl be broken, or the pitcher broken at the fountain, or the wheel broken at the cistern.

Then shall the dust return to the earth as it was: and the spirit shall return unto God who gave it.

Ecc. xii. 1–7.

As we all know, the ancient Hebrews were forbidden by their religion to make graven images of persons or animals. This may have been the first Puritanical prohibition against the arts of painting and sculpture. But unlike many of our Puritanical prohibitions against the arts, it may have served a good purpose. The Hebrews were a small people, numerically, living in a small country, surrounded by other peoples whose worship was sensual and crude. Perhaps they worshipped Jahveh more spiritually and cleanly because they were not permitted to make an image of Him, or of the creatures made in His image. Perhaps that is one reason why the Hebrews gave the world a monotheistic religion, a religion spiritually perceived. We must remember that the ancient world had no science comparable to ours, and strong enough to strike a lance of light through the dark fabric of ignorance and superstition, and to shatter the gross, material gods behind it. And for this reason, and for other reasons, the development of monotheistic religion might have come much later in history if the ancient Hebrews had been allowed to make graven images and worship them after the manner of other nations of their time.

Now in all strong races the desire to give form and substance to ideas and emotions is strong and keenly felt. The Hebrews were no exception to this rule, and the images which they were not allowed to make with their fingers they made with their minds and gave to the world in a literature strong and clear and beautiful. The reader can not find, I suppose, in all of the literature written or rewritten in our language, a more excellent description of old age than that quoted from Ecclesiastes. It is a superb description because it is a universal truth stated in symbols that are absolutely true and appropriate. The majesty of these metaphors has given this passage everlasting life.

Let us take a single verse of this chapter and translate it into plain prose statement. Instead of saying "In the days when the keepers of the house shall tremble," let us say, "In the days when a man's arms have grown weak"; instead of "and the strong men shall bow themselves," let us say, "when the legs are bent"; instead of "and the grinders shall cease because they are few," "when a man is losing his teeth and his ability to masticate"; and instead of "and those that look out of the windows be darkened," "when a man grows blind." Having done this we find that we have stated a scientific fact. But we have stated it quite unfeelingly. And therefore, when we say it in this fashion, we awaken no sense of wistfulness, fear, tenderness, regret or compassion in the reader. Whereas the great original, by its transcendent beauty and truth imaginatively expressed, reaches our minds and hearts and abides with us. It induces sympathy.

Images and symbols, then, are valuable in literature because they present truth far more concisely, vividly, memorably and emotionally than literal statement.

The more we think about it the more certain we become that the use of images and symbols in poetry has an importance that is far more than literary or decorative. It is structural. It takes issue from a poet's realization of life. The sense impressions which go into the making of a poet's images and symbols are the result of what his nimble five wits have taught him. True images and symbols are not worked out intellectually and tacked upon the surface of a poem superficially, as a ribbon bow is tacked to a piece of lingerie in a department store. Like good rhythms, good images and symbols are the direct and truthful record of a poet's emotions and ideas and are capable of giving the reader a share in these ideas.

Whenever images and symbols have been devised by the "surface intellect" for the superficial adornment of a work of art and for the love of mere cleverness, analysis is likely to reveal weakness and æsthetic insincerity. Sometimes poems by very clever moderns fall short of being good poems simply because the symbols used in them could never have been realized and profoundly felt and are, therefore, rather more clever than true. Says Wallace Stevens, in "Tattoo"

> "The light is like a spider.
> It crawls over the water.
> It crawls over the edges of the snow.
> It crawls under your eyelids
> And spreads its webs there—
> Its two webs."

Read casually that sounds well enough. But it will not bear analysis. A spider is a small, dark, rayed object moving in darts and jerks. Is light a spider in form, color, texture, movement, power? Do spiders *crawl* over water, over the edges of snow, under our eyelids? It sounds improbable. To read these lines thoughtfully is to be convinced that light is not at all like a spider. It is difficult to conceive of any interpretation of the poem that would reveal truth in this symbol.

Let us compare it with another little poem, by Carl Sandburg. The poem is called "Fog" and the new symbol used to make us feel a sense of the fog is what makes all the sum and substance of it.

> "The fog comes
> on little cat feet.
>
> It sits looking
> over harbor and city
> on silent haunches
> and then moves on."

Evidently Mr. Sandburg wishes to give us a sense of the quietness that is always in a fog. Nothing else but a cat moves so silently as a fog. The symbolism is daring, but it is quite true and has been truthfully felt. If we know what a fog is like, we can feel it for ourselves. It is whimsical, to be sure, and these lines have nothing more to recommend them than the honesty and suggestive power of this symbol or image. But having that, they justify themselves.

All images and symbols used in poetry can be tested by the reader. For a lover of poetry with a sympathetic imagination will be able to discriminate between sincere craftsmanship and that which is spurious. He will learn for himself why a nightingale is not a real bird in the poem of a man who has never heard one sing, but feels called upon to maunder about a nightingale's song. He will learn why an English primrose, beloved of Wordsworth, becomes a false flower in a poem by an American mimic who has never seen one, who would be wiser to write about goldenrod. He will understand why it is a heinous æsthetic sin to bring heather into a poem as a rhyme for weather, when the word is not only irrelevant, but only half understood through the literature of others. And if he will contrast enough good poems with enough bad ones, the reader will come to feel that poets capable of such artistic immoralities are only clowns wearing laurel wreaths that they have snatched from brows more reverend than their own.

The poet's purpose is not utilitarian, to be sure. He is no lawyer making a contract. But he must be as loyal to his own code as the lawyer to the law. It is his power and privilege to surround facts with beauty, or with such impressive qualities as are relevant to those facts. But he must serve as a priest celebrates a sacrament. His images and symbols must be the true outward and visible signs of the grace given him.

Now the poets in the period immediately preceding our own used images and symbols—poets always have used them, for it is well nigh impossible to make a readable poem without them—but they were not content simply to show the picture and suggest the meaning. At least, many of them were not content with this. They wanted to explain their own symbols. They wanted to moralize with them. They poured a good deal of water into the nectar they offered us. And sometimes it tasted like a thin and feeble gruel.

In our time, however, the best poets have given emphatic evidence of the belief that it is almost enough, if not quite enough, to present images and symbols adequately and let them work their own spell. This accounts, in part, for the brevity of much of our contemporary poetry and for the consciseness of it. It accounts, in part, for the beauty of it. But it makes it necessary for images and symbols to be, in and of themselves, true and valuable in relation to the mood of the poem, since the poet will not explain them or direct our attention to their meaning.

Let us read and discuss first a few poems in which mental images are used simply for the sake of the picture they present and for the sense impressions which can be shared with the reader. And then let us read and discuss other poems in which images are used for their value as symbols.

The poets who have called themselves Imagists are more emphatic than other poets in affirming their belief in the use of images. They are as emphatic as it is possible to be and keep sanity. Briefly stated, this is their ideal of what a poem should be:—an image, or series of related images, presented in organic rhythm and suggesting a mood. For the simple and direct lyric cry, for the philosophical suggestions that show the soul of the folk, for the plain earth-wisdom of simple men and women, for that proud and prescient sense of the meaning of life which has been the glory of English poetry in the work of many masters, the Imagists seem to care very little. And their best work is often done when they forget to be Imagists and become poets. But there is a measure of truth in their credo. And it has value as an antithetical remedy for the ills of Victorian diffuseness, vagueness and sentimentality. Almost any of the poems of H. D. are admirable illustrations of Imagism. The poem quoted at the end of this chapter, "Sea Gods," depends for its effect upon *our ability to see and smell and feel and share intellectually* what is told in it.

"But we bring violets,
Great masses, single, sweet,
Wood-violets, stream-violets,
Violets from a wet marsh.

This lyric, and many of the other lyrics by H. D., Richard Aldington, and the other Imagists, have undeniable beauty, for which we should be thankful. But we do not want all poetry to be of this kind. We need a more robust spiritual food. We can not live on candied flowers. And Imagists should use more verbs if they would stir us deeply. On the other hand, although it is clear that, if the tenets of Imagism became dogmas for any great number of poets, we should need a reaction against them as much as ever we needed reaction against the minor Victorians, we should not allow ourselves to belittle their very real achievements. Imagists are seldom guilty of trite phrases and dull similes. They have brought new color into poetry and new impressions of the beauty of the external world.

Many critics have come to believe that Amy Lowell is the

greatest of the Imagists, indeed more than an Imagist. Certainly she can do marvellous things with images and symbols. Like Aholiab, son of Ahisamech, she is "an engraver, and a cunning workman, and an embroiderer in blue, and in purple, and in scarlet, and fine linen." Other poets must lay the floor plans and rear the props that uphold our tabernacle of poetry; others must fashion an ark to keep sacred forever the covenant that we make with beauty and virtue. Others, to speak more briefly, must be our realists and idealists. Miss Lowell is primarily a cunning workman, an artificer in brilliant colors, an engraver of fine designs.

No one can rightly evaluate Miss Lowell's work who will not accept the fact that she is always a conscious artist. She goes far afield, sometimes, for the materials of her poems. But she selects them with care. She uses the lives of people who live on New England farms to-day, or the lives of quaint swashbucklers who lived a century ago and half a world away. She shows pictures of strange and vivid things that she has seen in a wide and vivid world. She makes these pictures out of the juxtaposition of odd trifles with scents and hues and textures that she likes. And in her best work she gives us frosty designs in thought as clear as glass, flashing patterns of feeling as warmly colored as glossy skeins of embroidery silk—blue and purple and scarlet, silver and gold. She distills sensations that sting like fiery liqueur. She threads together impressions as frail as a flutter of old lace. She is a poet of vigorous, penetrative and incessantly communicative imagination.

In her "Malmaison" and "1777," as in all of the poems in her recent book, "Can Grande's Castle," Miss Lowell has given us clearly and copiously imagined pictures from history. Here is an admirable picture of an English inn taken from her poem, "Hedge Island." It is simply a series of related images, but we see the picture. *We have been in that inn!*

"A long oak corridor. Then a burst of sunshine through leaded windows, spangling a floor, iris-tinting rounds of beef, and flaked veal pies, and rose-marbled hams, and great succulent cheeses. Wine-glasses take it and break it, and it quivers away over the table-cloth in faint rainbows; or, straight and sudden, stamps a startling silver whorl on the polished side of a teapot of hot bohea. A tortoise-shell cat naps between red geraniums, and myrtle sprigs tap the stuccoed wall, gently blowing to and fro."

This is the Imagist method, just the same method used in the poem by H. D. from which we quoted. But this poem is a narrative and that was a lyric.

To be sure, Miss Lowell's rampant imagination sometimes runs away with itself for sheer joy in the clatter it can make in passing. When this happens she gives us lurid little bits of clever mental agony like "Red Slippers." Or perhaps she finds forms and qualities in Nature for which Nature herself would seek in vain. In a recent poem about the war and the sugar-beet industry she made delightful red and yellow and globular pictures of a vegetable that looks like a long, grayish turnip. But since her imagination yields the real moonshine of poetry we should be willing to forgive the occasional babble. For a magical imagination Miss Lowell assuredly has.

None of her poems is a better illustration of the Imagist method than her "Cornucopia of Red and Green Comfits," a "Phantasm" of the great war recently published in *The Independent*. It is also typical of her genius.

It sometimes happens that poets who are not Imagists write poems that have a beauty of the kind Imagists often seek in vain, because they seek too intellectually and self-consciously. Such a poem is "Silver," by Walter de la Mare. It is a color study, delighting us as a fine painting would. It has the additional charm of a cool, liquid rhythm. Few poems of our day have so great a beauty of imagery. For every image is true. Anyone can see the same thing at the right place and time.

"Couched in his kennel, like a log,
With paws of silver sleeps the dog;
From their shadowy cote the white breasts peep
Of doves in a silver-feathered sleep."

This is all said in magical words. Millions of men and women and children have seen this silver symphony on moonlit nights. Now it is poetry.

In his "Old Woman of The Roads" Padraic Colum uses images in a lyrical fashion of his own to express the homely emotions of a poor and homeless old woman. They are all true images of things that belong in simple cottages and hold the love of simple women everywhere. The "white and blue and speckled store" of "shining delph," the "hearth and stool and all," the "clock with weights and chains," the "pile of turf," are all pictures of the desire in the old woman's heart. They come very near to being symbols.

Francis Carlin's quatrain, "The Cuckoo," is good imagery, deftly made of sound and color.

> "A Sound but from an Echo made
> And a body wrought of colored Shade,
> Have blent themselves into a bird
> But seldom seen and scarcely heard."

Very beautiful poetry can be made by the use of images. But a more subtle skill is required of the poet who would make us perceive, through his imagery, something greater and more important than the images presented. And the beauty of symbolism leads the human spirit farther than the beauty of imagery. Many of the best contemporary poets have written poems remarkable for beautiful symbolism, poems that are, in reality, large, compound, and subtly amplified metaphors. One of the most notable of these is Rupert Brooke's "The Great Lover."

It is descriptive of the hearty love of life, nothing more difficult and complex than that. And Rupert Brooke, who was a very keen and sentient poet, has used admirably chosen images of familiar things to symbolize his theme. When he enumerated the many things that made life blessed for him, he was speaking truly, doubtless, of each one of them. But he was doing more than that. In the strongest way in the world, and in a very beautiful way, he was saying over and over again that he loved life and found it good. This poem may well be considered the loveliest thing he ever wrote, although patriotism has made his sonnets more popular. Here is a short passage which gives but a taste of the flavor of the whole:

> "These have I loved:
> White plates and cups, clean-gleaming,
> Ringed with blue lines; and feathery, faery dust;
> Wet roofs, beneath the lamp-light; the strong crust
> Of friendly bread; and many-tasting food;
> Rainbows; and the blue, bitter smoke of wood;"

William H. Davies is another English poet who has written poems remarkable for their beautiful symbolism. In one famous little lyric he makes the thunderstorm the symbol of his own moods. In another poem, which is a brilliant narrative about two women whose lives were none too good, he uses the bird of paradise—an amazingly accurate, vivid and ironical symbol—to stand for something sacred which poor Nell Barnes had loved and cherished.

> "Not for the world! Take care!
> Don't touch that bird of paradise,
> Perched on the bed post there!"

A lesser artist might have explained in detail just what the bird of paradise meant to poor Nell. He might have moralized about the state of her conscience. He might have been sentimental. He might have wetted the feathers of his own symbol with his own tears and washed out their lovely color. But with fine, clean, sharp art Mr. Davies does none of these things. He lets the symbol stand out clearly and arouses in us a more profound pity than could ever have been aroused by many stanzas of explanation.

Still another fine use of symbols is to be found in "Frost To-night" by Edith M. Thomas. The symbols themselves are old, frost meaning death, flowers meaning the harvest of life, but they are used with a grave and sincere simplicity which makes them the poet's own. For this is quite enough to prevent the possibility of a trite effect, and to insure a sense of beautiful authenticity.

Similarly Adelaide Crapsey uses an old symbol, the wind, meaning fear and sorrow, but uses it masterfully in one of her little "Cinquains," "Night Winds."

> "The old,
> Old winds that blew
> When chaos was, what do
> They tell the clattered trees that I
> Should weep?"

The truth seems to be that through all the ages the same symbols have been used again and again. Wherever men and women have been led by life to think and feel certain things in a certain way, they have used certain symbols as the inevitable way of expressing themselves. In hot countries everlasting heat is the symbol of damnation; in cold countries, everlasting cold. Again and again the seasons, spring, summer, autumn and winter are made to mean birth, growth, maturity, death. A winding river is life. The seed of the man is the child. The banner is the nation. The summit is success. The uphill climb is effort. The tree is the race, the family, the strong man.

The use of the tree as a symbol of the strong man is particularly noticeable in poems about our American strong man, Abraham Lincoln. Many poems liken Lincoln to a tree. John Gould Fletcher calls him a "gaunt scraggly pine." The phrase is meaningful. Edwin Markham, writing with a similar idea in mind, says:

> "And when he fell in whirlwind, he went down
> As when a kingly cedar green with boughs
> Goes down with a great shout upon the hills,
> And leaves a lonesome place against the sky."

This is probably the best of all poems about Lincoln. And it is a very fine study for those interested in symbolism. For in it the qualities of natural objects, rocks, rain, and other works of external nature, are used as symbols of spiritual qualities in the great man.

If such symbols are old, as old as the ages, how is it that they retain their strength and freshness? The answer to that question is one word—Realization. They will seem trite and ineffectual, these symbols, or any symbols, if they are used artificially and insincerely or as the result of feeble, puerile, ineffectual realization. But when a poet feels the force of any symbol in relation to his own mood and emotion, the symbol will take, through the medium of his personality, a new individuality and authenticity. To be insincere in the world of action is to be less than ethical. To be insincere in the world of poetry is to be less than artistic.

Just before the war a book was published purporting to be a book of poems by founders of a new school of poetry. It was called "Spectra" and signed by collaborators, Emanuel Morgan and Anne Knish. In it were cleverly preposterous verses—a sort of symbolic gibberish—which deceived many clever persons—clever persons, mind—into taking the book seriously. Well known poets and well known critics wrote about that book and even wrote to the authors of it, telling them that the poor, stupid old world would understand them some day. But insincerity of conception and execution was so patent in every line that one wonders how anyone could have been deceived. Certainly the stupid old World was not deceived, although it howled with laughter at lines like the following:

"Two cocktails around a smile,
A grape-fruit after grace,
Flowers in an aisle
. . . Were your face!"

The stupid old World was right. Laughter was what the authors longed for and expected. "Spectra" was simply an elaborate spoof, a book made in ridicule of the insincerities of many of the "saffron schools." The attempt to show by exaggeration how absurd such literary insincerities can become was worth while. It is a noteworthy fact that the wise—in current opinion—were deceived. The simple and sincere were not. "Spectra" was written by two very good poets, Arthur Davison Ficke and Witter Bynner.

We have often been told that the masters of symbolism come from the Orient. This may be because the making of strong symbols is a task for leisure and meditation, and the Orient loves leisure and meditation as the Occident loves action and thought.

But whatever the reason may be, it is fairly probable that no poet of our time is a greater master of symbolism than Sir Rabindranath Tagore. As has been said in a previous chapter, symbolism is the very structure and symmetry of design in his poems written in English. We can pick up his books and open them almost at random, to find strong, sure symbolism on any page.

"The current in which I drifted ran rapid and strong when I was young. The spring breeze was spendthrift of itself, the trees were on fire with flowers; and the birds never slept from singing."

Pages could give no better idea of youth. There he goes on to to say,

"Now that youth has ebbed and I am stranded on the bank, I can hear the deep music of all things, and the sky opens to me its heart of stars."

Pages could give no better idea of age with its spiritual compensations.

The poetry of Kahlil Gibran, too, is almost entirely a poetry of symbolism. His poems are parables, not designs in rhyme, rhythm or imagery, although his rhythms are clear and pleasing. In his book, "The Madman," we have the best parables that can be found in contemporary poetry. And each may be interpreted according to the whimsy of the reader. "The Fox" is a sage little parable. It may mean ambition—illusion—the usual trend of human life—fate—or what you will.

"A fox looked at his shadow at sunrise and said, 'I will have a camel for lunch to-day.' And all morning he went about looking for camels. But at noon he saw his shadow again—and he said, 'A mouse will do.'"

But great poets of the Occident are also masters of symbolism. One of the most beautiful modern poems made out of a symbol is "Cargoes" by John Masefield. Only one symbol is used—the cargo. But in terms of that symbol, and in three short stanzas, Mr. Masefield describes commerce in three great periods of the world's history. And he contrives to give us a sense of the world's growth in democracy without saying a word about it.

The greatest piece of imagery and symbolism in contemporary poetry, however, may well be "The Bull" by Ralph Hodgson. This animal epic is warm, brilliant, magnificent. Each image in the rich sequence of stanzas has its own glistening pomp. All, taken together, are symbols that suggest the crescive power of life and the wistfulness of its waning into darkness.

CARGOES

Quinquireme of Nineveh from distant Ophir,
Rowing home to haven in sunny Palestine,
  With a cargo of ivory
  And apes and peacocks,
Sandalwood, cedarwood, and sweet, white wine.

Stately Spanish galleon coming from the Isthmus,
Dipping through the Tropics by the palm-green shores
  With a cargo of diamonds,
  Emeralds, amethysts,
Topazes, and cinnamon, and gold moidores.

Dirty British coaster with a salt-caked smoke stack,
Butting through the channel in the mad March days
  With a cargo of Tyne coal,
  Road rails, pig lead,
Firewood, ironware, and cheap tin trays.

THE BULL

See an old unhappy bull,
Sick in soul and body both,
Slouching in the undergrowth
Of the forest beautiful,
Banished from the herd he led,
Bulls and cows a thousand head.

Cranes and gaudy parrots go
Up and down the burning sky;
Tree-top cats purr drowsily
In the dim-day green below;
And troops of monkeys, nutting, some,
All disputing, go and come;

And things abominable sit
Picking offal buck or swine,
On the mess and over it
Burnished flies and beetles shine,
And spiders big as bladders lie
Under hemlocks ten foot high;

And a dotted serpent curled
Round and round and round a tree,
Yellowing its greenery,
Keeps a watch on all the world,
All the world and this old bull
In the forest beautiful.

Bravely by his fall he came:
One he led, a bull of blood
Newly come to lustihood,
Fought and put his prince to shame,
Snuffed and pawed the prostrate head
Tameless even while it bled.

There they left him, every one,
Left him there without a lick,

Left him for the birds to pick,
Left him there for carrion,
Vilely from their bosom cast
Wisdom, worth and love at last.

When the lion left his lair
And roared his beauty through the hills,
And the vultures pecked their quills
And flew into the middle air,
Then this prince no more to reign
Came to life and lived again.

He snuffed the herd in far retreat,
He saw the blood upon the ground,
And snuffed the burning airs around
Still with beevish odours sweet,
While the blood ran down his head
And his mouth ran slaver red.

Pity him, this fallen chief,
All his splendour, all his strength,
All his body's breadth and length
Dwindled down with shame and grief,
Half the bull he was before,
Bones and leather, nothing more.

See him standing dewlap-deep
In the rushes at the lake,
Surly, stupid, half asleep,
Waiting for his heart to break
And the birds to join the flies
Feasting at his bloodshot eyes,—

Standing with his head hung down
In a stupor, dreaming things:
Green savannas, jungles brown,
Battlefields and bellowings,
Bulls undone and lions dead
And vultures flapping overhead.

Dreaming things: of days he spent
With his mother gaunt and lean
In the valley warm and green,
Full of baby wonderment,
Blinking out of silly eyes
At a hundred mysteries;

Dreaming over once again
How he wandered with a throng
Of bulls and cows a thousand strong,
Wandered on from plain to plain,
Up the hill and down the dale,
Always at his mother's tail;

How he lagged behind the herd,
Lagged and tottered, weak of limb,
And she turned and ran to him
Blaring at the loathly bird
Stationed always in the skies,
Waiting for the flesh that dies.

Dreaming maybe of a day
When her drained and drying paps
Turned him to the sweets and saps,
Richer fountains by the way,
And she left the bull she bore
And he looked to her no more;

And his little frame grew stout,
And his little legs grew strong,
And the way was not so long;
And his little horns came out,
And he played at butting trees
And boulder-stones and tortoises,

Joined a game of knobby skulls
With the youngsters of his year,
All the other little bulls,
Learning both to bruise and bear,

Learning how to stand a shock
Like a little bull of rock.

Dreaming of a day less dim,
Dreaming of a time less far,
When the faint but certain star
Of destiny burned clear for him,
And a fierce and wild unrest
Broke the quiet of his breast,

And the gristles of his youth
Hardened in his comely pow,
And he came to fighting growth,
Beat his bull and won his cow,
And flew his tail and trampled off
Past the tallest, vain enough,

And curved about in splendour full
And curved again and snuffed the airs
As who should say Come out who dares!
And all beheld a bull, a Bull,
And knew that here was surely one
That backed for no bull, fearing none.

And the leader of the herd
Looked and saw, and beat the ground,
And shook the forest with his sound,
Bellowed at the loathly bird
Stationed always in the skies,
Waiting for the flesh that dies.

Dreaming, this old bull forlorn,
Surely dreaming of the hour
When he came to sultan power,
And they owned him master-horn,
Chiefest bull of all among
Bulls and cows a thousand strong.

And in all the tramping herd
Not a bull that barred his way,

Not a cow that said him nay,
Not a bull or cow that erred
In the furnace of his look
Dared a second, worse rebuke;

Not in all the forest wide,
Jungle, thicket, pasture, fen,
Not another dared him then,
Dared him and again defied;
Not a sovereign buck or boar
Came a second time for more.

Not a serpent that survived
Once the terrors of his hoof
Risked a second time reproof,
Came a second time and lived,
Not a serpent in its skin
Came again for discipline;

Not a leopard bright as flame,
Flashing fingerhooks of steel,
That a wooden tree might feel,
Met his fury once and came
For a second reprimand,
Not a leopard in the land.

Not a lion of them all,
Not a lion of the hills,
Hero of a thousand kills,
Dared a second fight and fall,
Dared that ram terrific twice,
Paid a second time the price. . . .

Pity him, this dupe of dream,
Leader of the herd again
Only in his daft old brain,
Once again the bull supreme
And bull enough to bear the part
Only in his tameless heart.

Pity him that he must wake;
Even now the swarm of flies
Blackening his bloodshot eyes
Bursts and blusters round the lake,
Scattered from the feast half-fed,
By great shadows overhead.

And the dreamer turns away
From his visionary herds
And his splendid yesterday,
Turns to meet the loathly birds
Flocking round him from the skies,
Waiting for the flesh that dies.

Ralph Hodgson

SEA GODS

I

They say there is no hope—
Sand—drift—rocks—rubble of the sea—
The broken hulk of a ship,
Hung with shreds of rope,
Pallid under the cracked pitch.

They say there is no hope
To conjure you—
No whip of the tongue to anger you—
No hate of words
You must rise to refute.

They say you are twisted by the sea,
You are cut apart
By wave-break upon wave-break,
That you are misshapen by the sharp rocks,
Broken by the rasp and after-rasp.

That you are cut, torn, mangled,
Torn by the stress and beat,
No stronger than the strips of sand
Along your ragged beach.

II

But we bring violets,
Great masses—single, sweet,
Wood-violets, stream-violets,
Violets from a wet marsh.

Violets in clumps from hills,
Tufts with earth at the roots,
Violets tugged from rocks,
Blue violets, moss, cliff, river-violets.

Yellow violets' gold,
Burnt with a rare tint—
Violets like red ash
Among tufts of grass.

We bring deep-purple
Bird-foot violets.
We bring the hyacinth-violet,
Sweet, bare, chill to the touch—
And violets whiter than the in-rush
Of your own white surf.

III

For you will come,
You will yet haunt men in ships,
You will trail across the fringe of strait
And circle the jagged rocks.

You will trail across the rocks
And wash them with your salt,
You will curl between sand-hills—
You will thunder along the cliff—
Break—retreat—get fresh strength—
Gather and pour weight upon the beach.

You will draw back,
And the ripple on the sand-shelf
Will be witness of your track.

O privet-white, you will paint
The lintel of wet sand with froth.
You will bring myrrh-bark
And drift laurel-wood from hot coasts.
When you hurl high—high—
We will answer with a shout.

For you will come,
You will come,
You will answer our taut hearts,
You will break the lie of men's thoughts,
And cherish and shelter us.

H. D.

ARIZONA

THE WINDMILLS

The windmills, like great sunflowers of steel,
Lift themselves proudly over the straggling houses;
And at their feet the deep blue-green alfalfa
Cuts the desert like the stroke of a sword.

Yellow melon flowers
Crawl beneath the withered peach-trees;
A date-palm throws its heavy fronds of steel
Against the scoured metallic sky.

The houses, double-roofed for coolness,
Cower amid the manzanita scrub.
A man with jingling spurs
Walks heavily out of a vine-bowered doorway,
Mounts his pony, rides away.

The windmills stare at the sun.
The yellow earth cracks and blisters.
Everything is still.

In the afternoon
The wind takes dry waves of heat and tosses them,
Mingled with dust, up and down the streets,
Against the belfry with its green bells:

And, after sunset, when the sky
Becomes a green and orange fan,
The windmills, like great sunflowers on dried stalks,
Stare hard at the sun they cannot follow.

Turning, turning, forever turning
In the chill night-wind that sweeps over the valley,
With the shriek and the clank of the pumps groaning beneath them,
And the choking gurgle of tepid water.

John Gould Fletcher

LINCOLN, THE MAN OF THE PEOPLE

When the Norn Mother saw the Whirlwind Hour
Greatening and darkening as it hurried on,
She left the Heaven of Heroes and came down
To make a man to meet the mortal need.
She took the tried clay of the common road—
Clay warm yet with the genial heat of Earth,
Dasht through it all a strain of prophecy;
Tempered the heap with thrill of human tears;
Then mixt a laughter with the serious stuff.
Into the shape she breathed a flame to light
That tender, tragic, ever-changing face;
And laid on him a sense of the Mystic Powers,
Moving—all husht—behind the mortal vail.
Here was a man to hold against the world,
A man to match the mountains and the sea.

The color of the ground was in him, the red earth;
The smack and tang of elemental things:
The rectitude and patience of the cliff;
The good-will of the rain that loves all leaves;
The friendly welcome of the wayside well;
The courage of the bird that dares the sea;
The gladness of the wind that shakes the corn;
The pity of the snow that hides all scars;
The secrecy of streams that make their way
Under the mountain to the rifted rock;
The tolerance and equity of light

That gives as freely to the shrinking flower
As to the great oak flaring to the wind—
To the grave's low hill as to the Matterhorn
That shoulders out the sky. Sprung from the West,
He drank the valorous youth of a new world.
The strength of virgin forests braced his mind,
The hush of spacious prairies stilled his soul.
His words were oaks in acorns; and his thoughts
Were roots that firmly gript the granite truth.

Up from log cabin to the Capitol,
One fire was on his spirit, one resolve—
To send the keen ax to the root of wrong,
Clearing a free way for the feet of God,
The eyes of conscience testing every stroke,
To make his deed the measure of a man.
With the fine gesture of a kingly soul,
He built the rail-pile and he built the State,
Pouring his splendid strength through every blow:
The grip that swung the ax in Illinois
Was on the pen that set a people free.

So came the Captain with the mighty heart;
And when the judgment thunders split the house,
Wrenching the rafters from their ancient rest,
He held the ridgepole up, and spikt again
The rafters of the Home. He held his place—
Held the long purpose like a growing tree—
Held on through blame and faltered not at praise.
And when he fell in whirlwind, he went down
As when a lordly cedar, green with boughs,
Goes down with a great shout upon the hills,
And leaves a lonesome place against the sky.

Edwin Markham

STANDARDS

White is the skimming gull on the sombre green of the fir-trees,
Black is the soaring gull on a snowy glimmer of cloud.

Charles Wharton Stork

PANDORA'S SONG

Of wounds and sore defeat
I made my battle stay;
Wingèd sandals for my feet
I wove of my delay;
Of weariness and fear,
I made my shouting spear;
Of loss, and doubt, and dread,
And swift oncoming doom
I made a helmet for my head
And a floating plume.
From the shutting mist of death,
And the failure of the breath,
I made a battle-horn to blow
Across the vales of overthrow.
O hearken, love, the battle-horn!
The triumph clear, the silver scorn!
O hearken where the echoes bring,
Down the grey disastrous morn,
Laughter and rallying!

William Vaughn Moody

A WHITE IRIS

Tall and clothed in samite,
Chaste and pure,
In smooth armor,—
Your head held high
In its helmet
Of silver:
Jean D'Arc riding
Among the sword blades!

Has Spring for you
Wrought visions,
As it did for her
In a garden?

Pauline B. Barrington

"FROST TO-NIGHT"

Apple-green west and an orange bar,
And the crystal eye of a lone, one star . . .
And, "Child, take the shears and cut what you will.
Frost to-night—so clear and dead-still."

Then I sally forth, half sad, half proud,
And I come to the velvet, imperial crowd,
The wine-red, the gold, the crimson, the pied,—
The dahlias that reign by the garden-side.

The dahlias I might not touch till to-night!
A gleam of the shears in the fading light,
And I gathered them all,—the splendid throng,
And in one great sheaf I bore them along.

In my garden of Life with its all-late flowers
I heed a Voice in the shrinking hours:
"Frost to-night—so clear and dead-still . . ."
Half sad, half proud, my arms I fill.

Edith M. Thomas.

SILVER

Slowly, silently, now the moon
Walks the night in her silver shoon;
This way, and that, she peers and sees
Silver fruit upon silver trees;
One by one the casements catch
Her beams beneath the silvery thatch;
Couched in his kennel, like a log,
With paws of silver sleeps the dog;
From their shadowy cote the white breasts peep
Of doves in a silver-feathered sleep;
A harvest mouse goes scampering by,
With silver claws, and a silver eye;
And moveless fish in the water gleam,
By silver reeds in a silver stream.

Walter de la Mare

FROM "VARIATIONS"

VI

You are as beautiful as white clouds
Flowing among bright stars at night:
You are as beautiful as pale clouds
Which the moon sets alight.

You are as lovely as golden stars
Which white clouds try to brush away:
You are as bright as golden stars
When they come out to play.

You are as glittering as those stairs
Of stone down which the blue brooks run:
You are as shining as sea-waves
All hastening to the sun.

Conrad Aiken

AN OLD WOMAN OF THE ROADS

O, to have a little house!
To own the hearth and stool and all!
The heaped up sods upon the fire,
The pile of turf against the wall!

To have a clock with weights and chains
And pendulum swinging up and down!
A dresser filled with shining delph,
Speckled and white and blue and brown!

I could be busy all the day
Clearing and sweeping hearth and floor,
And fixing on their shelf again
My white and blue and speckled store!

I could be quiet there at night
Beside the fire and by myself,
Sure of a bed and loth to leave
The ticking clock and the shining delph!

Och! but I'm weary of mist and dark,
And roads where there's never a house nor bush,
And tired I am of bog and road,
And the crying wind and the lonesome hush!

And I am praying to God on high,
And I am praying Him night and day,
For a little house—a house of my own—
Out of the wind's and the rain's way.

Padraic Colum

THE DARK CAVALIER

I am the Dark Cavalier; I am the Last Lover:
  My arms shall welcome you when other arms are tired;
I stand to wait for you, patient in the darkness,
  Offering forgetfulness of all that you desired.

I ask no merriment, no pretense of gladness,
  I can love heavy lids and lips without their rose;
Though you are sorrowful you will not weary me;
  I will not go from you when all the tired world goes.

I am the Dark Cavalier; I am the Last Lover;
  I promise faithfulness no other lips may keep;
Safe in my bridal place, comforted by darkness,
  You shall lie happily, smiling in your sleep.

Margaret Widdemer

SAID A BLADE OF GRASS

Said a blade of grass to an autumn leaf,
"You make such a noise falling! You scatter all my winter dreams."
Said the leaf indignant, "Low-born and low-dwelling!
Songless, peevish thing! You live not in the upper air and you can not tell the sound of singing."
Then the autumn leaf lay down upon the earth and slept.

And when Spring came she waked again—and she was a blade of grass.
And when it was autumn and her winter sleep was upon her, and above her through all the air the leaves were falling, she muttered to herself, "O these autumn leaves! They make such a noise! They scatter all my winter dreams."

Kahlil Gibran

SYMBOLS

I saw history in a poet's song,
In a river reach and a gallows-hill,
In a bridal bed, and a secret wrong,
In a crown of thorns: in a daffodil.

I imagined measureless time in a day,
And starry space in a wagon-road,
And the treasure of all good harvests lay
In a single seed that the sower sowed.

My garden-wind had driven and havened again
All ships that ever had gone to sea,
And I saw the glory of all dead men
In the shadow that went by the side of me.

John Drinkwater

THE DICTION OF CONTEMPORARY POETRY

"The new poetry strives for a concrete and immediate realization of life; it would discard the theory, the abstraction, the remoteness found in all classics not of the first order. It is less vague, less verbose, less eloquent, than most poetry of the Victorian period and much work of earlier periods. It has set before itself an ideal of absolute simplicity and sincerity—an ideal which implies an individual, unstereotyped diction; and an individual, unstereotyped rhythm."

Harriet Monroe in The New Poetry

The spirit of a poem may derive from any man and may belong to all mankind. But only a poet can give this spirit a body woven of rhythmical words. When the spirit of the poem has been clothed with this body, it becomes vocal. And that is the poet's achievement.

Therefore, to any poet who holds his vocation in honor, words are sacred. Practical men and women may use words chiefly for utility's sake, to make contracts, buy and sell, get food and give orders. Others use words humorously to make a kind of vivid and exaggerated fun which we call slang, which is sometimes akin to poetry—rather like poetry without any sense of proportion. But the poet must use words to make truth and beauty communicable. He must use them to share life bountifully and richly. Therefore he must have a sense of the sacredness of words. And it is worth while to remember that St. John, The Beloved, who was no mean poet, used "The Word" as the symbol of the Son of Man, who was to him also the Son of God.

A good poet must know words as other men and women seldom know them. He must know them as others know people. He must know that, like people, words do not always agree with one another and live in harmony when placed near together. In fact they have their own preferred associations. Therefore he must be a wise host, inviting such words to visit him together as will take pleasure in each other's society. He must know words in families, as we know our neighbors, understanding their relationships well so that he may be able to treat them tactfully. He must know their meanings—the minds that are in words. He must know their moods and the emotions that they excite—the hearts of words. And he must know and understand their sounds, long and short, rough and smooth, soft and resistant, bright and sombre—the beauty of words.

This is very important. For a loud, noisy word in a bit of quiet blank verse, will sometimes create such a disturbance that the beauty of the other words will pass unnoticed. It is like the entrance of a vulgar, ostentatious, self-made millionaire into a roomful of nuns or Quaker ladies. Or a prim, sedate little word introduced into a riotous lyric may seem to be as ill at ease as a staid New England dame at a marriage feast in Hawaii, where native drinks are drunk and native dances danced with abandon.

To any poet worthy the name, words are alive, and must be treated with the reverence due all living things. And perhaps the poets of to-day deserve more credit for their return to this ancient reverence for words, than they deserve for anything else. If there be any one way in which poetry has improved in the past ten years, it is in the matter of the judicious use of words. In the best poetry of recent years we have what Miss Monroe calls "an individual, unstereotyped diction," due to the poets' ideal of simplicity and sincerity.

William Butler Yeats (for whose poems and plays may Ireland be praised and blessed!) has been a strong influence for good in this matter of diction. It is now twenty years since he began preaching his gospel of the use of the words of the best contemporary speech in poetry. And nearly all of the best poets of our day have accepted this credo and live by its articles. John Masefield, Wilfrid Wilson Gibson and the other Georgians in England, Louis Untermeyer, Arthur Davison Ficke, Witter Bynner, and indeed all of the leading poets in this country, seem to have agreed that the language which is good enough for labor and love and marriage, for birth and death and the friendly breaking of bread, is good enough, if used with discrimination, for the making of poetry. And this accounts, in part, for the recent growth of popular interest in poetry. Our poets are not using a pedantic, unfriendly, top-loftical jargon, but the language of the common life. Their meanings do not have to be deciphered. They can be felt.

Because they believe in the use of the words of the best contemporary speech in poetry, poets of to-day are unwilling to use many of the archaic forms of English words. They seldom use the old-fashioned pronouns "thou" and "ye" and the verbal forms that end in "st" for the second person singular and in "th" for the third person singular. These forms were once used in daily speech. In those days poets could use them naturally and effectively in verse because they could *feel* them. But all too often, when modern poets have said "thou" in their verse, they have really felt "you" and translated it into "thou," because they have been taught that "thou" is in some inexplicable way more poetic. This is why recent poetry in which the old forms are too frequently used seems stilted, unnatural and remote from life. No modern man could stand before his sweetheart and address her as "O thou" without feeling a little bit ridiculous. That is why the "O thou" poems and the "hath-doth" poems (to quote my friends, the editors) seem ridiculous to contemporary critics.

Most of the modern lyrics in which such archaic forms occur could be improved by the substitution of modern forms. At the risk of being impertinent, even presumptuous, I am going to quote a poem by Dana Burnet (who has written much better and more vigorous verse), and, after quoting it, I am going to translate it into modern English. Here it is as he wrote it.

PAPER ROSES*

"How camest thou by thy roses, Child?"
"I toiled at them in a little room."
"Thy window flaming with the dawn?"
"Nay, master; 'twas in fearful gloom."

"What gave thy rose its color, then?"
"My cheek's blood, as I bent my head."
"Thy cheek is cold and lifeless, Child."
"Mayhap it was my heart that bled."

"One white rose in thy basket, Child?"
"Aye, master, that's to crown the whole."
"What is it, then, O Little Child?"
"Mayhap . . . mayhap it is my soul!"

To be sure, this is an imaginary dialogue, a spiritual rather than an actual conversation. And this fact may be used as an argument for the archaic language in it. But after much thought we come to believe that such spiritual dialogues have a more poignant appeal if they are written in simple, unobtrusive language. Moreover, this is a modern theme—child labor in great cities—and demands a modern treatment. Rewritten in modern English the poem is stronger. Here is what may be called a free translation:

"Where did you get your roses, Child?"
"I made them in a little room."
"Your window flaming with the dawn?"
"No, sir; in fearful gloom."

"What gave your roses color, then?"
"My heart's blood, as I bent my head."
"Your cheek is cold and lifeless, Child?"
"Perhaps my heart bled."

"One white rose in your basket, Child?"
"Yes, sir; it is to crown the whole."
"What is it, then, O little Child?"
"I think it is my soul."

The real danger in depending upon the use of archaic forms is that we may come to believe that there is peculiar merit in them and use them to get a conventionally poetic effect in lines that could not lay claim to being poetry by any other ruling. A comparison of two American poems by the same poet, will show how this sometimes happens. The poems are "Unconquered" and "Song" by Florence Earle Coates. The first poem is made out of a fine thought and feeling— a spiritual bravery. But it begins with these lines:

"Deem not, O Pain, that thou shalt vanquish me
Who know each treacherous pang, each last device,
Whereby thou barrest the way to Paradise!"

The second poem, also, is made out of a fine mood and a feeling of the greatness of human love. How much better it is!

"If love were but a little thing—
Strange love, which, more than all, is great—
One might not such devotion bring,
Early to serve and late.

If love were but a passing breath—
Wild love—which, as God knows, is sweet—
One might not make of life and death
A pillow for love's feet."

No one, in facing physical or spiritual agony, would be likely, nowadays, to say to himself, "Deem not, O Pain, that thou shalt vanquish me." But in thinking of the greatness and beauty of love anyone might rejoice to repeat the words of "Song." The first poem is stilted and artificial. The second is natural and lovely.

For every rule that critics make a few exceptions must be found. And it seems wise, sometimes, to set aside the modern prejudice against the old verbal and pronominal forms. Of course we must still say "thou" in devotional poetry if we wish to induce a feeling of worship, for the use of "thou" in addressing Deity is still a part of our folk speech. In churches people still say "thou" and they *feel* "thou." That is why Bliss Carman's beautiful religious lyric, "Lord of My Heart's Elation," would lose much of its grace and strength if "thou" were changed to "you" in it. The first stanza reads:

> "Lord of my heart's elation,
> Spirit of things unseen,
> Be thou my aspiration
> Consuming and serene!"

No one with any sense of æsthetic values would wish to substitute the modern pronoun here.

For a somewhat less obvious reason one would not wish to change "thou" to "you" in Constance Lindsay Skinner's poems of Indian life. The life of the American Indian is a tragic recessional. He is being thrust back into the past. Almost he seems to belong to the past. And when we think of his life and customs and folklore, we are thinking back into simpler and more naïve periods of history. Therefore, for the sake of that naïveté, that primitive feeling sometimes gained through the judicious use of old forms, Miss Skinner is justified.

The gist of the whole matter is that neither "thou" nor any other word should be used in poetry for conventional reasons or because it is supposed to be especially "literary." Any word strong enough to serve its purpose and convey meaning is poetic if used in the right place, in true and strong relation with other words, and as a result of the poet's sincere realization of the thing which he describes. The trouble is that unskilled poets sometimes use these antique forms because they suppose that, being antique, they have, in and of themselves, all the virtues of antiquity. Or else they use them inconsistently, mixed in with modern words and forms, to facilitate rhyming, or because they need extra syllables for their mechanically contrived meters. Poets who are not skillful enough to overcome the minor difficulties of rhyming and regular meter without recourse to ineffectual and false diction should be ashamed to show their clumsiness and to ply the great trade of Seanchan slothfully. To use "seemeth" in one line and "seems" in the next, "doth walk" in one line and "walks" in the next, is shoddy art. Such expressions are not variably used in good conversation. Poetry is the best conversation.

Perhaps just a word or two should be said about "poetic license," since many people have strange ideas about the liberties it permits poets. The first thing to be said is that it is mercifully obsolescent and that the sooner we forget it, the better. No good poet of to-day wants a license for any unfair dealing with words. No good poet wants license for any unfair dealing with meaning or rhythm or image. No good poet wants license to create any poetry which is less honest, craftsmanlike and beautiful than the most beautiful prose. Distortions of sentence structure, limp adjectives slipping downhill at the end of the line after their nouns, all ugly and awkward inversions and substitutions, are things that good contemporary poets despise. In an article written for *The Los Angeles Graphic*, Eunice Tietjens states the case against "poetic license" very well. What she says should be quoted with emphasis.

"If the modern poet gives himself greater liberty in the verse forms he uses—though even there he has only discarded one set of rules for another set quite as binding if not quite so easily defined—yet on the other hand he no longer permits himself to lay ruthless hands upon the language. The 'poetic' words which once besprinkled the pages of even the best poets are now laid aside, we hope forever, along with other outworn garments of an earlier civilization. Here again it is to be stated with certainty that the verse writer of to-day is not worthy of consideration who thinks himself licensed to use such words as 'e'en,' 'twixt,' ''mongst,' 'e'er,' and the rest of that ilk, or who resorts to such subterfuges as 'do swoon' and 'did come.'"

A few years ago the conventions of poetic language were held to be as unchanging as the laws of the Medes and Persians. In those days "azure" was considered a poetic word, "blue" a prosaic word, "beauteous" and "bounteous" were poetic words, "beautiful" and "bountiful" were prosaic words, "zephyr" was poetic, "breeze," prosaic. The modern poet favors the use of the words that used to be considered prosaic, for he finds that they are a part of our speech and therefore a part of our life. But he feels free, of course, to use any word as occasion demands. His only dogma is that there must be some sufficient reason of meaning or euphony which makes one word better than another.

Contemporary poetry, like great poetry of any period, owes much of its warmth and humanity to this freedom in the use of words. Time was when minor Victorians would have told us that such words as "greasy" and "pot" could never be made poetic and should never be used in a lyric. But Shakespeare, in a lyric that has lived for many generations as an admirable piece of picturing combined with genuine emotion, *used both of these words, in one line, in a repeated refrain!*

"While greasy Joan doth keel the pot."

If a modern innovator had written this poem with all its sharp beauty of homely picture, conservative critics would have made life miserable for him. They would have said, "That is not poetry." But it is perfect poetry of its kind. Every word in it is related to the meaning and mood of the whole. It is a sharing of life in vivid and unforgettable language. Shakespeare needed no rules. We need make none for him.

Contemporary poets permit themselves a large amount of freedom in their selection of words for poems, but they have a prejudice against a few words, and especially against a few tired adjectives that seem to have lost interest in life. Such adjectives as "vernal" and "supernal" are seldom used by our poets because they fail to make a quick and strong appeal to the modern mind. When we hear "heavenly or "lofty," most of us can make a mental picture of the meaning. When we say "spring," or "youthful," the same thing is true. But "supernal" and "vernal" bring no clear-cut conception. The life seems to have vanished out of them. And the good poet of to-day smiles when he remembers how they served to make life easy for the Post-Victorian minor poet who had left the adjective "eternal" all alone at the end of a line of verse and needed a rhyme for it.

Ten years ago the same poets who loved to rhyme "vernal" and "supernal" and "eternal" and "diurnal" had forgotten that words, for the poet, must be the fruit of realization. They filled their verses with words and phrases considered quite appropriate simply because they were customarily used and had become formulæ. They invented what might be called the rubber stamp method of writing poetry! But it was not poetry that they wrote.

To-day nothing wearies readers of poetry more than a trite and stereotyped diction. The public has learned that such diction is the result of laziness or mental sterility. Lilies are stately and violets modest yesterday, to-day and forever, truly. But lilies and violets have other qualities, also. And the poet of to-day knows that, in speaking of "the stately lily" or the "modest violet," he causes no animation in the modern mind, strikes no spark of emotion, shares no sense of life. Therefore, when we find such phrases in modern verse, we may be sure that the maker of the poem is rendering a mere lip-service, for hire or for vanity, that he is not rendering the strong and sincere soul-and-body service of the poet. For not until all poets and all readers have in mind the clean, hard honesty of words to the extent that each word must tally with experience, will these old phrases, once vitally and beautifully used, regain their value for occasional use in the mouths of the poets and of the people.

The use of trite phrases, oddly enough, is the besetting sin of academic poets and of other learned persons who read verses at meetings of scholarly societies. Humble persons who hear such verse read, or find it shamelessly exposed to view in the pages of parlor-table magazines, are troubled, saying to themselves, "It must be good poetry, for he is a very great man. If I knew enough I should like it." May Apollo speed the day when these humble persons will know for themselves that such metrical mimicries of a noble past are not poetry at all! Nor is poetry good because a *great man* has written it. It must be written by a *great poet.* A man may be a great philosopher, politician, teacher, novelist, historian, financier, and quite incapable of writing a single line of poetry. This should not have to be said.

While we wait for the millennium of the poets, which will be a rather jolly millennium when it comes—the evil goes on. At a meeting of very learned men in a very great city, and not very long ago, a piece of academic verse was read in which the following expressions were used: "mystery strange" (why not "strange mystery"?), "high supernal fiat" (note the tautology!), "red passion growths," "stately lily" (of course!), "purple mists," "lust of power," "love of gain," "balm of kindly counsel," "endless æons," "unseen, incredible, yet true," "memoried moods," "supine ease," "vibrant air," "wondrous past," "further parley," "verdure to the desert," "perilous peaks," "ardour of the soul," "pomp and pageant of the fall," "pitiful earth-ken," "vision far but fair," "thrills with purpose," "rainbow promises," and "heathen hearts." Why is it, by the way, that nobody ever mentions anything else about the heathen? Have they no eyes, ears, foreheads or feet?

The ghosts of the elder singers who were strong enough for realization and sincere expression might well haunt this man. But nothing happened to him when the poem was read. No one haled him to jail for his abuse of the language and his offer of counterfeit for the true coin of poetry. No one even demanded a bond of him to write no more verse. And yet, although he may be a good citizen and a good husband and father, he was, when he read that poem, a menace to American culture.

The diction of the poets who have styled themselves Imagists deserves especial attention, for theoretically they are arch-enemies of the trite phrase. And they are seldom guilty of the use of formulæ. This may be because the poets of this minor school are exceedingly intellectual poets and believe in making conscious use of sense impressions. Very often an Imagist poem is nothing but an exercise in imagining the pleasure to be had from certain textures, colors, sounds, sights, tastes and movements. The Imagists endeavor to be true to their "doctrine of the image" and use no abstractions, no vague suggestions. They present things in hard, concrete words. And, coming as they have, after a period of windy eloquence, bombastic piety, and flatulent sentimentality in poetry, they have done much to enable contemporary poets of all schools to focus their attention on the matter of diction.

But unfortunately, like many theorists, they have carried theory too far. They have been too much interested in their own æsthetic conceptions and in their theories of craftsmanship to remember that poetry, after all, is the sharing of life. And their diction has the stamp of Imagism upon it rather more frequently than the stamp of any individual poet's genius. The color words of this school have become a mannerism. Imagists are too fond of such lovely words as "chrome," "saffron," "mauve," especially "mauve." (One critic mentions "mauve Imagism")! And a certain modern poet, not an Imagist himself, has been so much influenced by this school that he even speaks of the wounds of Christ as "mauve." In fixing his mind upon a sense impression that he wishes to create for his reader, he is heedless of the associations of the word "mauve" with department stores and dressmakers, associations which might prevent a great poet from using the word to describe the wounds of the World-Hero.

In criticizing the diction of contemporary poetry, or of any poetry, we must always keep in mind the type of poetry we are reading. Diction which would be strong and true in narrative or dramatic poetry might be ill-suited to the needs of the makers of lyrics. In a narrative poem, or in a dramatic poem, characters must be differentiated, and this requires of a poet a skill in catching the flavors of the speech of the people he is describing. Not only must the diction of the whole poem be true to the spirit of the whole poem, but it must also be true, in each individual case, to the character of the speaker on whose lips it is found. And furthermore, it must be true to the locality in which the events take place, or to the racial consciousness behind them. And in long poems the words used must contribute to the variety of design without which they become monotonous.

The diction of "The Everlasting Mercy" by John Masefield fulfills all of these requirements. When the poem was first published in this country, its very strength, its chiaroscuro of rough ugliness and serene beauty, aroused critics who were fast becoming accustomed to mild-mannered and innocuous verse, and there was not a little discussion of the words in it. The famous and ugly passage which describes the beginning of the quarrel between Bill and Saul seemed to many persons to be superfluous and coarse. But to-day most of us have accepted it as an essential ugliness in a great poem full of spiritual beauty, for it shows very clearly, vividly and concisely just the class and kind of men who are quarreling together. It shows their racial quality as lower class Britishers and it sharpens our interest in what is to follow.

If it had been smoothly and prettily said, the value of the poem would have been destroyed. But such lines and such expressions would have no proper place in a short lyric of the subjective kind. We have only to read them to realize this.

"'It's mine.'
'It ain't!'
'You put.'
'You liar.'
'You closhy put.'
'You bloody liar.'
'This is my field.'
'This is my wire.'
'I'm ruler here.'

> 'You ain't.'
> 'I am.'
> 'I'll fight you for it.'
> 'Right, by damn.'"

We could never tolerate many lines like these even in a long narrative poem. And one of the delights in reading "The Everlasting Mercy" is a delight in the freshness and variety of the words used from page to page. Another passage quite as true racially, and quite as true to the character of Saul in one of his nobler moods, is the passage that describes the love of running light-foot and swift along a country road at night.

> "The men who don't know to the root
> The joy of being swift of foot
> Have never known divine and fresh
> The glory of the gift of flesh,
> Nor felt the feet exult, nor gone
> Along a dim road, on and on,
> Knowing again the bursting glows,
> The mating hare in April knows,
> Who tingles to the pads with mirth
> At being the swiftest thing on earth."

This passage is in keeping with that great passage from Browning's "Saul" that begins "How good is man's life, the mere living."

Just as good in its own way is the diction of the passage that tells how Saul amused little Jimmy Jaggard with fairy tales about Tom-cats and mouse-meat. And, in the end, the poem's language reaches into a beauty that means the redemption of the sinner. The racial quality is not lost. The man's class and character are not lost. But he is fulfilled in his own kind. All the words that are used show the fulfillment. It is the homely salvation of the humble.

> "All earthly things that blessèd morning
> Were everlasting joy and warning.

The gate was Jesus' way made plain,
The mole was Satan foiled again,
Black blinded Satan snouting way
Along the red of Adam's clay;
The mist was error and damnation,
The lane the road unto salvation.
Out of the mist into the light,
O blessèd gift of inner sight.
The past was faded like a dream;
There came the jingling of a team,
A ploughman's voice, a clink of chain,
Slow hoofs, and harness under strain.
Up the slow slope a team came bowing,
Old Callow at his autumn ploughing,
Old Callow, stooped above the hales,
Ploughing the stubble into wales.
His grave eyes looking straight ahead,
Shearing a long straight furrow red;
His plough-foot high to give it earth
To bring new food for men to birth.
O wet red swathe of earth laid bare,
O truth, O strength, O gleaming share,
O patient eyes that watch the goal,
O ploughman of the sinner's soul.
O Jesus, drive the coulter deep
To plough my living man from sleep."

The wisdom used in choosing these words, the utter naturalness of them, is something that is too good to be conspicuous and will be discovered only by those who read the poem more than once and think about it quietly. One line alone for truth and vitality would make this passage memorable,—

"Up the slow slope a team came bowing."

Who that has ever seen ploughing will deny the truth of these words? Almost equally good are the lines,

"His grave eyes looking straight ahead,
Shearing a long straight furrow red;
His plough-foot high to give it earth."

It is hardly necessary to speak of the grave, strong symbolism of many parts of this passage, for that is something that any reader will feel.

Another narrative poem in which the use of words can be studied to good advantage is "Hoops," by Wilfrid Wilson Gibson. Mr. Gibson's work differs from Mr. Masefield's in that he does not attempt to use just the words that his characters would have spoken. He uses the words that their souls might have spoken if their lips had learned them. For that reason his diction, beautiful and austere though it is, at times seems to take his characters far away from us as real, living men and women, capable of reserves and intimacies, and leave them with us only as spirits speaking through Mr. Gibson. In "Hoops," for example, we find a circus clown and a tender of camels talking together on the ground near the entrance of the circus tent. The clown is Merry Andrew. The tender of camels is Gentleman John. What they say to each other has genuine importance as the speech of two souls revealing themselves. In it is wisdom, a sense of values in life, a sense of beauty and of ugliness, and of the characters shown in beasts and persons. But all of these things belong to Mr. Gibson, the poet, and are felt as belonging to him. They may belong to the souls of Merry Andrew and Gentleman John, but they do not belong on their lips in the words that Mr. Gibson has chosen. Says Gentleman John:

"And then consider camels: only think
Of camels long enough, and you'ld go mad—
With all their humps and lumps; their knobbly knees,
Splay feet and straddle legs; their sagging necks,
Flat flanks and scraggy tails, and monstrous teeth."

That is an admirable description of a camel, somewhat too admirable, perhaps, for the mouth of Gentleman John, a little too clever with its play of double consonants and short "a" sounds from line to line, even though Mr. Gibson does tell us later—perhaps to explain Gentleman John's gift of words—that Gentleman John wanted to be a poet. Still more admirable as Mr.

ROBERT FROST

Gibson's own description, still more improbable as Gentleman John's description, are the lines about the elephant.

> "The elephant is quite a comely brute,
> Compared with Satan camel,—trunk and all,
> His floppy ears and his inconsequent tail.
> He's stolid, but at least a gentleman.
> It doesn't hurt my pride to valet him,
> And bring his shaving-water. He's a lord.
> Only the bluest blood that has come down
> Through generations from the mastodon
> Could carry off that tail with dignity,
> That tail and trunk. He cannot look absurd,
> For all the monkey tricks you put him through,
> Your paper hoops and popguns. He just makes
> His masters look ridiculous, when his pomp's
> Butchered to make a bumpkin's holiday."

As an example of good diction to which locality as well as character contributes flavor and quality, nothing can be better than the diction of Robert Frost. Mr. Frost is not merely a new craftsman, he is a new personal force deep-rooted in locality. He belongs somewhere—in rural New England. And from that physical and spiritual environment he draws his strength. We can hardly call his characters fictitious. For they are real. We know that they, or their ghosts are all there, "North of Boston" still. Poems like "Blueberries" are fragrant with the scent of the New England countryside and full of the dry, delicious humor of the thrifty, quiet, kindly Yankee farmer. "A Hundred Collars" is one of the most delightfully ironical poems in the whole of American literature. In it the New England small town drunkard, who happens to be an agent for a country newspaper, and the New England schoolmaster, who has outgrown his own home town, are obliged to share a room in a country hotel. The exquisite tact and kindliness of the drunkard, who wears collars of the size eighteen, and the awkward dislike, distrust, and discomfiture of the man of the world are shown in inimitable fashion. In "The Code: Heroics" we learn the silent pride of the New England "hired man" and his Yankee audacity in defending that pride. And in many and many a poem we have heart-breaking stories of lonely women on the farms who are servants to hired men as well as to their families. To get the best out of these narratives they must be read as a whole, as we would read the story of New England. In each of them the diction is the diction of the people described. Mr. Frost has been absolutely true to the characters as individuals and to the spiritual atmosphere of the locality. And he has not allowed any showy eccentricities to mar his style. No doubt many persons would prefer to have more catchwords and a peculiar jargon instead of the plain familiar English which his characters use. But Mr. Frost does not put dialect in the mouths of these people, because he does not hear them use it.

Even Mr. Frost's abbreviations are true to contemporary speech and to character. He does not use the old-fashioned "o'er," "twixt" and "'tis" of the conventional versifier. But he does use the common modern abbreviations, "doesn't," "isn't," "I'd" and the like. He is quite unmindful of literary conventionalities and very faithful to reality. And in spite of the plainness of the speech he uses—or because of it—his characters are intensely alive with passions that even reserves and humor can not hide.

Vachel Lindsay is another poet who shares life with us in every word. He puts it in the turn of every sentence. His phrases growl and flirt, smirk and glare, point fingers and make faces, sputter and fizzle and splash color broadly upon the universe. We come to realize gradually that he is a man with the imagination and sensitivity of the bards of Greece and the prophets of Israel, living in an immense modern world, where life is multiform and multi-colored, graver and more humorous, more complex and more varied than ever it was in the days of the ancient Greeks or Hebrews. And we realize, also, that he has lived in that state of social and spiritual consciousness which we call the United States of America.

In this fact we find one reason for his vitality as a poet. He is deeply rooted in our civilization. Our folklore, our customs, our ethics, our idealism and our reasons for laughter are well known to him. The time that he spent upon the open highways of our country, preaching his gospel of beauty,—"Bad public taste is mob law—good public taste is democracy"—that time was also a time of learning. In those days our people gave him many secrets. Perhaps they taught him not to scorn the simple and homely virtues which they value. Perhaps they helped not a little to make him what he has certainly become, the spiritual descendent of Mark Twain and James Whitcomb Riley, as American as Riley's pumpkins or the whitewash on Tom Sawyer's fence.

But his artistic heritage comes to him from long, long ago, from the troubadours and bards and minnesingers and minstrels, from the makers of sagas and runes. To sum it all up, he is something that has never been before—an American minstrel.

In "General William Booth Enters Into Heaven" we have a poem which is a masterpiece of powerful phraseology set to the tune of "The Blood of The Lamb." In this hotly human poem we are permitted to watch the transfiguration of Booth's "vermin-eaten saints with mouldy breath" when they are led into the courts of Heaven to the beating of Booth's drum. In the light of the beatific vision of King Jesus they become

"Sages and sybils now and athletes clean,
Rulers of empires and of forests green!"

The finest workmanship, however, in the making of this poem, is in the description of the forlorn army before the transfiguration.

In his greatest poem, "The Chinese Nightingale," all the strong, quaint, original qualities that have won fame for Vachel Lindsay are to be found at their best. Gracious rhythms, delicious imaginings and exquisite phraseology all belong to this fantasy in a Chinese laundry.

"Then this did the noble lady say:
'Bird, do you dream of our home-coming day
When you flew like a courier on before
From the dragon-peak to our palace-door,
And we drove the steed in your singing path—
The ramping dragon of laughter and wrath:
And found our city all aglow,
And knighted this joss that decked it so?
There were golden fishes in the purple river
And silver fishes and rainbow fishes.
There were golden junks in the laughing river
And silver junks and rainbow junks:
There were golden lilies by the bay and river,
And silver lilies and tiger-lilies,
And tinkling wind-bells in the gardens of the town
By the black-lacquer gate
Where walked in state
The kind king Chang
And his sweetheart mate . . .'"

In the making of the short, subjective lyric the words should be simple, fluent, melodious, such words as can be sung easily. Words like those that contributed to the force and vividness of long narratives like "The Everlasting Mercy" and "Hoops"—such words as "closhy," "snouting," "knobbly," "straddle," "humps," "popguns," "bumpkin" and the like, are seldom appropriate in lyrics! They would be quite out of place in such songs as Sara Teasdale gives us, or even in her supple and magnetic blank verse. Nor do we find any words of this kind in her work. Her diction, like her meaning and emotion, is limpid and simple. As an example, let us read five lines from her "Sappho."

"There is a quiet at the heart of love,
And I have pierced the pain and come to peace.
I hold my peace, my Cleïs, on my heart;
And softer than a little wild bird's wing
Are kisses that she pours upon my mouth."

These lines are perfect in chaste and fluent beauty. But we should realize that a very long poem of the dramatic or narrative type would lack variety and cloy upon us if made wholly of lines like these.

We must demand of all poets, then, that their diction be in harmony with the spirit of their creation. Poems that blaze with the soul of an individual, or of mankind, take to themselves, in the labor of great poets, a flesh of words of one kind with the spirit that flashes through it. In poetry, as in life, let the fool wear his motley, let Caliban be known in the coarse body of Caliban, let the Madonna wear her white beauty and her mantle of blue.

HER WORDS

My mother has the prettiest tricks
  Of words and words and words.
Her talk comes out as smooth and sleek
  As breasts of singing birds.

She shapes her speech all silver fine
  Because she loves it so.
And her own eyes begin to shine
  To hear her stories grow.

And if she goes to make a call
  Or out to take a walk
We leave our work when she returns
  And run to hear her talk.

We had not dreamed these things were so
  Of sorrow and of mirth.
Her speech is as a thousand eyes
  Through which we see the earth.

God wove a web of loveliness,
  Of clouds and stars and birds,
But made not any thing at all
  So beautiful as words.

They shine around our simple earth
  With golden shadowings,
And every common thing they touch
  Is exquisite with wings.

There's nothing poor and nothing small
  But is made fair with them.
They are the hands of living faith
  That touch the garment's hem.

They are as fair as bloom or air,
  They shine like any star,
And I am rich who learned from her
  How beautiful they are.

Anna Hempstead Branch.

THE SONG OF WANDERING AENGUS

I went out to the hazel wood
Because a fire was in my head,
And cut and peeled a hazel wand,
And hooked a berry to a thread;
And when white moths were on the wing,
And moth-like stars were flickering out,
I dropped the berry in a stream,
And caught a little silver trout.

When I had laid it on the floor,
I went to blow the fire a-flame,
But something rustled on the floor,
And some one called me by my name:
It had become a glimmering girl,
With apple-blossom in her hair,
Who called me by my name and ran
And faded through the brightening air.

Though I am old with wandering
Through hollow lands and hilly lands,
I will find out where she has gone,
And kiss her lips and take her hands;

And walk among long dappled grass,
And pluck till time and times are done
The silver apples of the moon,
The golden apples of the sun.

William Butler Yeats

GRIEVE NOT FOR BEAUTY

Grieve not for the invisible, transported brow
On which like leaves the dark hair grew,
Nor for the lips of laughter that are now
Laughing inaudibly in sun and dew,
Nor for those limbs that, fallen low
And seeming faint and slow,
Shall yet pursue
More ways of swiftness than the swallow dips
Among . . . and find more winds than ever blew
The straining sails of unimpeded ships!
Mourn not!—yield only happy tears
To deeper beauty than appears!

Witter Bynner

OLD AGE

Old Age, the irrigator,
Digs our bosoms straighter,
More workable and deeper still
To turn the ever-running mill
Of nights and days. He makes a trough
To drain our passions off,
That used so beautiful to lie
Variegated to the sky,
On waste moorlands of the heart—
Haunts of idleness, and art
Still half-dreaming. All their piedness,
Rank and wild and shallow wideness,
Desultory splendors, he
Straightens conscientiously
To a practicable sluice
Meant for workaday, plain use.

All the mists of early dawn,
Twilit marshes, being gone
With their glamor, and their stench,
There is left—a narrow trench.

Percy Mackaye

THE END OF THE WORLD

The snow had fallen many nights and days;
The sky was come upon the earth at last,
Sifting thinly down as endlessly
As though within the system of blind planets
Something had been forgot or overdriven.
The dawn now seemed neglected in the grey
Where mountains were unbuilt and shadowless trees
Rootlessly paused or hung upon the air.
There was no wind, but now and then a sigh
Crossed that dry falling dust and rifted it
Through crevices of slate and door and casement.
Perhaps the new moon's time was even past.
Outside, the first white twilights were too void
Until a sheep called once, as to a lamb,
And tenderness crept everywhere from it;
But now the flock must have strayed far away.
The lights across the valley must be veiled,
The smoke lost in the greyness or the dusk.
For more than three days now the snow had thatched
That cow-house roof where it had ever melted
With yellow stains from the beasts' breath inside;
But yet a dog howled there, though not quite lately.
Someone passed down the valley swift and singing,
Yes, with locks spreaded like a son of morning;
But if he seemed too tall to be a man
It was that men had been so long unseen,
Or shapes loom larger through a moving snow.
And he was gone and food had not been given him.
When snow slid from an overweighted leaf,
Shaking the tree, it might have been a bird
Slipping in sleep or shelter, whirring wings;
Yet never bird fell out, save once a dead one—

And in two days the snow had covered it.
The dog had howled again—or thus it seemed
Until a lean fox passed and cried no more.
All was so safe indoors where life went on
Glad of the close enfolding snow—O glad
To be so safe and secret at its heart,
Watching the strangeness of familiar things.
They knew not what dim hours went on, went by,
For while they slept the clock stopt newly wound
As the cold hardened. Once they watched the road,
Thinking to be remembered. Once they doubted
If they had kept the sequence of the days,
Because they heard not any sound of bells.
A butterfly, that hid until the Spring
Under a ceiling's shadow, dropt, was dead.
The coldness seemed more nigh, the coldness deepened
As a sound deepens into silences;
It was of earth and came not by the air;
The earth was cooling and drew down the sky.
The air was crumbling. There was no more sky.
Rails of a broken bed charred in the grate,
And when he touched the bars he thought the sting
Came from their heat—he could not feel such cold . . .
She said "O, do not sleep,
Heart, heart of mine, keep near me. No, no; sleep.
I will not lift his fallen, quiet eyelids,
Although I know he would awaken then—
He closed them thus but now of his own will.
He can stay with me while I do not lift them."

Gordon Bottomley

THE OLD BED

Streaming beneath the eaves, the sunset light
Turns the white walls and ceiling to pure gold,
And gold, the quilt and pillows on the old
Fourposter bed—all day a cold drift-white—
As if, in a gold casket glistering bright,
The gleam of winter sunshine sought to hold
The sleeping child safe from the dark and cold
And creeping shadows of the coming night.

Slowly it fades: and stealing through the gloom
Home-coming shadows throng the quiet room,
Grey ghosts that move unrustling, without breath,
To their familiar rest, and closer creep
About the little dreamless child asleep
Upon the bed of bridal, birth and death.

Wilfrid Wilson Gibson

SUNRISE ON RYDAL WATER

To E. de S.

Come down at dawn from windless hills
  Into the valley of the lake,
Where yet a larger quiet fills
  The hour, and mist and water make
    With rocks and reeds and island boughs
    One silence and one element,
    Where wonder goes surely as once
    It went
      By Galilean prows.

Moveless the water and the mist,
  Moveless the secret air above,
Hushed, as upon some happy tryst
  The poised expectancy of love;
    What spirit is it that adores
    What mighty presence yet unseen?
    What consummation works apace
    Between
      These rapt enchanted shores?

Never did virgin beauty wake
  Devouter to the bridal feast
Than moves this hour upon the lake
  In adoration to the east.
  Here is the bride a god may know,
  The primal will, the young consent,
  Till surely upon the appointed mood
  Intent
    The god shall leap—and, lo,

Over the lake's end strikes the sun—
  White, flameless fire; some purity
Thrilling the mist, a splendor won
  Out of the world's heart. Let there be
    Thoughts, and atonements, and desires;
    Proud limbs, and undeliberate tongue;
    Where now we move with mortal care
    Among
      Immortal dews and fires.

So the old mating goes apace,
  Wind with the sea, and blood with thought,
Lover with lover; and the grace
  Of understanding comes unsought
    When stars into the twilight steer,
    Or thrushes build among the may,
    Or wonder moves between the hills,
    And day
      Comes up on Rydal mere.

John Drinkwater

LEAVES

One by one, like leaves from a tree,
All my faiths have forsaken me;
But the stars above my head
Burn in white and delicate red,
And beneath my feet the earth
Brings the sturdy grass to birth.
I who was content to be
But a silken-singing tree,
But a rustle of delight
In the wistful heart of night,
I have lost the leaves that knew
Touch of rain and weight of dew.
Blinded by a leafy crown
I looked neither up nor down—
But the leaves that fall and die
Have left me room to see the sky;
Now for the first time I know
Stars above and earth below.

Sara Teasdale

SPRING

At the first hour, it was as if one said, "Arise."
At the second hour, it was as if one said, "Go forth."
And the winter constellations that are like patient ox-eyes
Sank below the white horizon at the north.

At the third hour, it was as if one said, "I thirst";
At the fourth hour, all the earth was still:
Then the clouds suddenly swung over, stooped, and burst;
And the rain flooded valley, plain and hill.

At the fifth hour, darkness took the throne;
At the sixth hour, the earth shook and the wind cried;
At the seventh hour, the hidden seed was sown,
At the eighth hour, it gave up the ghost and died.

At the ninth hour, they sealed up the tomb;
And the earth was then silent for the space of three hours.
But at the twelfth hour, a single lily from the gloom
Shot forth, and was followed by a whole host of flowers.

John Gould Fletcher

IN THE POPPY FIELD

Mad Patsy said, he said to me,
That every morning he could see
An angel walking on the sky;
Across the sunny skies of morn
He threw great handfuls far and nigh
Of poppy seed among the corn;
And then, he said, the angels run
To see the poppies in the sun.

A poppy is a devil weed,
I said to him—he disagreed;
He said the devil had no hand
In spreading flowers tall and fair
Through corn and rye and meadow land,
By garth and barrow everywhere:
The devil has not any flower,
But only money in his power.

And then he stretched out in the sun
And rolled upon his back for fun:
He kicked his legs and roared for joy
Because the sun was shining down,
He said he was a little boy
And would not work for any clown:
He ran and laughed behind a bee,
And danced for very ecstasy.

James Stephens

INTERLUDE

I am not old, but old enough
To know that you are very young.
It might be said I am the leaf,
And you the blossom newly sprung.

So I shall grow a while with you,
And hear the bee and watch the cloud,
Before the dragon on the branch,
The caterpillar weaves a shroud.

Scudder Middleton

MYSTERY

If a star can grow
On a blade of grass,
If a rose can climb
Like a Romeo,
And a river flow
Through a granite wall—
Maybe a human heart,
Broken within a breast,
Can heal again
In the simple rain,
When a man is laid to rest.

Scudder Middleton

THE GUM-GATHERER

There overtook me and drew me in
To his down-hill, early-morning stride,
And set me five miles on my road
Better than if he had had me ride,

A man with a swinging bag for load
And half the bag wound round his hand.
We talked like barking above the din
Of water we walked along beside.
And for my telling him where I'd been
And where I lived in mountain land
To be coming home the way I was,
He told me a little about himself.
He came from higher up in the pass
Where the grist of the new-beginning brooks
Is blocks split off the mountain mass—
And hopeless grist enough it looks
Ever to grind to soil for grass.
(The way it is will do for moss.)
There he had built his stolen shack.
It had to be a stolen shack
Because of the fears of fire and loss
That trouble the sleep of lumber folk:
Visions of half the world burned black
And the sun shrunken yellow in smoke.
We know who when they come to town
Bring berries under the wagon seat,
Or a basket of eggs between their feet;
What this man brought in a cotton sack
Was gum, the gum of the mountain spruce.
He showed me lumps of the scented stuff.
Like uncut jewels, dull and rough.
It comes to market golden brown;
But turns to pink between the teeth.

I told him this is a pleasant life
To set your breast to the bark of trees
That all your days are dim beneath,
And reaching up with a little knife,
To loose the resin and take it down
And bring it to market when you please.

Robert Frost

THE COW IN APPLE TIME

Something inspires the only cow of late
To make no more of a wall than an open gate,
And think no more of wall-builders than fools.
Her face is flecked with pomace and she drools
A cider syrup. Having tasted fruit,
She scorns a pasture withering to the root.
She runs from tree to tree where lie and sweeten
The windfalls spiked with stubble and worm-eaten.
She leaves them bitten when she has to fly.
She bellows on a knoll against the sky.
Her udder shrivels and the milk goes dry.

Robert Frost

AT NIGHT (To W. M.)

Home, home from the horizon far and clear,
  Hither the soft wings sweep;
Flocks of the memories of the day draw near
  The dovecote doors of sleep.

Oh, which are they that come through sweetest light
  Of all these homing birds?
Which with the strangest and the swiftest flight
  Your words to me, your words!

Alice Meynell

FROM "VARIATIONS"

II

Green light, from the moon,
Pours over the dark blue trees,
Green light from the autumn moon
Pours on the grass . . .
Green light falls on the goblin fountain
Where hesitant lovers meet and pass.

They laugh in the moonlight, touching hands,
They move like leaves on the wind . . .

I remember an autumn night like this,
And not so long ago,
When other lovers were blown like leaves,
Before the coming of snow.

Conrad Aiken

DAYBREAK

Four years of night and nightmare, years of black
Hate and its murderous attack;
Four years of midnight terrors till the brain,
Beaten in the intolerable campaign,
Saw nothing but a world of driven men
And skies that never could be clean again;
Hot winds that tore the lungs, great gusts
Of rotting madness and forgotten lusts;
Hills draped with death; the beat of terrible wings;
Flowers that smelt of carrion; monstrous things
That crawled on iron bellies over trees
And swarmed in blood, till even the seas
Were one wet putrefaction, and the earth
A violated grave of trampled mirth.
What light there was, was only there to show
Intolerance delivering blow on blow,
Bigotry rampant, honor overborne,
And faith derided with a blast of scorn.
This was our daily darkness; we had thought
All freedom worthless and all beauty naught.
The eager, morning-hearted days were gone
When we took joy in small things: in the sun,
Tracing a delicate pattern through thick leaves,
With its long, yellow pencils; or blue eaves
Frosted with moonlight, and one ruddy star
Ringing against the night, a chime
Like an insistent, single rhyme;
Or see the full-blown moon stuck on a spar,
A puff-ball flower on a rigid stalk;
Or think of nothing better than to walk
With one small boy and listen to the war
Of waters pulling at a stubborn shore;

Or laugh to see the waves run out of bounds
Like boisterous and shaggy hounds;
Watching the stealthy rollers come alive,
And shake their silver manes and leap and dive;
Or listen with him to the voiceless talk
Of fireflies and daisies, feel the late
Dusk full of unheard music or vibrate
To a more actual magic, hear the notes
Of birds with sunset shaking on their throats;
Or watch the emerald and olive trees
Turn purple ghosts in dusty distances;
The city's kindling energy; the sweet
Pastoral of an empty street;
Foot-ball and friends; lyrics and daffodils;
The sovereign splendor of the marching hills—
These were all ours to choose from and enjoy
Until this foul disease came to destroy
The casual beneficence of life. . . .

But now a thin edge, like a merciful knife,
Pierces the shadows, and a chiseling ray
Cuts the thick folds away.
Murmurs of morning, glad, awakening cries,
Hints of majestic rhythms, rise.
Dawn will not be denied. The blackness shakes,
And here a brand and there a beacon breaks
Into the glory that will soon be hurled
Over a cleared, rejuvenated world—
A world of bright democracies, of fair
Disputes, desires, and tolerance everywhere,
With laughter loose again, and time enough
To feel the warm-lipped and cool-fingered love,
With kindly passion lifted from the dead;
Where daylight shall be bountifully spread,
And darkness but a wide and welcome bed.

Louis Untermeyer

VISTAS

As I walked through the rumorous streets
Of the wind-rustled, elm-shaded city
Where all of the houses were friends
And the trees were all lovers of her,
The spell of its old enchantment
Was woven again to subdue me
With magic of flickering shadows,
Blown branches and leafy stir.

Street after street, as I passed,
Lured me and beckoned me onward
With memories frail as the odor
Of lilac adrift on the air.
At the end of each breeze-blurred vista
She seemed to be watching and waiting,
With leaf shadows over her gown
And sunshine gilding her hair.

For there was a dream that the kind God
Withheld, while granting us many—
But surely, I think, we shall come
Sometime, at the end, she and I,
To the heaven He keeps for all tired souls,
The quiet suburban gardens
Where He Himself walks in the evening
Beneath the rose-dropping sky
And watches the balancing elm trees
Sway in the early starshine
When high in their murmurous arches
The night breeze ruffles by.

Odell Shepard

CERTAIN AMERICAN POETS

They cowered inert before the study fire
While mighty winds were ranging wide and free,
Urging their torpid fancies to aspire
With "Euhoe! Bacchus! Have a cup of tea."

They tripped demure from church to lecture-hall,
Shunning the snare of farthingales and curls.
Woman they thought half angel and half doll,
The Muses' temple a boarding-school for girls.

Quaffing Pierian draughts from Boston pump,
They toiled to prove their homiletic art
Could match with nasal twang and pulpit thump
In maxims glib of meeting-house and mart.

Serenely their ovine admirers graze.
Apollo wears frock-coats, the Muses stays.

Odell Shepard

AFTER SUNSET

I have an understanding with the hills
At evening, when the slanted radiance fills
Their hollows, and the great winds let them be,
And they are quiet and look down at me.
Oh, then I see the patience in their eyes
Out of the centuries that made them wise.
They lend me hoarded memory, and I learn
Their thoughts of granite and their whims of fern,
And why a dream of forests must endure
Though every tree be slain; and how the pure,
Invisible beauty has a word so brief,
A flower can say it, or a shaken leaf,
But few may ever snare it in a song,
Though for the quest a life is not too long.
When the blue hills grow tender, when they pull
The twilight close with gesture beautiful,
And shadows are their garments, and the air
Deepens, and the wild veery is at prayer,
Their arms are strong around me; and I know
That somehow I shall follow when they go
To the still land beyond the evening star,
Where everlasting hills and valleys are,
And silence may not hurt us any more,
And terror shall be past, and grief and war.

Grace Hazard Conkling

SHIPS

I cannot tell their wonder nor make known
Magic that once thrilled through me to the bone,
But all men praise some beauty, tell some tale,
Vent a high mood which makes the rest seem pale,
Pour their heart's blood to flourish one green leaf,
Follow some Helen for her gift of grief,
And fail in what they mean, whate'er they do:
You should have seen, man cannot tell to you
The beauty of the ships of that my city.
That beauty now is spoiled by the sea's pity;
For one may haunt the pier a score of times,
Hearing St. Nicholas bells ring out the chimes,
Yet never see those proud ones swaying home
With mainyards backed and bows a cream of foam,
Those bows so lovely-curving, cut so fine,
Those coulters of the many-bubbled brine,
As once, long since, when all the docks were filled
With that sea-beauty man has ceased to build.

Yet, though their splendor may have ceased to be
Each played her sovereign part in making me;
Now I return my thanks with heart and lips
For the great queenliness of all those ships.

And first the first bright memory, still so clear,
An autumn evening in a golden year,
When in the last lit moments before dark
The *Chepica*, a steel-gray lovely barque,
Came to an anchor near us on the flood,
Her trucks aloft in sun-glow red as blood.

Then come so many ships that I could fill
Three docks with their fair hulls remembered still,
Each with her special memory's special grace,
Riding the sea, making the waves give place
To delicate high beauty; man's best strength,
Noble in every line in all their length.
Ailsa, *Genista*, ships, with long jibbooms,
The *Wanderer* with great beauty and strange dooms,

Liverpool (mightiest then) superb, sublime,
The *California* huge, as slow as time.
The *Copley* swift, the perfect *J. T. North*,
The loveliest barque my city has sent forth,
Dainty *John Lockett* well remembered yet,
The splendid *Argus* with her skysail set,
Stalwart *Drumcliff*, white-blocked, majestic *Sierras*,
Divine bright ships, the water's standard-bearers;
Melpomene, *Euphrosyne*, and their sweet
Sea-troubling sisters of the Fernie fleet;
Corunna (in whom my friend died) and the old
Long since loved *Esmeralda* long since sold.
Centurion passed in Rio, *Glaucus* spoken,
Aladdin burnt, the *Bidston* water-broken,
Yola, in whom my friend sailed, *Dawpool* trim,
Fierce-bowed *Egeria* plunging to the swim,
Stanmore wide-sterned, sweet *Cupica*, tall *Bard*,
Queen in all harbors with her moon-sail yard.

Though I tell many, there must still be others,
McVickar Marshall's ships and Fernie Brother's,
Lochs, *Counties*, *Shires*, *Drums*, the countless lines
Whose house-flags all were once familiar signs
At high main-trucks on Mersey's windy ways
When sunlight made the wind-white water blaze.
Their names bring back old mornings, when the docks
Shone with their house-flags and their painted blocks,
Their raking masts below the Custom House
And all the marvellous beauty of their bows.

Familiar steamers, too, majestic steamers,
Shearing Atlantic roller-tops to streamers,
Umbria, *Etruria*, noble, still at sea,
The grandest, then, that man had brought to be.
Majestic, *City of Paris*, *City of Rome*,
Forever jealous racers, out and home.
The *Alfred Holt's* blue smoke-stacks down the stream,
The fair *Loanda* with her bows a-cream.
Booth liners, Anchor liners, Red Star liners,
The marks and styles of countless ship-designers,

The *Magdalena*, *Puno*, *Potosi*,
Lost *Cotopaxi*, all well known to me.

These splendid ships, each with her grace, her glory,
Her memory of old song or comrade's story,
Still in my mind the image of life's need,
Beauty in hardest action, beauty indeed.
"They built great ships and sailed them," sounds most brave,
Whatever arts we have or fail to have.
I touch my country's mind, I come to grips
With half her purpose, thinking of these ships:
That art untouched by softness, all that line
Drawn ringing hard to stand the test of brine;
That nobleness and grandeur, all that beauty
Born of a manly life and bitter duty,
That splendor of fine bows which yet could stand
The shock of rollers never checked by land;
That art of masts, sail-crowded, fit to break,
Yet stayed to strength and backstayed into rake;
The life demanded by that art, the keen
Eye-puckered, hard-case seamen, silent, lean.
They are grander things than all the art of towns;
Their tests are tempests and the sea that drowns.
They are my country's line, her great art done
By strong brains laboring on the thought unwon
They mark our passage as a race of men—
Earth will not see such ships as those again.

John Masefield

CERTAIN CONSERVATIVE POETS

Very likely it is a good thing that most people are conservative. If most of us were radicals the world might be a fatiguing place to live in. We should all suffer from nervous prostration most of the time as a result of breaking the speed laws of rapid progress. After all, the normal conservative is a very decent person, liberal enough to try all things in due season and with due persuasion, and wise enough to hold fast to that which is good.

But always there are people who are more than normally conservative. They are the ultra-conservatives. They believe in "the good old times." They believe that things should always be done the way they used to be done. They think that "things were better" in the days of their childhood, or in the times of their fathers, who, in turn, probably thought the same thing of the times before their own. Ultra-conservatives are people in whose minds the ages progress backwards in time to a lost and lamented golden age of impossible virtue and intolerable beauty.

In the poetry of to-day we have both conservative and ultra-conservative poets. The moderate conservatives, poets like Bliss Carman, Charles G. D. Roberts, Anna Hempstead Branch, Lizette Woodworth Reese, Ada Foster Murray, Katharine Lee Bates, and a number of others who have been mentioned in preceding pages, are content simply to hold fast to all that is good in the traditions of English poetry. They are men and women of genuine culture, the heirs of the ages claiming their heritage. They are not in the forefront of what is called "the new poetry movement," nor are they in sympathy with all of its manifestations. But their best work is done in accordance with the same underlying principles that are the credo of "the new poets," although they do not go to extremes in practice or in theory and although they do not bring into contemporary poetry anything "new" except what is new in their own personalities, the thing which makes all poets, as Lord Dunsany says, "incomparable." These moderate conservatives make beautiful original patterns in poetry and use images and symbols and rhythms that are the result of sincere reactions to stimuli and the sincere expression of emotions felt. They avoid artificial, stereotyped diction. They use the language of the best contemporary speech in most of their verse. They are seldom diffuse, vague, sentimental. They are capable of concise lyrical expression and do not revel in decoration simply for its own sake and without due regard to its structural importance.

The ultra-conservatives are poets of quite another kind. If it be fair to judge by their work, they must believe that great poets are dead poets and the old thoughts, the best thoughts, forever and ever, Amen. They must believe that the best thing poets can do is to write in the spirit of and after the manner of the ancients who never die. They seem to care little for contemporary life and thought and do not create their poems after the manner of contemporary poetry.

Most of these ultra-conservative poets are men and women of unquestioned culture, men and women whose minds are saturated with literature, especially the literature of the past. They are steeped in culture as a rum-cake is steeped in rum. They know more about it than most of the radical poets ever will know. But they are not so near to contemporary life. And the poems that they make often seem to be the result of a reaction to literature, not of a reaction to life. Much of what they write is lunar, not solar, a cool, glimmering reflection from other and stronger lights. This is not to say that their work is imitative in any childish way. It is derivative, not from the strength of any one genius of the past, but from thought's companionship with many geniuses. It is the poetry of the learned rather than the poetry of those with "small Latin and less Greek."

It is these poets who argue in poetry with modern theories

of life and the universe. It is these poets who prefer the old wisdoms and follies of the race to the new. It is these poets who create out of old mythologies and creeds the old recipes for truth and beauty in a world that is new. And it is these poets whose technique differs in kind from the technique of most of the poets whose work we have discussed.

In the first place it is difficult to discover in their poetry any intimacy of relationship between the emotion felt (the mood and meaning of the poem) and the pattern of the poem, its rhythm, imagery, and symbolism. Very often the ultra-conservatives seem to have chosen a rhythm which they consider beautiful in and of itself, and then to have fitted their thoughts and feelings into the pattern of the rhythm. They seldom invent forms of decided strength and originality, like the forms Mr. Kipling and Mr. Chesterton use, but choose their forms academically from those already invented. Their rhythms, therefore, are not always of one sort and substance with their moods. Their designs are like moulds into which they press what they wish to say. And strict symmetry of metrical structure is so important in their minds that they will go to all extremes to preserve it. Sometimes they will leave out words that are important grammatically or logically, words that would never be omitted in lines of good prose, in order to avoid a change in accent, a substitution of a long syllable for two short syllables, or the interpolation of an extra short syllable in the line. Sometimes they will insert superfluous adjectives at the ends of lines for the sake of rhyme. Or they will invert the order of words in sentences and rearrange phrases and clauses in a manner closely resembling that of the Teutons, to serve the end of rhyme. For to the ultra-conservatives rhyme is more than simply one way of adding to the resonance and charm of poetry. It is a convention never to be forgotten save in blank verse or when one is asleep.

The diction of the ultra-conservatives is sometimes modern and very beautiful, but often archaic and literary. It is usually the ultra-conservative poet who prefers the use of the old pronominal forms for direct address and begins his poem with "O Thou" or "Ye who." It is he who prefers the archaic forms of verbs—the "hast," "art," "wert" forms that go with the archaic pronouns. It is usually the ultra-conservative poet who will use a form like "careth" in one line, in the third person, and in another line, for the sake of rhyme, a form like "cares," also in the third person. It is the ultra-conservative poet who prefers the diction that used to be called "poetic," the diction that once belonged to life and was used by poets of other periods wisely and well because they found it close to life.

It is the ultra-conservative poet who appears to believe in imagery and symbolism as decorative additions to the poem rather than as structural parts of its truth and beauty.

For these reasons the poets and critics who belong to what is called "the new poetry movement" have been exceedingly cruel to the ultra-conservatives. They have not always been just. It is very hard to be just in the consideration of ideals which we are trying to displace, for which we are trying to substitute ideals that we consider better and higher. But in the interests of poetry we should be just. For the poems of the ultra-conservatives mean beauty to them, as the poems of the radicals mean beauty to radicals. Time alone can tell, in each individual case, who is right.

Chief among ultra-conservative poets in popularity and fame is Alfred Noyes, and many of the battles of contemporary criticism have been fought out on the question of the merit of his work. When his first poems were brought to the attention of the American public in the days before the "new poetry movement" was properly begun, it was quite the thing to like Mr. Noyes. Now, if one would be popular as a critic, one must decry him as Victorian. But strict justice demands neither out and out praise nor out and out censure for his work. Some of it is very much worth while. He can do certain things that other poets of to-day can not do so well, or at least have not done. He does other things very badly indeed. But it is the melancholy truth that he is as popular for the things he does badly as for the things he does well. This is why.

His ideas do not conflict in any way with those to which men and women trained in the schools of the past generation are accustomed. His emotions are always decorous. His tunes jingle happily. His colors are pretty. His verse is scented with rose and sweet with honey. What he says of Chopin, in his poem, "The Death of Chopin," is as true of himself. He has

> "Made Life as honey o'er the brink
> Of Death drip slow."

The poorest of his poems are those that are argumentative. Poets seldom make good poems when they argue. But sometimes they succeed in presenting their ideas with a certain terse skill and vividness that are interesting. Mr. Noyes does not. When he upbraids the scientist and confronts what he chooses to think of as unfortunate and benighted materialism with the conventional and ultra-conservative idea of religion, he makes it quite evident that he has not taken pains to know and understand the ideas and ideals of his imaginary opponent. Without any insincere intentions, I am sure, he misinterprets his adversary and then valiantly defies the misinterpretation. The poems in which Mr. Noyes slays straw men are quite without any quality of deep insight and without the imaginative felicity of which he is capable at his best. They serve to convey to the reader an idea for which no poet would care to be responsible, that it is better to be intellectually comfortable than intellectually candid. Take, as an example, "The Old Sceptic."

Very little better than these argumentative poems are his long and diffuse and sentimental lyrics and his epic, "Drake." His lyrics lack concentration and power. His epic lacks dignity and reality. When we stop to think of what the actualities of life must have been for that gallant mariner, Mr. Noyes' pages of romantic and velvety narrative verse and his suave interpolated lyrics seem as unreal as the landscape painted on the drop curtain of a theater.

It is superfluous, too, to say much of Mr. Noyes' sentimentality. Other critics have told the tale of it unkindly enough. There is too much said in his poetry of the "seas of dream" and the "shores of song." In the lyric called "The Last Battle" we find this stanza:

"Now all the plains of Europe smoke with marching hooves of thunder,
And through each ragged mountain-gorge the guns begin to gleam;
And round a hundred cities where the women watch and wonder,
The tramp of passing armies aches and faints into a dream."

This moves along very pleasantly and seems very good until we stop to analyze it. Analysis is cruel. But how can the plains of Europe "smoke" with "hooves"? And do hooves march like feet? And what are "hooves of thunder?" And why do the guns "begin to" gleam? Is it not because Mr. Noyes needs three more syllables to fill out the metrical scheme of the line? And how does the "tramp" of the armies "ache?" And is it emotionally honest to say that the tramp of armies "faints into a dream?" Is that the effect it has on consciousness? The daily newspapers print many paragraphs that give a truer and more vivid idea of warfare and the passing armies than this stanza gives.

But this is enough of censure. It remains to tell the story of the very real beauty in Mr. Noyes' work. For this is the beauty which is neglected or forgotten by many contemporary critics, simply because they do not like the qualities described in what we have already said and will not look for compensating virtues.

At his best Mr. Noyes is that very rare poet, the maker of fine ballads. Not to recognize this fact is to be altogether unjust to him and blind to values in poetry. He has the story teller's gift, the pleasant fancy, the sense of the dramatic incident, the light, quick touch, the facility with rhyme and rhythm, which go into the making of good ballads. Mr. Noyes makes such very good ballads that he should never do anything else. "The Highwayman," quick, fluent, dramatic, merits the popularity which many of his less admirable poems have won. And what can be said that will detract from the charm of that delightful, rollicking, ringing ballad, "Forty Singing Seamen"?

"Forty Singing Seamen" is a very fine poem of its kind, a masterpiece among modern ballads. It is a poem of dual nature, never very far from reality, never very far from a world that is purely imaginary. The sailors, after drinking the grog of the ghosts, have preposterous visions, but they have the visions in a very real and human way. The sailor-talk seems to have the right flavor.

"Across the seas of Wonderland to Mogadore we plodded,
 Forty singing seamen in an old black barque,
And we landed in the twilight where a Polyphemus nodded
 With his battered moon-eye winking red and yellow through the dark!
  For his eye was growing mellow,
  Rich and ripe and red and yellow,
 As was time, since Old Ulysses made him bellow in the dark!
Cho.—Since Ulysses bunged his eye up with a pine-torch in the dark!"

That is the first stanza and every other stanza is as good, as rich and lively and entertaining. Only very dull people, or very sophisticated people, of whom there are too many nowadays, can fail to get fun out of a ballad like that.

Moreover the technique of it is admirable. The rhythm is the true accompaniment of the story and the spirit, and just what a ballad rhythm ought to be. The imagery is admirable and always important in the life and structure of the poem. It is not a poem for the learned and sober. It is not a poem for the æsthete of the saffron schools. It is a poem for normal, wholesome, red-blooded human beings. And in this day and age when few poets can make ballads that are even readable, we should be the more grateful for this achievement.

Mr. Noyes has written other poems, in a similar vein, that are not to be despised. His "Song of a Wooden-Legged Fiddler" is one of them.

There are good passages, also, in "The Forest of Wild Thyme," and especially in Part II, called "The First Discovery." From this poem are taken the following delicately imagined lines:

> "If you could suddenly become
> As small a thing as they,
> A midget child, a new Tom Thumb,
> A little gauze-winged fay,
> Oh then, as through the mighty shades
> Of wild thyme woods and violet glades
> You groped your forest-way,
> How fraught each fragrant bough would be
> With dark o'er-hanging mystery."

Another well known poet of the ultra-conservative type is George Edward Woodberry. His finest achievement in poetry may well be his sonnet sequence called "Ideal Passion." Many critics have praised it lavishly. Writing in the Bulletin of The Poetry Society of America, Jessie B. Rittenhouse said, "It is doubtful if Mr. Woodberry has done anything finer than these sonnets which invoke again the spirit of the 'Vita Nuova' and other great expressions of love sublimated to an unattainable ideal." That is an exact statement of the quality of these sonnets. But, if we think of them in a purely human way, and without regard to the spirit of other literature, which they may be said to invoke, we miss something which would give them vitality. They are rare, but attenuated. They lack the Antæan strength that comes only from the earth. The Hercules of idealism has strangled them in mid air. They make us feel an obligation to rise beyond gravitation, to breathe without oxygen. After all, is it not true that ideals, to be most serviceable to mankind, must grow out of the common racial experience of mankind and fulfill themselves in the most lovely flowering of that experience? There is beauty in the lines that say,

> "in a flying marble fold
> Of Hellas once I saw eternity

> Flutter about her form; all nature she
> Inspirits, but round her being there is rolled
> The inextinguishable beauty old
> Of the far shining mountains and the sea."

but it is chilly beauty. This sonnet sequence, however, is an intellectual achievement.

A poet hardly less conservative in type, but with a warmth and quaintness of manner not to be found in Mr. Woodberry's poetry, is Olive Tilford Dargan. She has the gift of saying, sometimes, the simple, inevitable words that make the unforgettable picture. She does this more than once in that quiet-toned, freely rhythmical poem called "Old Fairingdown," in lines like these:

> "Each mute old house is more old than the other,
> And each wears its vines like ragged hair
> Round the half-blind windows."

That is authentic poetry, original and true.

How greatly it differs from lines like the following taken from "The Magdalen to Her Poet"!

> "Take back thy song; or let me hear what thou
> Heardst anciently from me,
> The woman; now
> This wassail drift on boughless shore;
> Once lyre-veined leading thee
> To swinging doors
> Out of the coiling dark."

Such lines as these are not only obscure but uninteresting. And a comparison of these two passages will serve to show the kind of thing conservatives do at their best, and when they are not at their best, the typical excellences and faults of the group.

Mrs. Dargan's best work, like the best work of Mr. Noyes, has been done in the making of a ballad. If she would only make more ballads as charming as "Path Flower," how happy we should be! "Path Flower" is at once very simple and very conventional. It uses one of the typical stanzas of balladry. It deals with the simplest of incidents, something that might happen at any time in the life of any kindly person, the giving of a small coin to a young girl who looked ragged and hungry! But this poem is so magically made that we are as much interested in this little incident as we could be in an event more important. The interest is admirably sustained from line to line and the poem is written with tact, refinement and delicacy of perception. The same quaintness of manner which is pleasing in "Old Fairingdown" is found in "Path Flower."

> "At foot each tiny blade grew big
> And taller stood to hear,
> And every leaf on every twig
> Was like a little ear."

Enough has been said about the work of the ultra-conservative poets to show that there are two ideals of poetry to-day, theirs, and the ideal of most of the other poets. To the ultra-conservatives, poetry is most intimately associated with literature. To the others it is most intimately associated with life. To the ultra-conservatives, it is something sacrosanct and precious, something a little too fragile for every day use. To the others it is spiritual bread and butter.

Now unfortunately, many ultra-conservatives never realize that, by giving to poetry this quality of the sacrosanct and the precious, they are keeping it away from all that makes it most meaningful and lovable to the people of the every day world. Not that the standard of poetry should be lowered that it may be brought close to human hearts—the end is not achieved in that way! Rather the standard should be raised in spirit and in technique so that poetry achieves a simple greatness and a great simplicity worthy of the people. Poetry written in a special literary language with prescribed rhythms and conventional ideas and set patterns may have beauty of a kind, and sometimes does have. But it is a beauty of tapestries, not a beauty of wildflowers and bird-song. And it is when they escape from the bondage of conventional verbiage and meter, and become, for the nonce, simple, natural and human, that we delight to name the men and women of this type, not ultra-conservatives, but poets.

SONG

For me the jasmine buds unfold
And silver daisies star the lea,
The crocus hoards the sunset gold,
And the wild rose breathes for me.
I feel the sap through the bough returning,
I share the skylark's transport fine,
I know the fountain's wayward yearning,
I love, and the world is mine!

I love, and thoughts that sometime grieved,
Still well remembered, grieve not me;
From all that darkened and deceived
Upsoars my spirit free.
For soft the hours repeat one story,
Sings the sea one strain divine;
My clouds arise all flushed with glory—
I love, and the world is mine!

Florence Earle Coates

FORTY SINGING SEAMEN*

"In our lands be Beeres and Lyons of dyvers colours as ye redd, grene, black, and white. And in our land be also unicornes and these Unicornes slee many Lyons. . . . Also there dare no man make a lye in our lande, for if he dyde he sholde incontynent be sleyn." *Mediaeval Epistle, of Pope Prester John.*

I

Across the seas of Wonderland to Mogadore we plodded,
Forty singing seamen in an old black barque,

And we landed in the twilight where a Polyphemus nodded
With his battered moon-eye winking red and yellow through the dark!
For his eye was growing mellow,
Rich and ripe and red and yellow,
As was time, since old Ulysses made him bellow in the dark!

Cho.—Since Ulysses bunged his eye up with a pine-torch in the dark!

II

Were they mountains in the gloaming or the giant's ugly shoulders
Just beneath the rolling eyeball, with its bleared and vinous glow,
Red and yellow o'er the purple of the pines among the boulders
And the shaggy horror brooding on the sullen slopes below,
Were they pines among the boulders
Or the hair upon his shoulders?
We were only simple seamen, so of course we didn't know.

Cho.—We were simple singing seamen, so of course we couldn't know.

III

But we crossed a plain of poppies, and we came upon a fountain
Not of water, but of jewels, like a spray of leaping fire;
And behind it, in an emerald glade, beneath a golden mountain
There stood a crystal palace, for a sailor to admire;
For a troop of ghosts came round us,
Which with leaves of bay they crowned us,
Then with grog they well nigh drowned us, to the depth of our desire!

Cho.—And 'twas very friendly of them, as a sailor can admire!

IV

There was music all about us, we were growing quite forgetful
We were only singing seamen from the dirt of London-town,
Though the nectar that we swallowed seemed to vanish half regretful
As if we wasn't good enough to take such vittles down,
When we saw a sudden figure,
Tall and black as any nigger,
Like the devil—only bigger—drawing near us with a frown!

Cho.—Like the devil—but much bigger—and he wore a golden crown!

V

And "What's all this?" he growls at us! With dignity we chaunted,
"Forty singing seamen, sir, as won't be put upon!"
"What? Englishmen?" he cries, "Well, if ye don't mind being haunted,
Faith, you're welcome to my palace; I'm the famous Prester John!
Will ye walk into my palace?
I don't bear 'ee any malice!
One and all ye shall be welcome in the halls of Prester John!"

Cho.—So we walked into the palace and the halls of Prester John!

VI

Now the door was one great diamond and the hall a hollow ruby—
Big as Beachy Head, my lads, nay bigger by a half!
And I sees the mate wi' mouth agape, a-staring like a booby,
And the skipper close behind him, with his tongue out like a calf!
Now the way to take it rightly
Was to walk along politely
Just as if you didn't notice—so I couldn't help but laugh!

Cho.—For they both forgot their manners and the crew was bound to laugh!

VII

But he took us through his palace and, my lads, as I'm a sinner,
We walked into an opal like a sunset-coloured cloud—
"My dining-room," he says, and, quick as light we saw a dinner
Spread before us by the fingers of a hidden fairy crowd;
And the skipper, swaying gently
After dinner, murmurs faintly,
"I looks to-wards you, Prester John, you've done us very proud!"

Cho.—And we drank his health with honours, for he *done* us *very* proud!

VIII

Then he walks us to his garden where we sees a feathered demon
Very splendid and important on a sort of spicy tree!
"That's the Phoenix," whispers Prester, "which all eddicated seamen

Knows the only one existent, and *he's* waiting for to flee!
When his hundred years expire
Then he'll set hisself afire
And another from his ashes rise most beautiful to see!"

Cho.—With wings of rose and emerald most beautiful to see!

IX

Then he says, "In yonder forest there's a little silver river,
And whosoever drinks of it, his youth shall never die!
The centuries go by, but Prester John endures forever
With his music in the mountains and his magic on the sky!
While *your* hearts are growing colder,
While your world is growing older,
There's a magic in the distance, where the sea-line meets the sky."

Cho.—It shall call to singing seamen till the fount o' song is dry!

X

So we thought we'd up and seek it, but that forest fair defied us,—
First a crimson leopard laughs at us most horrible to see,
Then a sea-green lion came and sniffed and licked his chops and eyed us,
While a red and yellow unicorn was dancing round a tree!
We was trying to look thinner
Which was hard, because our dinner
Must ha' made us very tempting to a cat o' high degree!

Cho.—Must ha' made us very tempting to the whole menarjeree!

XI

So we scuttled from that forest and across the poppy meadows
Where the awful shaggy horror brooded o'er us in the dark!
And we pushes out from shore again a-jumping at our shadows
And pulls away most joyful to the old black barque!
And home again we plodded
While the Polyphemus nodded
With his battered moon-eye winking red and yellow through the dark.

Cho.—Oh, the moon above the mountains, red and yellow through the dark!

XII

Across the seas of Wonderland to London-town we blundered,
Forty singing seamen as was puzzled for to know
If the visions that we saw was caused by—here again we pondered—
A tipple in a vision forty thousand years ago.
Could the grog we *dreamt* we swallowed
Make us *dream* of all that followed?
We were only simple seamen, so of course we didn't know!

Cho.—We were simple singing seamen, so of course we could not know!

Alfred Noyes

ASH WEDNESDAY

(*After hearing a lecture on the origins of religion*)

Here in the lonely chapel I will wait,
Here will I rest, if any rest may be;
So fair the day is, and the hour so late,
I shall have few to share the blessed calm with me.
Calm and soft light, sweet inarticulate calls!
One shallow dish of eerie golden fire
By molten chains above the altar swinging,
Draws my eyes up from the shadowed stalls
To the warm chancel-dome;
Crag-like the clustered organs loom,
Yet from their thunder-threatening choir
Flows but a ghostly singing—
Half-human voices reaching home
In infinite, tremulous surge and falls.
Light on his stops and keys,
And pallor on the player's face,
Who, listening rapt, with finger-skill to seize
The pattern of a mood's elusive grace,
Captures his spirit in an airy lace
Of fading, fading harmonies.
Oh, let your coolness soothe
My weariness, frail music, where you keep
Tryst with the even-fall;
Where tone by tone you find a pathway smooth

To yonder gleaming cross, or nearer creep
Along the bronzèd wall,
Where shade by shade thro' deeps of brown
Comes the still twilight down.

Wilt thou not rest, my thought?
Wouldst thou go back to that pain-breeding room
Whence only by strong wrenchings thou wert brought?
O weary, weary questionings,
Will ye pursue me to the altar rail
Where my old faith for sanctuary clings,
And back again my heart reluctant hale
Yonder, where crushed against the cheerless wall
Tiptoe I glimpsed the tier on tier
Of faces unserene and startled eyes—
Such eyes as on grim surgeon-work are set,
On desperate outmaneuverings of doom?
Still must I hear
The boding voice with cautious rise and fall
Tracking relentless to its lair
Each fever-bred progenitor of faith,
Each fugitive ancestral fear?
Still must I follow, as the wraith
Of antique awe toward a wreck-making beach
Drives derelict?
Nay, rest, rest, my thought,
Where long-loved sound and shadow teach
Quietness to conscience overwrought.

Harken! The choristers, the white-robed priest
Move thro' the chapel dim
Sounding of warfare and the victor's palm,
Of valiant marchings, of the feast
Spread for the pilgrim in a haven'd calm.
How on the first lips of my steadfast race
Sounded that battle hymn,
Quaint heaven-vauntings, with God's gauntlet flung,
To me bequeathed, from age to age,
My challenge and my heritage!
"The Lord is in His holy place"—

How in their ears the herald voice has rung!
Now will I make bright their sword,
Will pilgrim in their ancient path,
Will haunt the temple of their Lord;
Truth that is neither variable nor hath
Shadow of turning, I will find
In the wise ploddings of their faithful mind;
Of finding not, as in this frustrate hour
By question hounded, waylaid by despair,
Yet in these uses shall I know His power
As the warm flesh by breathing knows the air.

O futile comfort! My faith-hungry heart
Still in your sweetness tastes a poisonous sour;
Far off, far off I quiver 'neath the smart
Of old indignities and obscure scorn
Indelibly on man's proud spirit laid,
That now in time's ironic masquerade
Minister healing to the hurt and worn!
What are those streams that from the altar pour
Where goat and ox and human captive bled
To feed the blood-lust of the murderous priest?
I cannot see where Christ's dear love is shed,
So deep the insatiate horrow washes red
Flesh-stains and frenzy-sears and gore.
Beneath that Cross, whereon His hands outspread,
What forest shades behold what shameful rites
Of maidenhood surrendered to the beast
In obscene worship on midsummer nights!
What imperturbable disguise
Enwraps these organs with a chaste restraint
To chant innocuous hymns and litanies
For sinner and adoring saint,
Which yet inherit like an old blood-taint
Some naked caperings in the godliest tune,—
Goat-songs and jests strong with the breath of Pan,
That charmed the easy cow-girl and her man
In uncouth tryst beneath a scandalous moon!
Ah, could I hearken with their trust,
Or see with their pure-seeing eyes

Who of the frame of these dear mysteries
Were not too wise!
Why cannot I, as in a stronger hour,
Outface the horror that defeats me now?
Have I not reaped complacent the rich power
That harvest from this praise and bowing low?
On this strong music have I mounted up,
At yonder rail broke bread, and shared the holy cup,
And on that cross have hung, and felt God's pain
Sorrowing, sorrowing, till the world shall end.

Not from these forms my questionings come
That serving truth are purified,
But from the truth itself, the way, the goal,
One challenge vast that strikes faith dumb—
If truth be fickle, who shall be our guide?
"Truth that is neither variable, nor hath
Shadow of turning?" Ah, where turns she not!
Where yesterday she stood,
Now the horizon empties—lo, her steps
Where yonder scholar woos, are hardly cold,
Yet shall he find her never, but the thought
Mantling within him like her blood
Shall from his eloquence fade, and leave his words
Flavor'd with vacant quaintness for his son.
What crafty patience, scholar, hast thou used,
Useless ere it was begun—
What headless waste of wing,
Beating vainly round and round!
In no one Babel were the tongues confused,
But they who handle truth, from sound to sound
Master another speech continuously.
Deaf to familiar words, our callous ear
Will quiver to the edge of utterance strange;
When truth to God's truth-weary sight draws near,
Cannot God see her till she suffer change?
Must ye then change, my vanished youth,
Home customs of my dreams?
Change and farewell!
Farewell, your lost phantasmic truth

That will not constant dwell,
But flees the passion of our eyes
And leaves no hint behind her
Whence she dawns or whither dies,
Or if she live at all, or only for a moment seems.

Here tho' I only dream I find her,
Here will I watch the twilight darken.
Yonder the scholar's voice spins on
Mesh upon mesh of loveless fate;
Here will I rest while truth deserts him still.
What hath she left thee, Brother, but thy voice?
After her, have thy will,
And happy be thy choice!
Here rather will I rest, and harken
Voices longer dead but longer loved than thine.

Yet still my most of peace is more unrest,
As one who plods a summer road
Feels the coolness his own motion stirs,
But when he stops the dead heat smothers him.
Here in this calm my soul is weariest,
Each question with malicious goad
Pressing the choice that still my soul defers
To visioned hours not thus eclipsed and dim,
Lest in my haste I deem
That truth's invariable part
Is her eluding of man's heart.
Farewell, calm priest who pacest slow
After the stalwart-marching choir!
Have men thro' thee taught God their dear desire?
Hath God thro' thee absolvèd sin?
What is thy benediction, if I go
Sore perplexed and wrought within?
Open the chapel doors, and let
Boisterous music play us out
Toward the flaring molten west
Whither the nerve-racked day is set;
Let the loud world, flooding back,
Gulf us in its hungry rout;
Rest? What part have we in rest?

Boy with the happy face and hurrying feet,
Who with thy friendly cap's salute
Sendest bright hail across the college street,
If thou couldst see my answering lips, how mute,
How loth to take thy student courtesy!
What truth have I for thee?
Rather thy wisdom, lad, impart,
Share thy gift of strength with me.
Still with the past I wrestle, but the future girds thy heart.
Clutter of shriveled yesterdays that clothe us like a shell,
Thy spirit sloughs their bondage off, to walk newborn and free.
All things the human heart hath learned—God, heaven, earth, and
hell—
Thou weighest not for what they were, but what they still may be.
Whether the scholar delve and mine for faith-wreck buried deep.
Or the priest his rules and holy rites, letter and spirit, keep;
Toil or trust in breathless dust, they shall starve at last for truth;
Scholar and priest shall live from thee, who art eternal youth.
Holier if thou dost tread it, every path the prophets trod;
Clearer where thou dost worship, rise the ancient hymns to God;
Not by the priest but by thy prayers are altars sanctified;
Strong with new love where thou dost kneel, the cross whereon Christ
died.

John Erskine

AROUND THE SUN *

The weazen planet Mercury,
Whose song is done,—
Rash heart that drew too near
His dazzling lord the Sun!—
Forgets that life was dear,
So shrivelled now and sere
The goblin planet Mercury.

But Venus, thou mysterious,
Enveilèd one,
Fairest of lights that fleet
Around the radiant Sun,

* From "The Retinue and Other Poems," copyright, 1918, by E. P. Dutton & Co.

Do not thy pulses beat
To music blithe and sweet,
O Venus, veiled, mysterious?

And Earth, our shadow-haunted Earth,
  Hast thou, too, won
The graces of a star
  From the glory of the Sun?
Do poets dream afar
That here all lustres are,
Upon our blind, bewildered Earth?

We dream that mighty forms on Mars,
  With wisdom spun
From subtler brain than man's,
  Are hoarding snow and sun,
Wringing a few more spans
Of life, fierce artisans,
From their deep-grooved, worn planet Mars.

But thou, colossal Jupiter,
  World just begun,
Wild globe of golden steam,
  Chief nursling of the Sun,
Transcendest human dream,
That faints before the gleam
Of thy vast splendor, Jupiter.

And for what rare delight,
  Of woes to shun,
Of races increate,
  New lovers of the Sun,
Was Saturn ringed with great
Rivers illuminate,
Ethereal jewel of delight?

Far from his fellows, Uranus
  Doth lonely run
In his appointed ways
  Around the sovereign Sun,—

Wide journeys that amaze
Our weak and toiling gaze,
Searching the path of Uranus.

But on the awful verge
  Of voids that stun
The spirit, Neptune keeps
  The frontier of the Sun.
Over the deeps on deeps
He glows, a torch that sweeps
The circle of that shuddering verge.

On each bright planet waits
  Oblivion,
Who casts beneath her feet
  Ashes of star and sun;
But when all ruby heat
Is frost, a Heart shall beat,
Where God within the darkness waits.

Katharine Lee Bates

THE FLIGHT

O Wild Heart, track the land's perfume,
  Beach-roses and moor-heather!
All fragrances of herb and bloom
  Fail, out at sea, together.
O follow where aloft find room
  Lark-song and eagle-feather!
All ecstasies of throat and plume
  Melt, high on yon blue weather.

O leave on sky and ocean lost
  The flight creation dareth;
Take wings of love, that mounts the most;
  Find fame, that furthest fareth!
Thy flight, albeit amid her host
  Thee, too, night star-like beareth,
Flying, thy breath on heaven's coast,
  The infinite outweareth.

II

"Dead o'er us roll celestial fires;
  Mute stand Earth's ancient beaches;
Old thoughts, old instincts, old desires,
  The passing hour outreaches;
The soul creative never tires—
  Evokes, adores, beseeches;
And that heart most the god inspires
  Whom most its wildness teaches.

"For I will course through falling years,
  And stars and cities burning;
And I will march through dying cheers
  Past empires unreturning;
Ever the world-flame reappears
  Where mankind power is earning,
The nations' hopes, the people's tears,
  One with the wild heart yearning."

George Edward Woodberry

My lady ne'er hath given herself to me
  In mortal ways, nor on my eyes to hold
  Her image; in a flying marble fold
Of Hellas once I saw eternity
Flutter about her form; all nature she
  Inspirits, but round her being there is rolled
  The inextinguishable beauty old
Of the far shining mountains and the sea.

Now all my manhood doth enrich her shrine
  Where first the young boy stored all hope, all fear.
Fortune and fame and love be never mine,
  Since, seeking those, to her I were less dear!
Albeit she hides herself in the divine,
  Always and everywhere I feel her near.

George Edward Woodberry

PATH FLOWER *

A red-cap sang in Bishop's wood,
  A lark o'er Golder's lane,
As I the April pathway trod
  Bound west for Willesden.

At foot each tiny blade grew big
  And taller stood to hear,
And every leaf on every twig
  Was like a little ear.

As I too paused, and both ways tried
  To catch the rippling rain,—
So still, a hare kept at my side
  His tussock of disdain,—

Behind me close I heard a step,
  A soft pit-pat surprise,
And looking round my eyes fell deep
  Into sweet other eyes;

The eyes like wells, where sun lies too,
  So clear and trustful brown,
Without a bubble warning you
  That here's a place to drown.

"How many miles?" Her broken shoes
  Had told of more than one.
She answered like a dreaming Muse,
  "I came from Islington."

"So long a tramp?" Two gentle nods
  Then seemed to lift a wing,
And words fell soft as willow-buds,
  "I came to find the Spring."

A timid voice, yet not afraid
  In ways so sweet to roam,
As it with honey bees had played
  And could no more go home.

Her home! I saw the human lair,
  I heard the hucksters bawl,
I stifled with the thickened air
  Of bickering mart and stall.

Without a tuppence for a ride,
  Her feet had set her free.
Her rags, that decency defied,
  Seemed new with liberty.

But she was frail. Who would might note
  The trail of hungering
That for an hour she had forgot
  In wonder of the Spring.

So shriven by her joy she glowed
  It seemed a sin to chat.
(A tea-shop snuggled off the road;
  Why did I think of that?)

Oh, frail, so frail! I could have wept,—
  But she was passing on,
And I but muddled "You'll accept
  A penny for a bun?"

Then up her little throat a spray
  Of rose climbed for it must;
A wilding lost till safe it lay
  Hid by her curls of rust;

And I saw modesties at fence
  With pride that bore no name;
So old it was she knew not whence
  It sudden woke and came;

But that which shone of all most clear
  Was startled, sadder thought
That I should give her back the fear
  Of life she had forgot.

And I blushed for the world we'd made,
  Putting God's hand aside,
Till for the want of sun and shade
  His little children died;

And blushed that I who every year
  With Spring went up and down,
Must greet a soul that ached for her
  With "penny for a bun!"

Struck as a thief in holy place
  Whose sin upon him cries,
I watched the flowers leave her face,
  The song go from her eyes.

Then she, sweet heart, she saw my rout,
  And of her charity
A hand of grace put softly out
  And took the coin from me.

A red-cap sang in Bishop's wood,
  A lark o'er Golder's lane;
But I, alone, still glooming stood,
  And April plucked in vain;

Till living words rang in my ears
  And sudden music played:
Out of such sacred thirst as hers
  The world shall be remade.

Afar she turned her head and smiled
  As might have smiled the Spring,
And humble as a wondering child
  I watched her vanishing.

Olive Tilford Dargan

CERTAIN RADICAL POETS

An old rhetoric, used in schoolrooms about twenty years ago, defines a figure of speech as "an intentional departure from the ordinary form, order, construction or meaning of words, intended to give emphasis, clearness, variety or beauty." This definition might be paraphrased to define the radical poetry of the moderns. Indeed a radical poet, like his poetry, may be called a figure of speech! For he departs intentionally from the ordinary form, order, construction or meaning of words in poetry, intending to give his work a new emphasis, clearness, variety and beauty.

Conservatives say that departures of this kind are fatal mistakes. They even hint that radical poets do not depart intentionally, but perforce, because the traditional ways of English poetry are too strait for their errant temperaments. This is easy to say, but difficult to prove. We shall learn too little good of radicals from the conversation of conservatives. To learn about radical poets we must read their poems and ask ourselves whether we can find the new "emphasis, clearness, variety and beauty."

Who, then, are the radical poets? As defined for purposes of this discussion, they are the poets whose craftsmanship is new and experimental. They may be, also, poets whose ideas on social problems are radical. Or they may be conservatives in their thought of life, and radicals only in their ways of making poems. That sometimes happens. Sometimes, also, it happens that poets who use the traditional forms of English verse are as radical in their social beliefs as their brothers who write free verse. What is said here is intended to apply only to poets who make their poems in the new or radical ways.

It is impossible to discuss them all. Many of them, moreover, have been mentioned in other chapters. Amy Lowell, of whom much has been said already, is an arch-radical. The Imagists, whose work was described in association with the discussion of images and symbols, have founded their important radical school. But no introduction to contemporary poetry would be complete without comment on the work of several other groups of radical poets.

The chief poets of the radical movement who are not Imagists can be classified together as oratorical, humanitarian radicals. They have much in common. Most of them are strong social democrats and to a certain extent propagandists in their poetry. They all seem to love life—even violently. They are possessed of strong emotions to which they give direct, eloquent, sometimes fulsome expression. To a certain extent they are iconoclasts. Their images and symbols are often vivid and impressive. Their diction is sometimes very good and sometimes very bad. Their rhythms are long, undulating, often broken and uncertain, sometimes very tiresome, at their best sonorous and beautiful. But all too often, in trying to create poems without using the traditional patterns, they have tried to create poems with no perceptible patterns. When they have tried to do this they have usually failed to make poetry.

The artistic ideal of the humanitarian radicals, if one can guess it from their work, is the ideal of oratory—a man pouring out his heart before his fellows. They would overwhelm us with torrents of emotion. They use language that the crowd understands. They are as eloquent as good political speakers. But they are seldom designers, makers. If their work is to live, it must be by virtue of the truth in it, by virtue of the value of the thoughts and emotions expressed (which value will be tested by time), not by virtue of pattern or melody.

The following lines taken from Clement Wood's perfervid apostrophe to the world in "Spring" are typical of much of the least interesting work of this group:

"Hey, old world, old lazy-bones, wake to the Spring-tune!
The music of the spheres is quickened to a jig,—
Wobble a one-step along your flashing orbit, with the moon for your
light-tripping partner!"

Such lines as these, without melody, without coherent beauty of design, tossed off at random, apparently, attempt a crude sublimity, but succeed only in being saucy. They slap Life jocosely on the shoulder and chuck the Universe under the chin.

It is only fair to Mr. Wood to say that he has done much better things than this. He has written interesting poems and he says some things worth saying, like these lines from "A Prayer:"

> "Keep me from dream-ridden indolence,
> That softens the sinews of my spirit.
>
> Send me forth, adventuring,
> From the quick mud of the gutter
> To the clasp of the thin golden fingers of the stars.
>
> Let me will life,
> And its freshening, hearty struggles."

James Oppenheim, also a humanitarian radical, is a more mature poet than Clement Wood and his work has been before the public longer. There is more of it to be considered and it deserves more careful consideration. Mr. Oppenheim thinks. He feels. And he speaks. As he himself says, in the poem called "Before Starting" in "Songs For The New Age,"

> "It was as if myself sat down beside me,
> And at last I could speak out to my dear friend,
> And tell him, day after day, of the things that were reshaping me."

In this calm of sincere and profound soliloquy Mr. Oppenheim's best poems seem to have been written, for they carry the atmosphere of calm soliloquy with them. It sometimes happens that they are very short. Such a poem is "The Runner in The Skies."

> "Who is the runner in the skies,
> With her blowing scarf of stars,
> And our Earth and sun hovering like bees about her blossoming heart?
> Her feet are on the winds, where space is deep,
> Her eyes are nebulous and veiled,
> She hurries through the night to a far lover."

The same virtue is in "The Greatest," "Quick As a Humming-bird," "No End of Song," "Larkspur" and "Said The Sun."

"Said the sun: I that am immense and shaggy flame,
Sustain the small ones yonder:
But what do they do when their half of the Earth is turned from me?
Poor dark ones, denied my light.

A little brain, however, was on that other half of the planet . . .
And so there were lamps."

Many of these short poems reveal Mr. Oppenheim at his best. They are concise, thoughtful, imaginative, and have the quiet charm of meditative speech. They make places for themselves in the minds of readers, and remain.

But Mr. Oppenheim does not always seem to be chatting quietly with himself about the things that are reshaping him. Often he is so vociferous that it is easy to picture him pacing a platform, talking with undeniable vigor to himself or to the multitude and making himself heard. In "Civilization" he is far more the orator than the poet. He is talking loud and scornfully.

"Civilization!
Everybody kind and gentle, and men giving up their seats in the car
for the women . . .
What an ideal!
How bracing!

Is this what we want?
Have so many generations lived and died for this?
There have been Crusades, persecutions, wars, and majestic arts,
There have been murders and passions and horrors since man was in
the jungle . . .
What was this blood-toll for?
Just so that everybody could have a full belly and be well-mannered?"

This is very interesting, but is it poetry? Here we have stimulating thought and honest feeling put into lengths of exclamatory language. But that is about all. We find no pattern in rhythm, imagery, or symbolism. We are glad of the stimulating thought and honest emotion. They are refreshing and much better for us than an æsthetic composition in which specious thoughts and shallow feelings are masked. Such lines may serve to arouse us from intellectual and spiritual lethargy. But the chances are that we shall never repeat them to ourselves for the joy of repeating them. We shall not cherish and remember lines like these as we should cherish and remember poems by William Vaughn Moody, Vachel Lindsay or Robert Frost. They will not make their own places and abide with us as Mr. Oppenheim's best poems will.

By far the finest piece of literature that James Oppenheim has produced is a dramatic poem called "Night." At night a priest, a scientist and a poet are met together under the stars and they confer together, telling one another what they think of the universe and all that therein is. Then a woman enters, carrying a burden, her dead baby in her arms, and seeks of each of them in turn the answer to the riddle of pain and sorrow. She is not satisfied with any answer and turns away from them all to defy the Power that lets such things be. Then comes the man, her husband, and, because he needs her, she turns away from death and goes back to life with him. Her maternal pity takes her mate to be her child. The priest says, "Forgive these children, Lord God!" The scientist says, "Ignorance is indeed bliss!" The poet says:

> "The secret of life?
> He gives it to her, she gives it to him . . .
> But who shall tell of it? Who shall know it?"

That is the story, a very simple story. The beauty of the poem is in the fact that it is an admirable piece of sympathetic imagination. Mr. Oppenheim knows the thought of the priest, the scientist and the poet; he has shown very clearly how these three typical personalities see life. He has known the emotions of the man. He has fathomed the sorrow of the woman. He has faithfully revealed truths that can be considered universal.

"Night" is very well written. The rhythm of the speeches is dignified. And the oratorical style, not well adapted, as a rule, to the uses of subjective, lyrical poetry, is quite appropriate in this dramatic poem in which are several speakers, in which each speaker is a type, a part of a pattern worked out in ideas. The language is warm and rich, simple and human and suggestive of subtle meanings. The priest's first question and the woman's answer are masterly. Says the priest, "Your child has died. . ." The woman answers, "My baby is dead. . ." The priest uses the general and impersonal word, "child." The woman uses the personal and more intimate word, "baby." The priest refers to an event that has taken place, "has died." The woman uses the present tense of her own sorrow, "is dead." Mr. Oppenheim ought to write more poems of this kind.

Probably one of the greatest of radical poets is Carl Sandburg. His manner is oratorical, like Mr. Oppenheim's, but he varies his rhythms with greater cunning and he is a greater artist. Some of his poems are very shapely in their clean-cut power of design. At their best his poems make one think of Rodin. They are the words that correspond to Rodin's lines. And in all of Mr. Sandburg's work we are conscious of a big, kind personality, a man speaking, a person present in language. He is the man who talks. In reading his books we are conscious of faith and virility, wise scorn, buoyant anger and great tenderness. Even those who read Mr. Sandburg's work without agreement, without much sympathy, are likely to say, "Well, anyway, he is a man." So true is this that a cautious critic is likely to ask himself, "Do I like this because it is poetry or because a manly personality is speaking?" Sometimes it is wise to ask this question. One may well ask whether the eloquent lines called "I Am The People, The Mob," are the lines of a poem or the lines of an impassioned speech on the destiny of the masses.

"I am the people—the mob—the crowd—the mass.
Do you know that all the great work of the world is done through me?
I am the workingman, the inventor, the maker of the world's food and
clothes.
I am the audience that witnesses history."

This is rather more eloquent than poetic. It has value as an expression of personality. It has a rhythm of staccato speech. But it is plain statement, after all. It lacks the lifting power of poetry. Nor do the lines about Chicago, the harangue "To A Contemporary Bunkshooter," and the curse spoken against Becker seem to be poems, although poetic phrases are plentiful in them and although, in a certain sense, they do vividly share life.

But this only tells a part of the story. Often, very often indeed, Mr. Sandburg is a poet of rhythm, symbol, and magical design. A poet he was when he wrote "Uplands in May," "Jan Kubelik," "Sheep," "Cool Tombs," "Back Yard," "The Harbor," "River Roads," "Early Moon," "Have Me," "Handfuls," "Bringers" and many other poems.

More than any other poet who has found a public, Mr. Sandburg uses the speech of the common people of America, with its colloquialisms and its slang. In "Wilderness" is the following paragraph.

"O, I got a zoo, I got a menagerie, inside my ribs, under my bony head, under my red-valve heart—and I got something else: it is a man-child heart, a woman-child heart: it is a father and mother and lover: it came from God-Knows-Where: it is going to God-Knows-Where—For I am the keeper of the zoo: I say yes and no: I sing and kill and work: I am a pal of the world: I came from the wilderness."

Only the common people and children sometimes use "got' in that way. It is the familiar folk speech to which words like "zoo" and "pal" belong. Such words would not be taboo for conservative poets in narrative or dramatic poetry, but no conservative poet would take them upon his own lips in his own speech or song. Similarly Mr. Sandburg, in his poem about those who "go forth before daybreak" (strangely called a "psalm"), says that the policeman buys shoes "slow and careful." The use of the adjective for the adverb is another part of the homely talk of the common people. Sometimes one wonders why Mr. Sandburg uses these colloquialisms. As part of the talk of a character in a story, they would be piquant and flavorous. But why should Mr. Sandburg, the poet, use them when he himself is speaking to his readers? If one might hazard a guess, it is simply because he likes the folk speech, the plain man's way of saying things, so much that he would rather be picturesque and colloquial than keep the venerable beauty of pure English.

Mr. Sandburg has written poems of several kinds, as we have seen already, oratorical poems, picture poems, brief lyrical poems. His work is growing in power and in beauty. At first much of it was loud and brash. Now much of it is quaint and full of gentleness. And best of all it is close to the heart of the folk, whence the best poetry comes.

Almost as much as radicals differ from conservatives do radicals like T. S. Eliot and Ezra Pound differ from radicals like Carl Sandburg and James Oppenheim. Their emotions are not redundant, but spare. Their style is not oratorical. Their voices are not orotund, but sly, insinuating, satirical, and, occasionally, shrill. They are poets of the world and very far from the folk. They are undeniably alarmingly clever. Notice these lines from "The Love Song of J. Alfred Prufrock" by T. S. Eliot:

> "Let us go then, you and I,
> When the evening is spread out against the sky
> Like a patient etherized upon a table."

The comparison would never come into the mind of a stupid man, of an unsophisticated man. It is clever, also, to speak of the "damp souls of housemaids." It is clever to say that the laughter of a certain Mr. Apollinax "was submarine and profound."

It is such cleverness that one finds in Mr. Eliot's work. It is for such things, as much as for anything else, that his admirers praise him. His sketches of personality are dry and hard. His comment on the complex lives of worldlings is all entertaining. But a poet must be more than clever and entertaining to merit the attention of many readers. A brittle æstheticism is not enough.

As for Mr. Pound, it is difficult to write about him. He is so clever that one mentions him with trepidation, knowing how much amused he would be at the wrong thing said. The truth of the matter is that Mr. Pound is too clever to be a poet. He ought to spend his time in discovering geniuses and explaining talent and genius to a less clever world. For whether one agrees with him or not, he is frequently interesting as a critic.

Now in Mr. Pound's poetry, as in his prose criticism, we find a very keen-edged intellect cutting and slashing at stupidity. In criticism this may be all very well. But in poetry it is irritating. A poem subtly charged with conscious superiority will hardly give pleasure to many readers, because they themselves never have cause to know what conscious superiority is like, and therefore can not share the mood. Very likely Mr. Pound does not expect nor even wish his poems to give pleasure to many readers. He would prefer, probably, to please a few hundred carefully selected intellects. Or perhaps he would please only himself and is content to amuse the dull world. Most of his poems are no better than clever. Take these lines, for example, from "Further Instructions:"

"You are very idle, my songs;
I fear you will come to a bad end.

You stand about the streets. You loiter at the corners and busstops,
You do next to nothing at all.
You do not even express our inner nobility;
You will come to a very bad end.

* * * *

> But you, newest song of the lot,
> You are not old enough to have done much mischief.
> I will get you a green coat out of China
> With dragons worked upon it.
> I will get you the scarlet silk trousers
> From the statue of the infant Christ at Santa Maria Novella;
> Lest they say we are lacking in taste,
> Or that there is no caste in this family."

The ordinary person is bewildered by lines like these. It disturbs him to have a poet self-consciously address his poems and make fun of his readers at the same time. Louis Untermeyer, our shrewd American critic, has made a series of amusing parodies of Mr. Pound's style which the ordinary person will enjoy rather more than the originals. They are included in his book of parodies "—And Other Poets," a book which will be a delight to students of the style of contemporary poets.

But if all his works were of this kind, it would not be worth while to discuss Mr. Pound as a poet at all. Sometimes he is guilty of a catcall from the top gallery. But there are serene musical interludes. His translations from the Chinese are interesting. His "Ballad For Gloom" has a certain gallantry which the brave, who have known bitterness, will understand and feel. The rhythm of it is strong, the feeling is strong. His "Ballad of The Goodly Fere" is one of the finest poems about Christ that contemporary poets have given us. In this poem Christ is the brave man, the hero.

> "A master of men was the Goodly Fere,
> A mate of the wind and sea.
> If they think they ha' slain our Goodly Fere
> They are fools eternally.
>
> "I ha' seen him eat o' the honey-comb
> Sin' they nailed him to the tree."

Very beautiful, also, are some of the lines in his "Dance Figure," a poem written "For the Marriage in Cana of Galilee."

"Dark-eyed,
O woman of my dreams,
Ivory sandaled,
There is none like thee among the dancers,
None with swift feet.

I have not found thee in the tents,
In the broken darkness.
I have not found thee at the well-head
Among the women with pitchers.

Thine arms are as young saplings under the bark;
Thy face as a river with lights."

The scriptural style of these lines is worthy of note. If only Mr. Pound were less clever, he might be a very good poet.

Alfred Kreymborg, the leader in the group of poets generally called "The Others" from the name of their magazine and their anthology, is a poet of another kind. He is a whimsical radical, the leader of the whimsical radicals. His poems are like the little oddments one finds while rummaging in an old curiosity shop. Some of them are ridiculous and valueless, some quaint and amusing; a few are beautiful. His poorer poems are shadowy and trivial. They lack symmetry of design, charm of rhythm and vitality of emotion. But his best poems make up for certain deficiencies of rhythm and design and rather slight emotion —the most serious lack—by their charm of really delicate fancy and by their quaint symbolism. Their beauty is minute and fragile, like the beauty of a miniature. Some of the best of his poems are "Idealists," "Old Manuscript," "Earth Wisdom," and "Improvisation."

Mr. Kreymborg is the author of "Six Plays For Poet Mimes," six entertaining little dramas in free verse. They have been played with success at a number of the "Little Theaters" and by groups of students. Each of these plays, however, may be considered as a pattern in which the words are only an outline. Or perhaps it would be truer to say that the words are intended to be a running comment on the action. Certainly the words are not complete alone, without action. Very likely that should augur well for them as plays. In much that is called "poetic drama" the words are decidedly in the way of all that happens on the stage; they hinder and retard the action. In Mr. Kreymborg's plays that could not be true. For to the reader they seem to need the action that they may fulfill themselves. As poems to be read they are incomplete.

The same thing might be said of another play by another poet, "Grotesques: A Decoration In Black And White," by Cloyd Head. This is a more serious work than the plays of Alfred Kreymborg, and of greater importance. But it is a poetic drama to be played rather than a dramatic poem to be read. Mr. Head has been merciless and unflinching in cutting out every bit of language that is unnecessary in the play when it is acted. Perhaps that is why "Grotesques" won the enthusiastic praise of Harriet Monroe and of many competent critics when it was first played in Chicago at the Chicago Little Theater. But it should not be underestimated as a poem. Grim in its philosophy, an ironical comment on human achievement and destiny, it is one of the most interesting radical poems of the period. But it is too long to be reprinted as a whole and it is difficult to do it justice by quotation, since it is, as has been said, a poetic play, a conventionalized "decoration" to be seen with the eyes and heard with the ears at the same time. It is only fair to say of Mr. Head that he has undeniable talent and is a scrupulous and uncompromising artist. He is likely to contribute much genuine beauty to contemporary literature.

Of the radical poets in general it may be said that most of their work will die, and die very soon. But that may be said just as truly of conservative poets. Nearly all of the work of nearly all poets dies, and dies soon. And it is never possible for any generation to know which of its achievements will endure and become immortal. Contemporary criticism is always a mere preliminary test before the final examination, a straw vote taken before election day.

But the history of the arts and of mankind seems to show that often it is the *great* radicals of one generation who survive and become types of the achievement of that generation, and are considered conservative by succeeding generations. Therefore radical tendencies should be studied carefully. It is not necessary, of course, to ponder the inanities and insanities of all seekers after novelty and sensationalism, any more than it is necessary to give thoughtful consideration to poems that are, obviously, feeble imitations of Tennyson and Keats. The greatest scholars can not understand the chatter of daws, the shrieking of jays. But wherever a radical poet can be found who is giving something good out of himself and giving it sincerely, he should have as good a hearing as conservatives are certain to get, even if his way of giving expression to his feelings be a new way with which we are not familiar. Perhaps he should have a rather better hearing than the conservative for the simple reason that he brings something new which is not generally understood. Our fair-minded readers and just critics should be sure that they know what the new poet is trying to do before they respond to it with harsh censure. For radical poets are poets who are making experiments that may lead to new adventures in beauty for us all.

For other reasons we should be generous with the strongest radical poets. Much poetry that has no value for posterity may have value for us in showing us the countenance of our own generation as in a mirror. Much that is lax, errant, wilful, slovenly, in the thought and feeling of this generation, will be shown in the work of our radical poets, just as much that is smug, complacent, drab, commonplace, will be reflected in the work of conservatives. Perhaps, after all, it is between the two extremes of conservatism and radicalism that we usually find the genius of beauty, the genius of truth and the genius of holiness.

FROM "NIGHT"

A Priest, A Poet, A Scientist.
Hilltop, in October: the stars shining.
[*The Priest kneels; the Scientist looks at the heavens through a telescope; the Poet writes in a little note-book.*]

THE PRIEST

When I consider Thy heavens, the work of Thy fingers, the moon and the stars, which Thou hast ordained;
What is man, that Thou art mindful of him,
And the son of man, that Thou visitest him?

THE SCIENTIST

Algol which is dim, becomes again a star of the second magnitude.

THE POET

My beloved is far from this hilltop, where the firs breathe heavily, and the needles fall;
But from the middle of the sea
She, too, gazes on the lustrous stars of calm October, and in her heart
She stands with me beneath these heavens—daintily blows
Breath of the sighing pines, and from the loaded and bowed-down orchards and from the fields
With smokes of the valley, peace steps up on this hill.

THE PRIEST

Thou art the Shepherd that strides down the Milky Way;
Thou art the Lord, our God: glorified be Thy name and Thy works.
I see Thee with Thy staff driving the star-sheep to the fold of dawn.

THE SCIENTIST

The Spiral Nebula in Ursa Major, that forever turns
Slowly like a flaming pin-wheel . . . thus are worlds born;
Thus was the sun and all the planets a handful of million years ago.

THE POET

She is far from me . . . but in the cradle of the sea
Sleepless she rocks, calling her beloved: he heeds her call:
On this hilltop he picks the North Star for his beacon . . .
For by that star the sailors steer, and beneath that star
She and I are one in the gaze of the heavens.

THE PRIEST

[*Slowly rising and turning to the others*]
Let us glorify the Creator of this magnificence of infinite Night,
His footstool is the Earth, and we are but the sheep of this Shepherd.

THE SCIENTIST

Thus shall we only glorify ourselves,
That of this energy that rolls and drives in suns and planets
Are but the split-off forces with cunning brains,
And questioning consciousness . . . Pray if you must—
Only your own ears hear you, and only the heart in your breast
Responds to the grandiose emotion. . . . See yonder star?
That is the great Aldebaran, great in the night,
Needing a whole sky, as a vat and a reservoir, which he fills with his flame. . .
But no astronomer with his eye to his lenses
Has seen ears on the monster.

THE PRIEST

Thou that hast never seen an atom, nor the ether thou pratest of,
Thou that hast never seen the consciousness of man,
What knowest thou of the invisible arms about this sky,
And the Father that leans above us?

THE POET

We need know nothing of any Father
When the grasses themselves, withering in October, stand up and sing their own dirges in the great west wind,
And every pine is like a winter lodging house where the needles may remember the greenness of the world,
And the great shadow is jagged at its top with stars,

And the heart of man is as a wanderer looking for the light in a window,
And the kiss and warm joy of his beloved.

THE PRIEST

Man of Song and Man of Science,
Truly you are as people on the outside of a house,
And one of you only sees that it is made of stone, and its windows of glass, and that fire burns in the hearth,
And the other of you sees that the house is beautiful and very human,
But I have gone inside the house,
And I live with the host in that house
And have broken bread with him, and drunk his wine,
And seen the transfiguration that love and awe make in the brain. . . .
For that house is the world, and the Lord is my host and my father:
It is my father's house.

THE SCIENTIST

He that has gone mad and insane may call himself a king,
And behold himself in a king's palace, with feasting, and dancing women, and with captains,
And none can convince him that he is mad,
Slave of hallucination. . . .
We that weigh the atom and weigh a world in the night, and we
Who probe down into the brain, and see how desire discolors reality,
And we that see how chemical energy changes and transforms the molecule,
So that one thing and another changes and so man arises—
With neither microscope, nor telescope, nor spectroscope, nor finest violet ray
Have we found any Father lurking in the intricate unreasonable drive of things
And the strange chances of nature.

THE POET

O Priest, is it not enough that the world and a Woman are very beautiful,
And that the works and tragic lives of men are terribly glorious?

There is a dance of miracles, of miracles holding hands in a chain around the Earth and out through space to the moon, and to the stars, and beyond the stars,
And to behold this dance is enough;
So much laughter, and secret looking, and glimpses of wonder, and dreams of terror. . . .
It is enough! it is enough!

THE PRIEST

Enough? I see what is enough!
Machinery is enough for a Scientist,
And Beauty is enough for a Poet;
But in the hearts of men and women, and in the thirsty hearts of little children
There is a hunger, and there is an unappeasable longing,
For a Father and for the love of a Father . . .
For the root of a soul is mystery,
And the Night is mystery,
And in that mystery men would open inward into Eternity,
And know love, the Lord.
Blessed be his works, and his angels, and his sons crowned with his glory!
[*A pause. The Woman with a burden in her arms comes in slowly.*]

James Oppenheim

CLAY HILLS

It is easy to mould the yielding clay.
And many shapes grow into beauty
Under the facile hand.
But forms of clay are lightly broken;
They will lie shattered and forgotten in a dingy corner.

But underneath the slipping clay
Is rock. . . .
I would rather work in stubborn rock
All the years of my life,
And make one strong thing
And set it in a high, clean place,
To recall the granite strength of my desire.

Jean Starr Untermeyer

COOL TOMBS

When Abraham Lincoln was shoveled into the tombs, he forgot the copperheads and the assassin . . . in the dust, in the cool tombs.

And Ulysses Grant lost all thought of con men and Wall Street, cash and collateral turned ashes . . . in the dust, in the cool tombs.

Pocahontas body, lovely as a poplar, sweet as a red haw in November or a pawpaw in May, did she wonder? does she remember? . . . in the dust, in the cool tombs?

Take any streetful of people buying clothes and groceries, cheering a hero or throwing confetti and blowing tin horns . . . tell me if the lovers are losers . . . tell me if any get more than the lovers . . . in the dust . . . in the cool tombs.

Carl Sandburg

LOAM

In the loam we sleep,
In the cool moist loam,
To the lull of years that pass
And the break of stars,

From the loam, then,
The soft warm loam,
We rise:
To shape of rose leaf,
Of face and shoulder.

We stand, then,
To a whiff of life,
Lifted to the silver of the sun
Over and out of the loam
A day.

Carl Sandburg

IDEALISTS

Brother Tree:
Why do you reach and reach?
do you dream some day to touch the sky?
Brother Stream:
Why do you run and run?
do you dream some day to fill the sea?
Brother Bird:
Why do you sing and sing?
do you dream—

Young Man;
Why do you talk and talk and talk?

Alfred Kreymborg

OLD MANUSCRIPT

The sky
is that beautiful old parchment
in which the sun
and the moon
keep their diary.
To read it all,
one must be a linguist
more learned than Father Wisdom;
and a visionary
more clairvoyant than Mother Dream.
But to feel it,
one must be an apostle:
one who is more than intimate
in having been, always,
the only confidant—
like the earth
or the sea.

Alfred Kreymborg

HOW POEMS ARE MADE

"Si'l fait beau temps,"
Disait un papillon volage,
"S'il fait beau temps,
Je vais folâtrer dans les champs."
"Et moi," lui dit l'abeille sage,
"J'irai me mettre à mon ouvrage
S'il fait beau temps."

More than half of the people who think about poetry prefer to believe that the poet, like the butterfly, flutters gaily in the sunlight and sips honey. They like to think that because he is fed on the honey of inspiration his wings are glorious in flight. But poets themselves, and those who know most about them, tell us that they are as devout in labor as the proverbial bee. And unless poetry is a thing by itself, utterly unlike the other great arts, unlike music, sculpture, architecture, the dance, the drama, it is reasonable to suppose that labor must be a part of a poet's life and that there must be a travail before beauty is born.

Yet these two theories, which we may as well call the butterfly theory and the bee theory, are not necessarily irreconcilable. A poet does live creatively by virtue of inspiration. But inspiration is not a thing peculiar to poets. All mankind knows inspiration, and if it did not belong as truly to the housewife and the bricklayer and the stockbroker as to the poet, poets would have no understanding audience. But a poet is a poet by reason of his ability to do with inspiration what these others can not do with it or can not do so well. It is the poet who makes the delicate cell, the poem, in which the honey of inspiration is stored, to be a joy for all in the days when no flowers blossom and the world is dour and cold. That he may know how to make that cell the poet must work!

But fortunately, there are many ways of working, and sooner or later each poet finds his own best way. Some poets brood over poems a long time before they ever set down a word on paper, and then, when it is once set down, make very few changes. This is what Sara Teasdale does. And it is a method of work common to many makers of the best short lyrics. It is a difficult method for poets whose days are full of other things than poetry, for there is always the danger of losing the poem. But to hold a poem in the mind and let it grow there is a fine and natural way of making it. Other poets write rapidly and make few alterations, but they write many, many poems which they regard only as practice-work and throw away. When they are content they give the poem to the public, but not otherwise. Such poets must have a well-developed critical faculty and must be able to choose wisely from their own works the things that are best. Robert Frost works in this way and seldom gives the world a poem which the world is not glad to receive. Still other poets write in the first flush of inspiration and then revise again and again until the perfect poem emerges out of a chaos of self-expression. Vachel Lindsay works in this way. He sometimes re-writes his long poems thirty or forty times. And finally, there are poets who write very slowly and revise with great care. Such a poet is Carl Sandburg, a master of concise human speech.

Moreover, the fact that a great poet can write a masterpiece as John Masefield wrote his "Cargoes," in a few minutes one Sunday morning, should not lead any young poets to accept the butterfly theory of poetry. When Mr. Masefield achieved that miracle he was already a master poet. The masters can all do things that can not be done by the pupils, by beginners. They have learned their craft. When the idea comes, when the keen emotion is felt, when they have found inspiration, they are ready. They are amply equipped for the task of giving form to idea and mood and inspiration. And, moreover, in one way or another, the masters have earned that equipment by hard work. They have learned what they know. They have taught themselves how to do what they have done. Every poet, whether he realizes it or not (and often he does not realize it), has lived through what may be called a "vocational education." The more we learn about the lives of poets the more certain we are that this is true.

Fortunately very few poets were ever self-conscious about this vocational education. Very few have "taken courses" in the hope of learning "how to be poets." That would be almost criminal! But, if we could investigate, we should be likely to find out that nearly all good poets began, in childhood or early youth, to do certain things of their own volition and for their own satisfaction that were of undoubted value in preparation for poethood.

Perhaps the poet-child showed a keen zest for rhythm and a marked desire to experiment with rhythmical tunes. Perhaps he loved to dance or to move his hands in time to the rhythm of music, or to watch the movement of great machines and attempt to count the time and give the stresses by tapping, or perhaps he even attempted to tap the staccato rhythms of a strongly accented bit of conversation. Perhaps his sense of rhythm was pleased by certain forms of athletic play and perhaps he tried to translate these rhythms into words. All of these ways of playing with rhythmical tunes might justly be called a work of preparation for the making of poems. One poet, Margaret Widdemer, tells me that when she was a little girl she would go all alone into her grandmother's big parlor and dance there, without music, for sheer delight in the rhythms she could make.

Later came a more self-conscious preparation for the life of a poet. The poet-child began to write poems. He would set down on a piece of paper his rhymes and rhythms and ideas and emotions. And he would gloat over these effusions in secret. When he had just written a poem he probably thought it the finest poem in the world. A few days, a few weeks, or a few months later he would be in despair about it. Then he would write another. Sometimes he would solemnly vow by Apollo and all the Muses to give up poetry and become a real estate agent, or keep chickens. Then he would find out that it was impossible to give up poetry. It simply could not be done. And he would return to his first love and vow by Apollo and all the Muses that he would become a great poet. And this also was a part of the vocational education of the poet. For all good poets learn, sooner or later, that they can not give up poetry, that they must make it, and that they should make it as well as they possibly can.

Another part of a poet's vocational education is learning to love the masterpieces of other poets. William Rose Benét, an accomplished poet and an experienced editor, says:

"I shall never forget walking the streets of Oakland, California, in the belief that I was another Francis Thompson selling matches or something, just after I had read his poem, 'Any Saint.' Of course I wasn't, but it did my poetic impulse untold good. I became such a lunatic on the subject of Francis Thompson that if I found ten words about him in any magazine—and there have been nearer a million written—I would gloat over them in ecstasy. I used to haunt the old Mercantile Library in San Francisco before it moved down town. I was then studying stenography in a business college. One noon I discovered in a back number of *The English Review* John Masefield's song about

> 'A bosun in a blue coat bawling at the railing,
> Piping through a silver call that had a chain of gold.'

That was a number of years before he was famous. The hour was enchanted for me till I got that stave by heart."

Mr. Benét says it is the best thing in the world for young poets to "get drunk on the poetry of other poets, but they must be great poets, and the young poet must pick them out for himself and because they meet the needs of his particular temperament." But he is careful to add this word of advice, "Don't write the way they do! Imitate them outright if you like, *for practice, but recognize it as imitation.* Don't reflect the minds and usages of other people, no matter how much it seems the only way to write. It isn't. There are a thousand thousand ways to write. When you write, try to express *yourself*, not someone else."

Such elder-brotherly advice from poets is hard to get except in personal conversation between old friends. As a general thing when anyone asks a poet how poems are made the poet looks up with pained bewilderment and says he does not know. Usually he is telling the truth. When he is making a poem he is so absorbed in the creative labor that he can not watch the process carefully, or as one poet says, "hear his own clock tick." And when the poem is finished the process of its creation interests him very little. He has climbed into Paradise. Good. He will kick away the ladder by which he climbed.

The poet's stock answer for inquisitive ladies and other prying persons who wish to know how his poems are made is, "I don't know. They make themselves." This is a half-truth, and like most half-truths, it sounds very fine. True, the poet seldom does know just how his poems began to grow in his mind, whether they were suggested by a scent or color of the external world or by an inward conflict of emotions. True, he seldom knows just how he performs the glorious, concentrated intellectual labor that makes his moods vocal and communicable. And to say that poems make themselves is not a bad way of explaining all this. For unless poems do, in a certain sense, make themselves, they should not be made at all. Certainly they should never be written to please a friend or an editor. If they are written simply as a result of some such suggestion from the outside, they are likely to be dull and lifeless. This accounts for the insipid quality of most "occasional poems." When people ask poets to be "occasional" they should permit them to be humorous and write mere verse.

But we can hardly suppose that poems are made without the instrumentality of the human intellect! Indeed the more we know about poems the more certain we become that they are made by the whole personality of the poet. The mere fact that they are ever made implies the process of creation! And any process is interesting if we can find out about it from those who have watched it and understood it and are able to analyze and describe.

For this reason it is a great pleasure and privilege to be able to present Sara Teasdale's ideas on the subject of how poems are made. Sara Teasdale is well known for her brief, simple lyrics wherever English poetry is read, and what she has to say can be accepted safely as authoritative. She realizes, of course, that other kinds of poetry can be made by other poets in other ways. But this is one way and the results justify a careful consideration of the method. She says:

"My theory is that poems are written because of a state of emotional irritation. It may be present for some time before the poet is conscious of what is tormenting him. The emotional irritation springs, probably, from subconscious combinations of partly forgotten thoughts and feelings. Coming together, like electrical currents in a thunder storm, they produce a poem. A poem springs from emotions produced by an actual experience, or, almost as forcefully, from those produced by an imaginary experience. In either case, the poem is written to free the poet from an emotional burden. Any poem not so written is only a piece of craftsmanship.

"Most poets find it easier to write about themselves than about anything else because they know more about themselves than about anything else. If a poet has a great gift, he may be able to speak for a whole race, creed or class simply by speaking for himself. But for a poet consciously to appoint himself the mouthpiece of a certain class or creed *en masse*, is dangerous business. If each poet will try to get himself down in black and white as concisely and honestly as he can, every kind of reaction to beauty and pain will finally be recorded. Each poet will make a record different from that of any of his fellows, and yet the record of each will be true.

"Out of the fog of emotional restlessness from which a poem springs, the basic idea emerges sometimes slowly, sometimes in a flash. This idea is known at once to be the light toward which the poet was groping. He now walks round and round it, so to speak, looking at it from all sides, trying to see which aspect of it is the most vivid. When he has hit upon what he believes is his peculiar angle of vision, the poem is fairly begun. The first line comes floating toward him with a charming definiteness of color and music. In my own case the rhythm of a poem usually follows, in a general way, the rhythm of the first line. [This is what Lanier thought should be true. Author.] The form of the poem should be a clear window-pane through which you see the poem's heart. The form, as form, should be engrossing neither to the poet nor to the reader, who should be barely conscious of the form, the rhymes, or the rhythm. He should be conscious only of emotions given him, and unconscious of the medium by which they are transmitted.

"For generations readers have been accustomed to certain forms of rhythms and to certain rhyme-schemes. These are familiar. They carry the reader swiftly and easily to the heart of the poem. They do not astonish or bewilder him. The poet who chooses this older, more melodic music, and the regular chiming of the rhymes that usually goes with it, should use great care to vary these deftly and spontaneously. Otherwise his poem will be an unconvincing sing-song.

"Brief lyrical poems should be moulded in the poet's mind. They are far more fluid before they touch ink and paper than they ever are afterward. The warmth of the idea that generated the poem should make it clear, ductile, a finished creation, before it touches cold white paper. In the process of moulding his idea into a poem the poet will be at white heat of intellectual and emotional activity, bearing in mind that every word, every syllable, must be an unobtrusive and yet an indispensable part of his creation. Every beat of his rhythm, the color of each word, the ring of each rhyme, must carry his poem, as a well-laid railway track carries a train of cars, smoothly to its destination. The poet must put far from him the amazing word, the learned allusion, the facile inversion, the clever twist of thought, for all of these things will blur his poem and distract his reader. He must not overcrowd his lines with figures of speech, because, in piling these one upon another, he defeats his own purpose. The mind of the reader can not hold many impressions at one time. The poet should try to give his poem the quiet swiftness of flame, so that the reader will feel and not think while he is reading. But the thinking will come afterwards."

William Rose Benét is another poet who has consented to say what he knows about how poems are made. His own poetry is not at all like Sara Teasdale's, although he has written a few fine subjective lyrics. His best poems have always a certain narrative interest and seem like stories of spiritual adventure. He carries us into far countries of the imagination to see strange sights and hear wild, engaging talk. He has a genius for the making of ballads and his poem, "The Horse Thief," half realism and half flambuoyant fancy, is one of the finest of the kind in recent literature.

Mr. Benét's suggestions constitute a program for an intellectual athlete. This is part of what he says:

"Sidney Lanier was of the belief that a poet should have sound scientific knowledge, should know biology, geology, archæology as well as etymology. I should add psychology, sociology, and all the other ologies there are. This is almost ridiculous, you say. There is nothing ridiculous about it. A poet should swallow the encyclopædia, and then after that the dictionary. He should be a linguist if possible. He should be a business man. He should be able to meet any type of man on his own ground and understand what he is talking about. The poet should be able, also, to relate the thing discussed to the cosmos in general as the highly specialized individual is not able to relate it. A poet should know history inside and out and should take as much interest in the days of Nebuchadnezzar as in the days of Pierpont Morgan. Don't get the idea that you can only write about fairies—but there are plenty of fairies even on the Stock Exchange if you are attractive to fairies. They are whimsical people, you know. But get interested in everything, and stay interested."

If young poets were to accept this advice at its face value they would be nourishing impossible ambitions. But the thing that Mr. Benét means, the thing he is trying to emphasize in this paragraph, is a thing that young poets can achieve if they will, a certain breadth of sympathy and understanding that reaches through all pursuits and vocations to the common heart of mankind, and a certain breadth of interest in all that happens in the world, all that has happened or is likely to happen.

When Mr. Benét goes on to talk of the actual process of making poems, we find that what he has to say is very interesting in relation to the kind of poems he writes, which ought to be the case, of course. He suggests, first of all, the acquisition of a good vocabulary, then a practice in visualization. "Hunt up all the great paintings ancient or modern that you can see and saturate yourself in their mysteries of color. That will help your visualization to be more than a cheap lithograph. Then, when you come to make a poem, visualize intensely. Try to see it as if it were a living scene with more than 'shadow shapes that come and go' moving through it. Then think of your visualization in terms of the greatest music you know. Hold that thought! Wrestle with it until you feel that somehow—God alone knows how —you can express it in words."

Mr. Benét offers young poets several other bits of excellent advice. "Get your poems by heart," he says, "and go around annoying people by mouthing to yourself." This is really very important, for it is almost the only way that the young poet has of learning how words sound in sequences. Mr. Benét has some good things to say, also, about writing for the love of expression and writing for money.

"If you want to write for money, all right. I have written for money and served God and Mammon. It is pleasanter serving God, but Mammon is more remunerative—possibly. I'm not yet sure. One thing I am sure of. A poem that is not written

EDWIN MARKHAM

out of an enthusiasm quite above the consideration of personal gain, though that element may figure, can never be a great poem. Poets have never made money at poetry. I don't believe they ever will. That means—when you are writing poetry try to write great poetry—don't try to write verse. Don't mix the two things. You can write verse also if you like. But don't make shandygaff of your poetry. There is no pleasure like the writing of poetry, and no despair like it."

Mr. Benét's last bit of advice is this: "Do not be didactic in words if you can help it. If your poem is a great poem it will be powerfully didactic in effect. And that is all that is worth anything. If you preach outright in words the chances are that you will weaken the 'drive' of your poem and circumscribe the scope of its influence."

Another poet who is careful to warn young poets of the dangers of didacticism is Edwin Markham, the famous maker of "The Man With The Hoe." His warning is the more valuable because indiscriminating people sometimes call "The Man With The Hoe" didactic poetry, failing to understand that everything that might have been dry and didactic in such a poem was consumed in this poet's great social passion, transmuted into pure flame of emotion before it was expressed in virile poetry. No poet in America is better known or better loved than Mr. Markham. His advice will surely be welcomed by young poets of to-morrow. This is what he says:

"The poet comes to behold and to express the hidden loveliness of the world, to point out the ideal that is ever seeking to push through the husk of things and to reveal the inner spiritual reality. So all of life is material for his seeing eye and his thinking heart, as he makes the wonderful familiar and makes the familiar wonderful.

"Young poet, I command you to be critical of your own work, to reach a ground where you can not be easily satisfied. Make a serious study of the art of poetry and become acquainted at first hand with the best poetry of the world. Read constantly the great masters; dwell with loving heart upon their great lines, their great passages, their great poems. These will become touchstones for testing the value of your own verse. There is nothing that takes the place of work. The kingdom of song can be taken only by industry, by patient resolve led on by the wings of inspiration.

"Listen to a few warnings: the greatest of all poetic heresies is the heresy of the Didactic. We who have a serious purpose in our poetry, must, as far as possible, beware of the bare-bones of moral preachment. We must not be so intent on capturing the truth as to forget the beauty that is the veil of truth. Indeed, beauty is so essential to truth that we do not really possess the truth unless we have the beauty. So we are forced to keep seeking until we find some symbol that will express the beauty that is the eternal vesture of truth. This is not always an easy task, yet it is the stern task that is laid upon the poet by the austere Muse.

"The poet must avoid the threadbare, the commonplace, and the scientifically exact. He seeks to rise on the wings of words to that high level where the kindled imagination can create forms of ideal loveliness and find space for unhindered flight. To this end the poet must avoid words like 'visualize' as being too precise for his purpose, too cold for his emotion. As far as possible he must use words that have been long lavendered by time and are therefore surrounded by an atmosphere of association and suggestiveness.

"Be especially careful, then, to avoid all worn-out phrases and clauses. I have just come upon one in a recent poet's work: 'Things are not what they seem.' Hackneyed expression is the death of poesy. Seek for the fresh phrase that will send upon the mind the surprise of unexpected beauty.

"There are three planes in the poet's work—the ground of imagination, the highest of all grounds; the ground of winsome fancy; and the yet lower ground of freakish conceit. A flash of imagination gives you the sense of the ultimate truth, a glimpse of the universe as God sees it. An airy bubble of fancy gives you a pleasing glitter; if it is not the truth, it is at least an illusion that charms us. But a conceit is a forced fancy: we feel no livingness in it, no illusion of poetic reality.

"And now, young poet, I am sending you my lyric blessing and wishing you many happy adventures on the hills of Helicon."

Another poet whose opinions many young readers will be glad to know is Harriet Monroe. This is what she has been kind enough to say:

"As editor of *Poetry, A Magazine of Verse*, I have had the pleasure—or pain—of reading in typed manuscript vast numbers of modern poems. This severe and educative discipline has made me very weary of certain faults which are, in the last analysis, insincerities—the use of another man's or another period's, words, phrases or ideas instead of the poet's own.

"We have almost vowed never to print in *Poetry* such words as 'surcease,' "erstwhile,' 'anon,' 'forsooth,' 'doth,' 'thou,' and 'thee,' and countless phrases similarly archaic; except on the rare occasions when subject and mood demand an archaic effect. Also we have grown extremely tired of Pan and other such talked-of gods of Greece; of Babylon and Arcadia and other more or less fabulous places; of Guinevere and Helen of Troy and Cleopatra—all the long-celebrated fascinators. It requires a special and peculiar magic to touch any of these enshrined idols without disaster, and with most modern poets the effort to do so is merely a pathetic appeal from the poverty of their own imaginations to the wealth that has been accumulated by the poets and artists of the past. It is essentially an insincerity, because it uses other people's experience and imagining instead of the poet's own. And a stern and stripped sincerity is a first essential of good art.

"Sincerity of rhythm—a technique evolved from within, from the poet's own need, and not adopted ready-made, is another essential which the modern poet should demand of himself. If he is not satisfied with merely stringing iambics or anapæsts, he may discover that each person's most intimate possession is the intensely personal rhythm to which he attunes the world.

If he doesn't find his own, he will be saved the agony of more slowly discovering that he is no poet.

"I know of no rules but this for writing poems, and this presupposes a human soul overcharged with emotion, with love of life, and impelled to utter it in words. Be sincere—present your own emotional experience, not anyone else's, in your own carefully chosen words and intensely felt rhythms, not anyone else's."

It is easy to tell how poems should not be made. That is what is usually done. And there the instruction given usually stops. Few indeed are the poets who, like Sara Teasdale, can give a really helpful account of how poems actually are made, or are willing to do it if they can. But, one and all, the poets agree in this matter of sincerity. Padraic Colum, the young Irish poet now resident in this country, reiterates the same idea with a charming humor that is part of his Celtic inheritance, no doubt:

"The best way of making a play, according to Bernard Shaw, is to take over a portion of another play. This process can not be commended as regards the making of poetry. In the first place the available amount of poetry is better and more publicly known than the available material in plays: one would have to put in passages that someone would recognize and the recognition would cause a loss of attention!"

Reinforcing his humorous Irish reason, Mr. Colum says that poems must be the result of intensity of feeling.

"Now intensity of feeling can only come from personal, from novel experience. Without personal, without novel experience, we may say that there will be no liveliness of movement in the poem. We have to be sure, then, that we have some intensity of feeling about the matter that is in our mind to be projected as a poem. It is personal, that is to say, it is not something that has been reported to you, but something that belongs to yourself: also it means more to you than anything else of the ten thousand happenings of the day. Feeling like this about the matter you may start to make your poem.

Remember, if your poem is to be a short one that the poem is in the first line.—

"She walks in beauty like the night."

Everything is said in that first line, and what follows only holds up the mood that that first line has evoked.

"The rest has all been said by Gautier.—

'Leave to the tyro's hands
The loose, unlabored style:
Choose thou that which demands
The labor of the file.'

"Do not let your little poem run about too soon or it may become bandy-legged. Nurse it in your mind for many days and give it the blessing of the sun and moon and air and of the silence of the night."

The same warning against insincerity is tacitly suggested in what Robert Frost has said about realism and idealism in literature. The dry, homely humor of the following paragraph merits repetition.

"A man who makes really good literature," says Mr. Frost, "is like a fellow who goes into the fields to pull carrots. He keeps on pulling them patiently enough until he finds a carrot that suggests something else to him. It is not shaped like other carrots. He takes out his knife and notches it here and there, until the two pronged roots become legs and the carrot takes on something of the semblance of a man. The real genius takes hold of that bit of life which is suggestive to him and gives it form. But the man who is merely a realist, and not a genius, will leave the carrot just as he finds it. The man who is merely an idealist and not a genius, will try to carve a donkey where no donkey is suggested by the carrot he pulls."

Two other things a young poet should always remember as well as he remembers a poet's sincerity, and they are a poet's pride and a poet's humility. The poet's pride is a pride in his vocation, not in himself, a pride in his art, not in his own artistry. It is a pride that can make him of one heart and mind with "makers" of old, no matter how humble he may be. The primitive singer of the cavemen, the first bards and minstrels, the epic masters, all have passed on to him a part of their gift of the Word.

This pride, furthermore, will not permit even the youngest and humblest of the poets to hear poetry underrated without protest. His protest may be humorous, but he will make it, gently, in a thoughtless world, whenever it may be necessary. Then mankind, as a whole, will come at last to perceive something of the grandeur of poetry. The story of a poet's pride in poetry is most magically told in "At The King's Threshold" by William Butler Yeats. Mr. Yeats tells the story of Seanchan, poet of ancient Ireland, who lay down to die of starvation on the threshhold of the king, to cast shame upon him, because that unwise king had denied to him, a representative of poetry, a place with the bishops and the lawgivers at the royal table. That unwise king had to learn that poetry must be respected. He humbled himself before Seanchan. To-day the people are kings. It is for poets to command their respect.

But for himself the poet must be humble. Fame is something which may come to him with its advantage of association with the world's great folk and its disadvantages of stress and burdensome publicity and misunderstanding and the unkindness of many commentators. But fame is not what should be hungrily sought. The thing to be hungrily sought is beauty of expression. When a poet is seeking that he will be content to say, very humbly, with Robert Bridges, Laureate of England,

> "I have loved flowers that fade
> Within whose magic tents
> Rich hues have marriage made
> With sweet unmemoried scents:
> A honeymoon delight,—
> A joy of love at sight,
> That ages in an hour:—
> My song be like a flower!"

PART II

THE SPIRIT OF CONTEMPORARY POETRY

DEMOCRACY AND THE NEW THEMES

At the Author's Congress of The Panama-Pacific International Exposition in 1915, Edwin Markham, who is often called "The Dean of American Poetry," gave an address on the subject of contemporary verse. Those who listened felt that, in spite of his venerable appearance, he was one of the youngest and most promising poets present. In the course of his discussion he told the following story. A young man once went to Mr. Markham and said, "Mr. Markham, I feel sure that I have it in me to write a great poem. I know that I can do it. But I have not been able to think of a subject worthy of my powers. Now, Mr. Markham, if you will suggest the subject, I will write the poem." Mr. Markham fumbled in his pocket, and, after a moment's deliberation, drew thence a rusty nail. "This is as good a subject as any," said he to the young man. And the young man was properly rebuked.

For a man who, in a world of physical and spiritual miracles, could think of no subject "worthy of his powers," would write no better of the grand march of the galaxies in the milky way than of a little piece of metal covered with rust. After all, the little piece of iron has been a part of the procession of stars and planets. And, if our minds are so dull and unimaginative that we find no cause for wonder in near and familiar objects, why should we dare to suppose that we can fathom, describe, and interpret marvels vast and remote? Mr. Markham knew very well that a rusty nail in the pocket of a genius may be anything that the genius wishes it to be. It may be the very nail that held down the first plank in the floor of the house that Jack built. Or a leprachaun may have used it in cobbling the boot of a giant. But in the pocket of a dull, uninteresting man a rusty nail becomes a dull, uninteresting object. Now the moral of Mr. Markham's story is simply this: *It is the poet who makes the poem, not the theme!* A poor poetaster will make poor poetry, or slipshod verse out of the greatest theme of all—if there be any greatest theme. And indeed his inadequacy will be the more apparent when he strains after that which his intellect can not reach. A great poet, on the other hand, will make great poems out of things that others pass by heedlessly. The beauty of the poem is not in the theme but in the poet's power to present it.

This truth can be convincingly illustrated by reading and comparing good and bad poems on the same subject. Let us read and compare three poems on the same theme, the mature woman who has known the sorrows and joys of life and found her serene fulfillment. Probably the three men who wrote these poems had felt the same feeling. Probably they had the same ideal in mind. They differ from one another in their skill as poets.

The first stanzas quoted are dull and prosy, directly stated abstractions. We are willing to believe that the worthy woman Roscoe Gilmore Stott describes has lived a worthy life and merits praise. But we do not care. We are not interested.

THE STRONG WOMAN

Somehow her very delicacy was strength,
With which she met the tempest-tide of life;
Frail craft that did not fear the journey's length
Nor dread the billow's strife.

Somehow her gentle tenderness was pow'r,
With which she did the larger task alone;—
Frail toiler fashioned for the leisure hour,
A sturdy workman grown.

Somehow her unfeigned purity was rule,
With which she wrought in meek yet regal mien;—
Frail monarch acting as her Maker's tool—
Unknown, uncrowned, unseen!

Hundreds of verses like this are written daily. It does no harm provided no one is led to suppose that they are poetry.

This particular set of verses is not even clearly thought and phrased. We notice that the lady changes incredibly from line to line. In the first stanza she is a "frail craft," in the second a "frail toiler" and a "sturdy workman," in the third a "frail monarch" and her "Maker's tool." Imagine a tool that is "unknown, uncrowned, unseen." Note the silly spelling of "power," the redundancy of "gentle tenderness," the tiresome triteness of the use of the symbol chosen for life, the tempest, and the triteness of the rhymes. This all indicates inability. Mr. Stott has not made a poem. But that is not the fault of the theme chosen.

Scudder Middleton has made a poem out of the same theme. It is written quietly and sincerely, in good English, with no absurdities and incongruities. It gives us a glimpse of a real personality and a sense of pleasure in the woman described. It is called "A Woman."

A WOMAN

She had an understanding with the years;
For always in her eyes there was a light
As though she kept a secret none might guess—
Some confidence that Time had made her heart.
So calmly did she bear the weight of pain,
With such serenity accept the joy,
It seemed she had a mother love for life,
And all the days were children at her breast.

But even better than this poem is Joseph Campbell's lyric, "The Old Woman." In it not a word embarrasses the meaning. Every line fits into a perfect picture which the poet has freshly seen and felt and presented. The symbolism is strong and true. The melody lives.

THE OLD WOMAN

As a white candle
In a holy place,
So is the beauty
Of an agèd face.

As the spent radiance
  Of the winter sun,
So is a woman
  With her travail done,

Her brood gone from her,
  And her thoughts as still
As the waters
  Under a ruined mill.

In these three poems, I think, we can all see clearly that it is the poet who gives value to the poem. And the natural corollary of this idea is the belief that there is no such thing as a "poetic subject." We are sometimes told, even yet, that stars and flowers are poetic, that kings and gods are poetic, but that men's labors and creations and the plain things of the earth are not poetic. A few dogmatic persons still tell us that poets should write about the past and about the traditions of the past, that they should never write about the crude and unassimilated present. Such persons bristle with other "shoulds" and "should nots." But poets are not likely to be greatly influenced by their opinions. For good poets of to-day, like good poets of all time, begin their work of creation wherever they touch life most closely. They build no partition between themselves and every day. And although this fact is sometimes responsible for much that is bizarre and awkward, sordid and trivial, in the lesser work of the minor poets, it is responsible, also, for the soundness and vigor, the fearless truth, keen irony, and brilliant beauty of our best poetry.

In our times the poet's choice of themes has been much influenced by the growth of the spirit of democracy in the world. A real poet is not a dilettante, an onlooker, but a full-fledged human being. He shares the spiritual life of his times. If we remember the Iliad, we remember that only one poor man was personally and individually mentioned in it, the wretch, Thersites, who was not favored of gods or men because he was neither beautiful nor good as were the heroes of Greek story. This, undoubtedly, was because the Homeric poets lived in a civilization that worshipped leaders, heroes, kings, gods. These great men were symbols of the achievement of the race. Poetry was for them and about them. But we no longer worship the strength that subdues the many to the selfish purposes of the few. English poetry, from the beginning, has kept on growing stronger and stronger in the spirit of democracy. And Walt Whitman, our American tidal wave of democracy, swept our beaches clear of the refuse of old preferences. In the old days poets sang of the princess in the tower, the paragon of beauty, the great lady of the court. To-day they are not ashamed to sing of little Miss Stitcher, the seamstress; of Mrs. Suds, the woman who takes in washing; of Polly Cornfields, wife of an Iowa farmer. For to-day all of these women are princesses. In the common woman of to-day the modern poet sees the Madonna. The poets of old sang of murdering knights and picturesque highwaymen. To-day poets sing of Timothy Green and John Ledger and Tom Sugar, the ordinary men who went "over there." They have found knighthood in the common man. Indeed, that witty critic, William Crary Brownell, seems to think that the reaction in favor of democracy has influenced literature too strongly. He complains that poets who are not "adoring the golden calf" are "incensing the under dog."

Now it should be understood that this broad, democratic interest in everybody which modern poets manifest is not a pose. Poets who write adequately about our workaday world are not well-to-do young persons who have made a few excursions into the slums to "see life" and are returning to share the piquant proletarian excitement with the upper classes. Verse-makers of that kind we have. They were fashionable five or ten years ago. But their work is negligible for it never rings true. Poets who write convincingly of the brave life of the great masses of mankind, and of the sharp pains of poverty, have learned their speech in the world of poverty and of the people. And although modern philanthropists sometimes patronize the poor, modern poets do not.

In that large and vigorous poem, "The Man With The Hoe,"

we find no condescension. Mr. Markham is not a polite and gentlemanly person, standing a little apart from his kind and wondering why the poor are often dirty and sometimes ugly. He knows that the bodies of the humble sometimes reveal the spiritual shortcomings of the proud and the great. The whole poem, which is so well known that I need not quote it, is a tremendous protest against the black causes of poverty and ugliness.

Vachel Lindsay, who travelled across the continent, "afoot and light hearted," trading his poems for bread and a night's lodging in the homes of the poor, shows an understanding of poverty which is just as keen and intimate in its own way. To him the pity of it all, the sorrow of sorrows is

> "Not that they starve, but starve so dreamlessly,
> Not that they sow, but that they seldom reap,
> Not that they serve, but have no gods to serve,
> Not that they die, but that they die like sheep."

Louis Untermeyer is another poet who has spoken bravely against the oppression of the poor. If it were not for the fact that Mr. Untermeyer uses regularly stressed rhythms and occasional rhymes, and is a maker of fine symmetrical patterns in poetry, one might almost classify him with the humanitarian radicals. For his thought is radical enough, and humanitarian enough. But he is never the orator, when he writes verse, always the poet, even in his most impassioned protests against what he conceives to be injustice. In one of his short poems he identifies himself spiritually, and for the purposes of the poem, with the miners about whom he is writing. In this way, by dramatizing his emotions and putting himself in the other man's place, he succeeds in giving us a subjective lyric through which the soul of a miner speaks:

> "God, we don't like to complain—
> We know that the mine is no lark—
> But—there's the pools from the rain;
> But—there's the cold and the dark."

"Caliban In The Coal Mines" is memorable.

VACHEL LINDSAY

LOUIS UNTERMEYER

A poem which is not directly concerned with the problem of poverty, but which belongs most decidedly to the spirit of brotherhood and democracy, is Witter Bynner's beautiful long poem, "The New World." It is expressive of a strange prescience of immortality and of a belief in the communion of saints. Mr. Bynner brings the light of the spirit of democracy to focus in the beautiful personality of one woman, Celia.

> "Once when we broke a loaf of bread
> And shared the honey, Celia said:
> 'To share all beauty as the interchanging dust,
> To be akin and kind and to entrust
> All men to one another for their good,
> Is to have heard and understood,
> And carried to the common enemy
> In you and me,
> The ultimatum of democracy.'"

Carl Sandburg, when he is not the orator making eloquent protests and demanding action, sometimes makes marvellously good little poems out of the thought that since we must all soon find places in the great democracy of the dead, where rich and poor, tyrant and slave, become one thing, dust, it would be well to bring more of the spirit of democratic loving-kindness into life. No other poet has taken just this way of pointing us toward democracy by writing about death. For that reason we are the more interested. Mr. Sandburg does it again and again. In "Cool Tombs" Mr. Sandburg tells us what Abraham Lincoln and Ulysses S. Grant forgot "in the dust, in the cool tombs." Then he says, "Take any streetful of people," and he asks "if any get more than the lovers" "in the dust . . . in the cool tombs." Similarly, speaking of John Brown's grave, he says, "Room for Gettysburg, Wilderness, Chickamauga, on a six foot stage of dust." And again in his terse poem, "Southern Pacific," he tells how Huntington, the great railroad man, now "sleeps in a house six feet long," dreaming of ten thousand men saying, "Yes, sir;" and how Blithery, one of the ten thousand, now sleeps "in a house six feet long," and dreams of saying "Yes, sir;" to Huntington. Then he closes with these words,

"Huntington,
Blithery, sleep in houses six feet long."

In "Illinois Farmer" Mr. Sandburg says, "Bury this Illinois farmer with respect," and he describes the farmer's long, epic struggle with the prairie wind. The description is brief, concise. Then says Mr. Sandburg,

"The same wind will now blow over the place here where his hands must dream of Illinois corn."

Again the idea is phrased with more lyrical magic in the lines from "Loam" which say,

"We stand then
To a whiff of life,
Lifted to the silver of the sun
Over and out of the loam
A day."

When nothing else will bring democracy to men the thought of death will bring it.

In his dramatic poem, "The Operation," Wilfrid Wilson Gibson shows us how the poor face the thought of pain and death. It is about a woman who lived years with a cancer in her body rather than tell her husband and go to the expense of having an operation. Her father had died of the disease and she knew it. She suffered excruciating pain. But she said nothing, nothing at all, until her little daughter was old enough to make a home for her father. Then the wife went to the doctor. That is the story. It is told as a dialogue between husband and wife after the visit to the doctor. The husband says,

"Eleven years! And never breathed a word,
Nor murmured once, but patiently . . ."

The wife answers,

> "I come of fisherfolk, who live on patience.
> It's little use for any man
> To be impatient with the sea."

The same spirit is manifested in the work of many another contemporary poet. Margaret Widdemer sings of "The Old Suffragist" and takes upon herself, as a representative of happy womanhood, a grim load of responsibility for the sins committed in factories. And yet she is a conservative poet in thought and style. James Oppenheim, a poet as radical as Margaret Widdemer is conservative, takes the realities of the common life in a great city and makes a luminous picture of them. His "Saturday Night" was written while he was a young poet and before his work was well known. He no longer likes it, but other people do. "Saturday Night" tells the story of the happy, nonchalant evening that comes only once a week to workers in great cities. Every stanza is beautiful. It must suffice, here, to quote only two.

"The lights of Saturday night beat golden, golden over the pillared street—
The long plate-glass of a Dream-World olden is as the footlights shining sweet—
Street-lamp—flambeau—glamour of trolley—comet-trail of the trains above,
Splash where the jostling crowds are jolly with echoing laughter and human love.

"This is the City of the Enchanted: and these are her Enchanted People:
Far and far is Daylight, haunted with whistle of mill and bell of steeple—
The Eastern tenements loose the women, the Western flats release the wives
To touch, where all the ways are common, a glory to their sweated lives."

Out of a very passionate love of the great industrial city, which, in spite of its sharp, tragic contrasts of riches and poverty, good and evil, all true moderns feel, have come many of the best and most beautiful of the songs of democracy.

But of all modern poets of the people John Masefield is probably the greatest. His story is no longer new, for journalists have told it often—the story of a young peer of Chaucer, indentured to a sea-captain in the days of his youth, when dreams were mighty, and sent out upon the great sea-paths of the world to use the holystone upon foul decks and to do his trick with the rest; the story of the man in him loving the salt taste of adventure; the story of the poet in him grown restless, demanding more than the "wash and thresh" of the sea foam, and bringing him, twenty-five years ago, to this country of ours, where, he had heard, a man might become what he liked; the story of his quest for that which he needed and of the bizarre but not meaningless trick which Fate played in letting him become, for a time, an assistant to a New York bar-keeper; the story of his return to England and of the publication of "The Everlasting Mercy" in 1911, of the strong chorus of acclaim that greeted it and of the fame blown as far as the sea winds he had loved and learned to celebrate. It is an old story, this story of John Masefield, but it is a great story, and will become a great tradition, for it is the life story of a master of the English speech, of the greatest living poet of the people.

Such words as "great" are not used with glib frequency by those to whom words are sacred, but, because they are light upon the lips of many persons who have no part in the love of sincere meanings, it becomes necessary, sometimes, to make the use of them go hand in hand with a definition. Therefore, to say that John Masefield is a great poet is to say that he has much of Chaucer's gift of catching and sharing the flavor of persons and circumstances, much of the delicate perception of beauty that was in Keats, much of the color of Coleridge and the plain earth-wisdom of Burns, much, even, of the sap and savor of life that was the power in Shakespeare. He has, moreover, a music of his own, and a sense of the significance of things, which, because it is modern, is more profound and searching in its own way than any philosophy of earlier times. The world has lived and died many times since the days of Chaucer, and has known many resurrections. John Masefield has shared the life and death and the rising again into light.

Since Chaucer's day the love and fear of potentates has been a dying cult. To-day no man seems splendid because he wears purple. A belief in the heroism and beauty of the common people has lightened perceptibly the blear darkness of the modern world. This growing faith in the people has been choked off again and again by greed and violence, but it can never be held by death. Always it breaks free of the dark bondage and comes back stronger than ever. And, even before the great war brought us a new sense of values, in a country that worshipped prosperity, many of us knew that no real hero will hew his way to success unless he can do it with a sword as clean as Excalibur.

In the poetry of John Masefield all the light of this belief shines proudly. Over and over again, in ringing words, words as clean as silver, firm as bronze, and ruddy as gold, he tells his times the value of that which was once called valueless. He is the spokesman of all defeats that have been better than victories, of all good losers who have been a gain to the race, of the weak and the poor and the humble whose bodies and souls have built stairs by which the strong might climb. For he knows that under the old systems of the past only a few could achieve a rich reward, a shining victory. He is the bard of the scientist who, for forty years, will study the legs of one insect, that a later scientist, profiting by his painfully acquired knowledge, may make a great discovery. He is the bard of other failures, of the terrible spawn of life that we so little understand—the sinner of the kind externally and obviously and vulgarly sinful—the sinner from whom most of us run away, with whom Christ remained. Such sinners are presented to us in poems like "The Everlasting Mercy" with such an amazing power that we think no more of the printed page and forget that the story is a written one which we have read. Having shared a master's understanding and devotion, we suppose that we have been a part of the tale.

Not once, but many times, does Mr. Masefield tell his story of pomp discredited, of valor and beauty triumphant in renunciation and apparent defeat. This is the underlying theme of his great book about the war, "Gallipoli," a glorious epic in prose, a book to make even jaded reviewers and sophisticated critics weep. It is the underlying theme of his great tale, "Dauber." It is everywhere in his narratives, like an immeasureable extension of Browning's thought,

> "What I aspired to be
> And was not, comforts me."

Mr. Masefield does more than tell stories that illustrate his great theme. He does what lesser poets could not do without becoming verbose and tiresome. He states the belief, formulates the credo of the new democracy. He sets it to work in the minds of his readers, like ferment. It is suggested tacitly or sounded clearly in nearly everything that he writes. It becomes resonant in that powerful lyric called "A Consecration" in which John Masefield takes the poor and the outcast to be his own people, and dedicates to them his life and his songs. It is a poem which can hardly be quoted too often.

> "Not of the princes and prelates with periwigged charioteers
> Riding triumphantly laurelled to lap the fat of the years,
> Rather the scorned—the rejected—the men hemmed in with the spears;
>
> * * * * * *
>
> "Theirs be the music, the color, the glory, the gold;
> Mine be a handful of ashes, a mouthful of mould.
> Of the maimed, of the halt and the blind in the rain and the cold—
> Of these shall my songs be fashioned, my tale be told. Amen."

To pass on from the love of man, as we find it in poetry, to the love of the things that man has made and done, as they are celebrated in the poems of our time, is to take but a short step. The spirit of democracy has enabled many poets to find a new kind of beauty in industrial civilization. It is not the beauty of stars and flowers, but the beauty of streets deep-cut between heights of honeycombed steel and concrete, streets like canyons through which flow the streams of life and deeds. The great industrial city is a new thing upon the earth, but already poets have sung the songs of skyscraper and subway, of seemingly endless miles of lighted windows at night, of the sun twinkling on thousands of flat roofs all day; they have sung the songs of great machines which are to our times what "the hanging gardens of Babylon" and the pyramids were to antiquity; they have sung the great creations of machines, the great engineering feats of the day. Most notable among poems of this kind are "The Steam Shovel," by Eunice Tietjens, and "The Turbine" and "Our Canal," by Harriet Monroe.

In the opening lines of Mrs. Tietjens' poem is the great declarative sentence of modernity which states man's triumph over nature.

> "Beneath my window in a city street
> A monster lairs, a creature huge and grim
> And only half believed: the strength of him—
> Steel-strung and fit to meet
> The strength of earth—
> Is mighty as men's dreams that conquer force."

Harriet Monroe's "The Turbine" is somewhat more elaborate and less direct, for in it she dramatizes the emotions of the man who manages the turbine. Great machinery always makes strangers in a factory grip themselves hard. It makes them tense with a peculiar emotion. That tense emotion is in the poem.

> "Look—if I but lay a wire
> Across the terminals of yonder switch
> She'll burst her windings, rip her casings off,
> And shriek till envious Hell shoots up its flames,
> Shattering her very throne."

"Our Canal" is more idealistic in tone, perhaps because it is written about a work of man's doing, rather than about the machines with which it was done. The poem was written just after the completion of the Panama Canal, at a time when we all saw a vision of the meeting of East and West and hoped that the canal might become an international highway to permanent peace. The poem is rich in the American idealism which we shared in the days before the great war showed us that the goals of peaceful service were set much farther away than we supposed and that we must strive longer and more sternly if we would reach them. The poem is valuable as a revelation of American spiritual life, and the following strophes, with which it ends, give a very good idea of the meaning of the whole.

"'What build we from coast to coast?
It's a path for the Holy Ghost.
Oh, To-morrow and Yesterday
At its gate clasp hands, touch lips;
We shall send men forth in ships
To find the perfect way.

'All that was writ shall be fulfilled at last.
Come—till we round the circle, end the story.
The west-bound sun leads forward to the past
The thundering cruisers and the caravels.
To-morrow you shall hear our song of glory
Rung in the chime of India's temple bells.'

O lazy laughing Panama!
O flutter of ribbon 'twixt the seas.
Pirate and king your colors wore
And stained with blood your golden keys.
Now what strange guest, on what mad quest,
Lifts up your trophy to the breeze!
O Panama, O ribbon-twist
That ties the continents together,
Now East and West shall slip your tether
And keep their ancient tryst!"

If the poets who write about the industrial world were all romanticists ready to cast a glamour over facts, we should not hear of any opposition to their belief that any subject may be a subject for a poem. They might write about guttering candles or about the Pleiades with the same certainty that they would have the enthusiasm of many readers and the somnolent negligence of others for their reward. But many modern poets are realists who cast no glamour over facts and bring into poetry elements of ugliness to which admirers of the Victorian poets are quite unaccustomed. The modern poet's reasons for giving ugliness a place in poetry should be explained, therefore, so that they need not be misunderstood.

Ugliness is very likely to be revealed in all modern poetry of a realistic kind which describes and shares life in which ugliness is found. The ugliness is in the poetry simply because the poet is sincere. He will not falsify values. No good poet loves ugliness for its own sake. But good poets do believe that ugliness, brought into poetry in its right relationships and because it is found in the life presented, is to poetry what occasional discords are to music; and therefore no discussion of the spirit of contemporary poetry is complete without mention of the element of ugliness.

To be sure, ugliness is no new thing in literature. Isaiah and Jeremiah were not afraid of it. They were very bold in their descriptive denunciations of moral evil and the symbols they used were strong and ugly symbols. Shakespeare permitted his characters the horrid delight of using very ugly language as occasion demanded. They availed themselves of this privilege with a glee and abandon almost unparalleled in the works of the moderns. Only a very naughty small boy can call names with the gusto of Shakespeare. Milton, stately poet of the sublime style, was not too nice and finicky to describe the horrors of the supposititious Hell in the life to come. Even the children in high schools know very well that he enjoyed creating the character of Satan. The poets of to-day are simply returning to these old ways of the poets, remembering the old traditions, when they describe in an ugly, but truthful way, the real little hells that we have near us here and now. They are showing us that the whole of life belongs to poetry. They are not picking out pretty bits of life for exploitation, forgetful of all the rest. Post-Victorian versifiers had eliminated ugliness and even when they wrote about sin they did not make it seem ugly. The poet of to-day believes that this is a mischievous way to write. Poets should not write covertly. They should not make any kind of ugliness seem smooth and pretty and romantic. That is why our best moderns sometimes seem like careful housewives running around after the charwoman, Civilization, mercilessly pointing out the dust that she has left hidden in cracks and corners.

Now so long as the poet keeps a sense of the proportion that should exist between beauty and ugliness, so long as he does not succumb to a pathological pleasure in the portrayal of unloveliness, the clear-eyed recognition of it is good for him and for his readers. But a reaction against Puritan repressions and against Victorian smoothness and prudery has carried a few moderns of the radical schools too far toward ugliness, so far indeed that their minds are not quite healthy. Such poems as seem to glorify and show pleasure in dirt, disease, sin, morbidity, animality, and abnormality are not great poetry no matter how cleverly they may be written. And, unfortunately, some of these poems are cleverly written. I have in mind a poem by a man capable of perceiving beauty, who has manifested the power in one or two poems that are reasonably good. It is called "K. McD." by William Carlos Williams. It begins in this fashion:

> "You exquisite chunk of mud,
> Kathleen—just like
> Any other chunk of mud
> —especially in April."

Of course this is not poetry. It is the reduction of a really sublime credo of ugliness to absurdity. It is a puerile effort to awaken sensations of surprise. It is novelty—not originality—

at its worst. And it is worse than all that, for it is banal and uninteresting.

But such ugliness as can be found in "The Widow In the Bye Street" or "The Everlasting Mercy," or is inherent in the realistic narratives of Mr. Gibson because it is inherent in the life described, such ugliness as makes characters real in plays like Mr. Bottomley's "King Lear's Wife," or serves to point an irony in the direction of truth as in certain poems by Rupert Brooke, such ugliness, in short, as insures quick recognition of itself and a sharp reaction, such ugliness as exists in its own true relations to life and for the sake of the larger beauty which includes it, is tonic and stimulating and a vitalizing force in poetry.

The poet of to-day takes from life anything which interests him and makes it the theme of a poem. He knows that he can never write well about anything which does not interest him keenly. Therefore, no matter how great and noble a theme may be, if he can not react toward it with fresh and vitalizing emotion, he will say nothing about it. For one man may write well about an organ grinder on the corner although he is bored by Phœbus Apollo. And the lights and shadows on the wall of a cheese factory may be more beautiful to another poet than an imagined sunset in Athens. The poet realizes, of course, that he shows his interests and enthusiasms and reveals himself through them whenever he writes a poem. And he knows that his own life and personality determine his choices. But he knows also, that in spite of literary fashions, which change with changing times, he can never write a good poem who does not feel it first. The theme must be the spark that kindles the warmth of his emotion. That is why we are sometimes tempted to believe that the contemporary poet, like Peter of old, has heard a voice crying from Heaven, "What God hath cleansed that call not thou common." For he seems to have accepted all of life, with its ugliness as well as its beauty, its defeat as well as its triumph. Having accepted life, he writes with fearless sincerity.

A CONSECRATION

Not of the princes and prelates with periwigged charioteers
Riding triumphantly laurelled to lap the fat of the years,
Rather the scorned—the rejected—the men hemmed in with the spears;

The men of the tattered battalion which fights till it dies,
Dazed with the dust of the battle, the din and the cries,
The men with the broken heads and the blood running into their eyes.

Not the be-medalled Commander, beloved of the throne,
Riding cock-horse to parade when the bugles are blown,
But the lads who carried the koppie and cannot be known.

Not the ruler for me, but the ranker, the tramp of the road,
The slave with the sack on his shoulders pricked on with the goad,
The man with too weighty a burden, too weary a load.

The sailor, the stoker of steamers, the man with the clout,
The chantyman bent at the halliards putting a tune to the shout,
The drowsy man at the wheel and the tired lookout.

Others may sing of the wine and the wealth and the mirth,
The portly presence of potentates goodly in girth;—
Mine be the dirt and the dross, the dust and scum of the earth!

Theirs be the music, the color, the glory, the gold;
Mine be a handful of ashes, a mouthful of mould.
Of the maimed, of the halt and the blind in the rain and the cold—

Of these shall my songs be fashioned, my tale be told. Amen.

John Masefield

THE LEADEN-EYED

Let not young souls be smothered out before
They do quaint deeds and fully flaunt their pride.
It is the world's one crime its babes grow dull,
Its poor are ox-like, limp and leaden-eyed.

Not that they starve, but starve so dreamlessly,
Not that they sow, but that they seldom reap,
Not that they serve, but have no gods to serve,
Not that they die, but that they die like sheep.

Vachel Lindsay

CALIBAN IN THE COAL MINES

God, we don't like to complain—
We know that the mine is no lark—
But—there's the pools from the rain;
But—there's the cold and the dark.

God, You don't know what it is—
You, in Your well-lighted sky,
Watching the meteors whizz;
Warm, with the sun always by.

God, if You had but the moon
Stuck in Your cap for a lamp,
Even You'd tire of it soon,
Down in the dark and the damp.

Nothing but blackness above,
And nothing that moves but the cars—
God, if You wish for our love,
Fling us a handful of stars!

Louis Untermeyer

THE COMMON STREET

The common street climbed up against the sky,
Gray meeting gray; and wearily to and fro
I saw the patient, common people go,
Each with his sordid burden trudging by.
And the rain dropped; there was not any sigh
Or stir of a live wind; dull, dull and slow
All motion; as a tale told long ago
The faded world; and creeping night drew nigh.

Then burst the sunset, flooding far and fleet,
Leavening the whole of life with magic leaven.
Suddenly down the long wet glistening hill
Pure splendor poured—and lo! the common street,
A golden highway into golden heaven,
With the dark shapes of men ascending still.

Helen Gray Cone

CHERRY WAY

Here, before the better streets begin,
Grimy backs of buildings wall it in,
Strident with the station's endless din,
And a yoke
Of dun smoke
Makes its title a dull joke.

Time was, once, long fled, when this slim street
Was all color-tremulous and sweet;
When the Sygne-Poste had a right to say
"Cherrie Waye,"
But to-day
It is palely bleak and gray.

Sometimes, when the moon is riding high,
Whitely, in a cold and cobalt sky,
From beneath their ancient graves close by,
Shadowed deep,
Ladies creep
Here to wring their hands and weep;

Holding up the flounced and flowered skirt
From the sordid ugliness and dirt,
With faint sighs and gesturings of hurt,
As to say—
"Lack-a-day!
Can thys be Oure Cherrie Waye?"

Ruth Comfort Mitchell

BROADWAY

How like the stars are these white, nameless faces—
These far innumerable burning coals!
This pale procession out of stellar spaces,
This Milky Way of souls!
Each in its own bright nebulæ enfurled,
Each face, dear God, a world!

I fling my gaze out through the silent night:
In those far stars, what gardens, what high halls,
Has mortal yearning built for its delight,
What chasms and what walls?
What quiet mansions where a soul may dwell?
What heaven and what hell?

Hermann Hagedorn

THE FLOWER FACTORY

Lisabetta, Marianina, Fiametta, Teresina,
They are winding stems of roses, one by one, one by one,
Little children, who have never learned to play;
Teresina softly crying that her fingers ache to-day;
Tiny Fiametta nodding when the twilight slips in, gray.
High above the clattering street, ambulance and fire-gong beat,
They sit, curling crimson petals, one by one, one by one.

Lisabetta, Marianina, Fiametta, Teresina,
They have never seen a rosebush nor a dewdrop in the sun.
They will dream of the vendetta, Teresina, Fiametta,
Of a Black Hand and a face behind a grating;
They will dream of cotton petals, endless, crimson, suffocating,
Never of a wild-rose thicket nor the singing of a cricket,
But the ambulance will bellow through the wanness of their dreams,
And their tired lids will flutter with the street's hysteric screams.
Lisabetta, Marianina, Fiametta, Teresina,
They are winding stems of roses, one by one, one by one.
Let them have a long long playtime, Lord of Toil, when toil is done,
Fill their baby hands with roses, joyous roses of the sun!

Florence Wilkinson

THE TIME-CLOCK

I

"Tick-Tock! Tick-Tock!"
Sings the great time-clock.
And the pale men hurry
And flurry and scurry
To punch their time
Ere the hour shall chime.
"Tick-tock! Tick-tock!"
Sings the stern time-clock.

"It—is—time—you—were—come!"
Says the pendulum.
"Tick-tock! Tick-tock!"
Moans the great time-clock.
They must leave the heaven
Of their beds. . . . It is seven,
And the sharp whistles blow
In the city below.
They can never delay—
If they're late, they must pay.
"God help them!" I say.
But the great time-clock
Only says, "Tick-tock!"

They are chained, they are slaves
From their birth to their graves!
And the clock
Seems to mock
With its awful "tick-tock!"
There it stands at the door
Like a brute, as they pour
Through the dark little way
Where they toil night and day.
They are goaded along
By the terrible song
Of whistle and gong,
And the endless "Tick-tock!"
Of the great time-clock.

"Tick-tock! Tick-tock!"
Runs the voice of the clock.

II

Some day it will cease!
They will all be at peace,
And dream a new dream
Far from shuttle and steam.
And whistles may blow,
And whistles may scream—
They will smile—even so,
And dream their new dream.

But the clock will tick on
When their bodies are gone;
And others will hurry,
And scurry and worry,
While "Tick-tock! Tick-tock!"
Whispers the clock.

"Tick-tock! Tick-tock!
Tick-tock! Tick-tock!"
Forever runs on the song of the clock!

Charles Hanson Towne

NIGHT'S MARDI GRAS

Night is the true democracy. When day
Like some great monarch with his train has passed,
In regal pomp and splendor to the last,
The stars troop forth along the Milky Way,
A jostling crowd, in radiant disarray,
On heaven's broad boulevard in pageants vast.
And things of earth, the hunted and outcast,
Come from their haunts and hiding-places; yea,
Even from the nooks and crannies of the mind
Visions uncouth and vagrant fancies start,
And specters of dead joy, that shun the light,

And impotent regrets and terrors blind,
  Each one, in form grotesque, playing its part
  In the fantastic Mardi Gras of Night.

Edward J. Wheeler

THE FUGITIVES

We are they that go, that go,
Plunging before the hidden blow.
We run the byways of the earth,
For we are fugitive from birth,
Blindfolded, with wide hands abroad
That sow, that sow the sullen sod.

We cannot wait, we cannot stop
For flushing field or quickened crop;
The orange bow of dusky dawn
Glimmers our smoking swath upon;
Blindfolded still we hurry on.

How do we know the ways we run
That are blindfolded from the sun?
We stagger swiftly to the call,
Our wide hands feeling for the wall.

Oh, ye who climb to some clear heaven,
By grace of day and leisure given,
Pity us, fugitive and driven—
The lithe whip curling on our track,
The headlong haste that looks not back!

Florence Wilkinson

ROSES IN THE SUBWAY*

A wan-cheeked girl with faded eyes
  Came stumbling down the crowded car,
Clutching her burden to her breast
  As though she held a star.

Roses, I swear it! Red and sweet
  And struggling from her pinched white hands,
Roses . . . like captured hostages
  From far and fairy lands!

The thunder of the rushing train
  Was like a hush. . . . The flower scent
Breathed faintly on the stale, whirled air
  Like some dim sacrament—

I saw a garden stretching out
  And morning on it like a crown—
And o'er a bed of crimson bloom
  My mother . . . stooping down.

Dana Burnet

THE MAN WITH THE HOE *

"God created man in his own image, in the image of God created He him."

Bowed by the weight of centuries, he leans
Upon his hoe and gazes on the ground,
The emptiness of ages in his face
And on his back the burden of the world.
Who made him dead to rapture and despair,
A thing that grieves not and that never hopes,
Stolid and stunned, a brother to the ox?
Who loosened and let down this brutal jaw?
Whose was the hand that slanted back this brow?
Whose breath blew out the light within this brain?

Is this the thing the Lord God made and gave
To have dominion over sea and land;
To trace the stars and search the heavens for power;
To feel the passion of eternity?
Is this the dream He dreamed who shaped the suns
And marked their ways upon the ancient deep?

*** Millet's painting, "The Man with the Hoe" was the inspiration for this poem.**

Down all the caverns of Hell to their last gulf
There is no shape more terrible than this—
More tongued with censure of the world's blind greed—
More filled with signs and portents for the soul—
More packt with danger to the universe.

What gulfs between him and the seraphim!
Slave of the wheel of labor, what to him
Are Plato and the swing of Pleiades?
What the long reaches of the peaks of song,
The rift of dawn, the reddening of the rose?
Through this dread shape the suffering ages look;
Time's tragedy is in that aching stoop;
Through this dread shape humanity betrayed,
Plundered, profaned and disinherited,
Cries protest to the Judges of the World,
A protest that is also prophecy.

O masters, lords and rulers in all lands,
Is this the handiwork you give to God,
This monstrous thing, distorted and soul-quenched?
How will you ever straighten up this shape;
Touch it again with immortality;
Give back the upward looking and the light;
Rebuild in it the music and the dream;
Make right the immemorial infamies,
Perfidious wrongs, immedicable woes?

O masters, lords and rulers in all lands,
How will the future reckon with this man?
How answer his brute question in that hour
When whirlwinds of rebellion shake the world?
How will it be with kingdoms and with kings—
With those who shaped him to the thing he is—
When this dumb terror shall appeal to God,
After the silence of the centuries?

Edwin Markham

"SCUM O' THE EARTH"

I

At the gate of the West I stand,
On the isle where the nations throng.
We call them "scum o' the earth";

Stay, are we doing you wrong,
Young fellow from Socrates' land?—
You, like a Hermes so lissome and strong
Fresh from the master Praxiteles' hand?
So you're of Spartan birth?
Descended, perhaps, from one of the band—
Deathless in story and song—
Who combed their long hair at Thermopylae's pass? . . .
Ah, I forget the straits, alas!
More tragic than theirs, more compassion-worth,
That have doomed you to march in our "immigrant class"
Where you're nothing but "scum o' the earth."

II

You Pole with the child on your knee,
What dower bring you to the land of the free?
Hark! does she croon
That sad little tune
That Chopin once found on his Polish lea
And mounted in gold for you and for me?
Now a ragged young fiddler answers
In wild Czech melody
That Dvořak took whole from the dancers.
And the heavy faces bloom
In the wonderful Slavic way;
The little, dull eyes, the brows a-gloom,
Suddenly dawn like the day.
While, watching these folk and their mystery,
I forget that they're nothing worth;
That Bohemians, Slovaks, Croatians,
And men of all Slavic nations
Are "polacks"—and "scum o' the earth."

III

Genoese boy of the level brow,
Lad of the lustrous, dreamy eyes
Astare at Manhattan's pinnacles now
In the first, sweet shock of a hushed surprise;
Within your far-rapt seer's eyes
I catch the glow of a wild surmise
That played on the Santa Maria's prow
In that still gray dawn,
Four centuries gone,
When a world from the wave began to rise.
Oh, it's hard to foretell what high emprise
Is the goal that gleams
When Italy's dreams
Spread wing and sweep into the skies.
Caesar dreamed him a world ruled well;
Dante dreamed Heaven out of Hell;
Angelo brought us there to dwell;
And you, are you of a different birth?—
You're only a "dago,"—and "scum o' the earth"!

IV

Stay, are we doing you wrong
Calling you "scum o' the earth,"
Man of the sorrow-bowed head,
Of the features tender yet strong,—
Man of the eyes full of wisdom and mystery
Mingled with patience and dread?
Have not I known you in history,
Sorrow-bowed head?
Were you the poet-king, worth
Treasures of Ophir unpriced?
Were you the prophet, perchance, whose art
Foretold how the rabble would mock
That shepherd of spirits, erelong,
Who should carry the lambs on his heart
And tenderly feed his flock?
Man—lift that sorrow-bowed head.
Lo! 'tis the face of the Christ!

The vision dies at its birth.
You're merely a butt for our mirth.
You're a "sheeny"—and therefore despised
And rejected as "scum o' the earth."

V

Countrymen, bend and invoke
Mercy for us blasphemers,
For that we spat on these marvelous folk,
Nations of darers and dreamers,
Scions of singers and seers,
Our peers, and more than our peers.
"Rabble and refuse," we name them
And "scum o' the earth" to shame them.
Mercy for us of the few, young years,
Of the culture so callow and crude,
Of the hands so grasping and rude,
The lips so ready for sneers
At the sons of our ancient more-than-peers.
Mercy for us who dare despise
Men in whose loins our Homer lies;
Mothers of men who shall bring to us
The glory of Titian, the grandeur of Huss;
Children in whose frail arms shall rest
Prophets and singers and saints of the West.

Newcomers all from the eastern seas,
Help us incarnate dreams like these.
Forget, and forgive, that we did you wrong.
Help us to father a nation, strong
In the comradeship of an equal birth,
In the wealth of the richest bloods of earth.

Robert Haven Schauffler

FROM "THE NEW WORLD"

Celia was laughing. Hopefully I said:
"How shall this beauty that we share,
This love, remain aware
Beyond our happy breathing of the air?

How shall it be fulfilled and perfected? . . .
If you were dead,
How then should I be comforted?"
  But Celia knew instead:
"He who finds beauty here, shall find it there."
  A halo gathered round her hair.
I looked and saw her wisdom bare
The living bosom of the countless dead.
. . . And there
I laid my head.

  Again when Celia laughed, I doubted her and said:
"Life must be led
In many ways more difficult to see
Than this immediate way
For you and me.
We stand together on our lake's edge, and the mystery
Of love has made us one, as day is made of night and night of day.
Aware of one identity
Within each other, we can say:
'I shall be everything you are.' . . .
We are uplifted till we touch a star.
We know that overhead
Is nothing more austere, more starry, or more deep to understand
Than is our union, human hand in hand.
. . . But over our lake come strangers—a crowded launch, a lonely sailing boy.
A mile away a train bends by. In every car
Strangers are travelling, each with particular
And unkind preference like ours, with privacy
Of understanding, with especial joy
Like ours. Celia, Celia, why should there be
Distrust between ourselves and them, disunity?
. . . How careful we have been
To trim this little circle that we tread,
To set a bar
To strangers and forbid them!—Are they not as we,
Our very likeness and our nearest kin?
How can we shut them out and let stars in?"

She looked along the lake. And when I heard her speak,
The sun fell on the boy's white sail and her white cheek.
"I touch them all through you," she said. "I cannot know them now
Deeply and truly as my very own, except through you,
Except through one or two
Interpreters.
But not a moment stirs
Here between us, binding and interweaving us,
That does not bind these others to our care."
The sunlight fell in glory on her hair. . . .
And then said Celia, radiant, when I held her near:
"They who find beauty there, shall find it here."
And on her brow,
When I heard Celia speak,
Cities were populous
With peace and oceans echoed glories in her ear
And from her risen thought
Her lips had brought,
As from some peak
Down through the clouds, a mountain-air
To guide the lonely and uplift the weak.
"Record it all," she told me, "more than merely this,
More than the shine of sunset on our heads, more than a kiss,
More than our rapt agreement and delight
Watching the mountain mingle with the night. . . .
Tell that the love of two incurs
The love of multitudes, makes way
And welcome for them, as a solitary star
Brings on the great array.
Go make a lovers' calendar,"
She said, "for every day."

And when the sun had put away
His dazzle, over the shadowy firs
The solitary star came out. . . . So on some night
To eyes of youth shall come my light
And hers.

Witter Bynner

PATRIOTISM AND THE GREAT WAR

Courage is the fundamental biological virtue, the necessary virtue without which the human race could never have survived on this planet. Long before people discussed the virtues and classified their names as abstract nouns, courage was a concrete and definite thing. If he would eat, the man of the stone age must have courage in hunting and fishing and fighting. If she would protect her young, the woman of the stone age must have courage to stand before them in the door of her cave. Therefore courage is probably planted deeper in us than any of the virtues acquired later in the history of the race and is probably the most common of all virtues. Certainly, whenever it is demanded of them, men and women with no very unusual qualities of any other kind manifest courage in a remarkable degree. And in almost all normal human beings, as the great war has proved, is a capacity for courage, even for heroism. In spite of the fact that many of us never rise very high above our sins and follies, it can be said justly that few of us are cowards.

Much of the power of the social and racial passion called patriotism is to be found in the fact that it calls upon the common woman and man to exercise this ancient virtue. It affords an opportunity for transfiguration. No matter what his faults may have been, when the time comes a man will be a man—and, in the same sense, a woman will be a woman. For once they will be godlike, giving everything, facing and enduring all things for the sake of the dear soil of the mother land, for the streets of the home town, and for the civilization in which they have been bred, which, in spite of all the criticisms leveled against it in times of peace, probably suits them better than any other which might be imposed upon them.

For it is the glory of poor errant human nature to love the

exercise of courage, or of any virtue. Nothing gives a man more happiness than the expression of that which is best in himself. Nothing, to speak colloquially, is more fun than being good. Let a man once get a good strong taste of any particular virtue and know what it is like to practise it and the chances are that he will enjoy it so much that Satan will have little power over him with the opposite vice. That man will have to be tempted in another way. When a rich man gives away large parts of his fortune in philanthropies of one kind or another, he is enjoying the virtue of generosity. When a man who could earn an excellent living in business continues to preach and teach at a low wage, he is enjoying his self-abnegation. The virtue which we have tried, the virtue in which we believe, that alone will content us. And it is only the person who has never made a fair trial of "being good" in one way or another, who does not like it. To be sure it is not always easy to be good in a world where goodness does not altogether control the popular imagination and where it is not always understood. But that fact makes it the more interesting.

Now courage is the virtue that most men and women know best. And patriotism is the greatest of social and racial passions. Therefore when patriotism calls men and women to the exercise of the ancient biological virtue, not in the dull, slow ways of peace, but in the quick and dramatic ways of war that stir the imagination and arouse the emotions, then the people respond. Out of that response came the first war songs. Out of it will come the last.

Nearly all living poets have written something about the great war. If we could have all of the thousands of poems written by recognized poets, with their dates, we should have a passionate record of all that mankind has felt about the war and of the several currents of changing emotion that have swept across the world since 1914. But the whole story of the poetry of the war can never be told in any one book. The best that can be done here is to tell what a few poets of our language have felt and how they have spoken, for themselves, for their people, for their times.

In 1914 many sober-minded persons here and abroad thought that there would never be another great war. In the United States, especially, we had begun to feel very secure in the thought of the world's peace. We are a nation made of people from many nations, "of many one." We were getting ready for world federation and internationalism. And then the greatest of all international wars began. For a while we stood aloof. We were annoyed with Europe. We were disgusted with Germany's behavior to Belgium, to be sure. We wanted to help the poor Belgians. We were willing to give generously. But for ourselves we did not believe in bloodshed unless it was necessary in self-defense. We thought things could and should be settled by arbitration. We did not want to take part in Europe's ugly family quarrel. In spite of our theoretical internationalism we did not feel that we were a part of the same world which the Europeans were disturbing. As in the days of Washington, we thought we were the "New World" and they were the "Old World." We did not understand that from now on there can be but one great family in the world, the human family, and that any vital quarrel will involve all members of that family sooner or later.

Therefore the first American poems about the great war were poems of peace. They were not very good. Perhaps, in so far as they touched the war, the American poems of that period may be called negligible. Most of them pointed out the wickedness of Europe or the wickedness of war. Most of them took issue in the minds of their makers from moral ideas, not from emotional realizations. Some of them expressed a generous sympathy with the sufferings of Europe. As poetry none of them were great.

But in England, at that same time, war was necessary. It was not a subject for academic discussion. It was a reality. And the first English poems were songs inciting men to valor, lyrics which called to the minds of Englishmen the heroism of

England's valiant dead. They made the old racial appeal to the common virtue of courage.

In England these first poems about the war seem to have been written by mature and famous poets, perhaps because the young poets were among those first called to the front. In a small volume called "Songs And Sonnets For England In War Time" (Lane) and published in 1914, we find no poems by the young fighting singers who have since brought beauty out of the Hell in which they lived. In this little book were poems by Thomas Hardy, G. K. Chesterton, Henry Newbolt and others as well known. But their contributions to this volume can hardly be set side by side with their best work in poetry. Very little in the book is more than manly journalism. The best poems in it are Laurence Binyon's generous lyric, "To Women," and Rudyard Kipling's "For All We Have And Are," a poem strong in the racial spirit.

"For all we have and are,
For all our children's fate,
Stand up and meet the war.
The Hun is at the gate!

* * * * * *

"There is but one task for all—
For each one life to give.
Who stands if freedom fall?
Who dies if England live?"

For the rest, none of the poets represented had, at that time, written a great poem about the war. It was not for any lack of genius. It was simply that it was too soon. The spiritual realities of the war were too stupendous to be quickly revealed. The issues of it could not be realized quickly. Never before in our times had men and women been called upon to witness such a pageant of the human spirit. Old wars gave no clue to the magnitude of this one. Poets needed to wait and learn, before they could speak.

The English learned sooner than we, for they stepped first

out of safety and peace into the valor and agony of the maelstrom. Then, when the first convulsion of pain shook the heart of a great people, their speech was heard, as English speech has always been heard, in the voices of poets worthy of England. John Masefield gave the world "August, 1914," and Rupert Brooke, the "Nineteen Fourteen" sonnets.

"August, 1914" is quiet and profound. It begins with the line,

> "How still this quiet cornfield is to-night!"

In every sweet-flowing line a depth of quietness is felt. Yet the poem is as moving as the beat of drums. In it is the essence of what one feels about one's own country and folk. Mr. Masefield thought and wrote of the Englishmen of all ages who had heard the news of war, who went home to think about it quietly at their own hearths,

> "With such dumb loving of the Berkshire loam
> As breaks the dumb hearts of the English kind,
>
> "Then sadly rose and left the well-loved Downs,
> And so by ship to sea, and knew no more
> The fields of home, the byres, the market towns,
> Nor the dear outline of the English shore,
>
> "But knew the misery of the soaking trench,
> The freezing in the rigging, the despair
> In the revolting second of the wrench
> When the blind soul is flung upon the air,
>
> "And died (uncouthly, most) in foreign lands
> For some idea but dimly understood
> Of an English city never built by hands
> Which love of England prompted and made good."

Three of the "Nineteen-Fourteen" sonnets of Rupert Brooke, "Peace," "The Dead" (one of two with that title), and "The Soldier" were published first in Chicago, in *Poetry, A Magazine of Verse*. These and the others in the same group are noble alike in conception and execution. They are thrilling in their exaltation.

> "Now, God be thanked who has matched us with this hour,
> And caught our youth and wakened us from sleeping!"

That was Rupert Brooke's answer, that was the answer of youth called to be a sacrifice for the sins of the world. The fine, white fire of this mood lights every line of these sonnets. Surely man is never greater than when he can give thanks for his own renunciations.

Rupert Brooke showed his love of life in his earlier poems. His occasional ironies, gritty and delightfully humorous, were the ironies of youth and without bitterness. They have done nothing to destroy our belief that he found joy in the things of the world. This makes the sonnets seem the more lovely since now, for Rupert Brooke, as for "The Dead" of whom he wrote,

> "Frost, with a gesture, stays the waves that dance
> And wandering loveliness. He leaves a white
> Unbroken glory, a gathered radiance,
> A width, a shining peace, under the night."

Rupert Brooke's sonnets are purely lyrical, the direct expression of great personal emotion. His friend, Wilfrid Wilson Gibson, who gave us the first good realistic poetry of the war, has dramatized the emotions of the common soldier, any soldier at the front. He tells us things that we all know very well might be in the heart of any decent, normal man not a soldier by trade and inclination, but for love of honor and home. The wonder about dying, the horror of killing, the great helpless sympathy for other suffering men, all the poignant pathos of warfare are to be found in these plain, homely little poems. They are like strong, true sketches in charcoal, done in a few lines, but unforgettable. And in the making of them Mr. Gibson is so much an artist that he has used always the exact, the vivid word. In "The Bayonet" he says:

"This bloody steel
Has killed a man,
I heard him squeal
As on I ran."

Only strong personal realization could have written that word "squeal." It brings home to us the horror of killing as no other word could.

Much of the beauty of these poems is in the absolute faithfulness to reality which seems to be Mr. Gibson's ideal. We read about the lad who lies in the trench thinking of home as he left it, and saying to himself,

"I wonder if the old cow died or not."

We read about another lad "back from the trenches more dead than alive," who is suffering mental torment because three of his chums dropped dead beside him in the trench and whispered their dying messages to him, and yet he "can not quite remember." We read about the feverish man in the ambulance who keeps other chaps awake all night muttering about his garden

"Two rows of cabbages,
Two of curly-greens,
Two rows of early peas,
Two of kidney beans."

Another realist, Siegfried Sassoon, writes of the war in much the same spirit, save that the edge of his irony is sharper and he is more bitter about the war and the destruction it has wrought. Mr. Sassoon knows war by actual experience. He can not write of it as the older poets wrote before the battle was on. Nor do any of the young poets who have fought write as men wrote of war in days gone by. In a very terrible short poem called "The Kiss," Mr. Sassoon expresses something which seems to be in the hearts of all of these young poets who have come to grips with war and suffered and fought most bravely. In this poem, with sensitive spirit, he prays for an insensate fury which will enable him to do his hideous duty. He says,

> "To these I turn, in these I trust;
> Brother Lead and Sister Steel."

and then he makes his prayer:

> "Sweet Sister, grant your soldier this;
> That in good fury he may feel
> The body where he sets his heel
> Quail from your downward darting kiss."

Terrible as such poems are, there is something essentially noble in the intellectual honesty that will cast no glamour over the thing which must be done, not because it is beautiful, but because, in an imperfect world, it is necessary. This same uncompromising bitterness is to be found in many another strong lyric, in "Golgotha," "When I'm Among A Blaze of Lights," "A Mystic As a Soldier," "Blighters" and "At Carnoy." Mr. Sassoon is a sincere and truth-loving poet of whom fine things may be expected.

His two friends, Robert Graves and Robert Nichols, are less bitter in their thought of the war. Robert Graves, if one can judge him by his book, "Fairies And Fusiliers," is not bitter at all, but a gay young singer, capable of impish mischief and insouciant fancy. His poems of the war are well made, true and beautiful with a boy's spirit of gallantry. In particular "The Assault Heroic" is a fine poem which tells how a young officer, worn out after five sleepless days and nights in the trenches, in that peculiar trance between sleep and wakefulness which sometimes comes to the very weary, must fight his own spiritual enemies within himself. When he has won his victory,

> "with my spear of Faith,
> Stout as an oaken rafter,
> With my round shield of laughter"

he hears once more the very real voices of his men in the trench, saying,

> *"Stand to! Stand to!*
> *Wake up, sir! Here's a new*
> *Attack! Stand to! Stand to!"*

Robert Nichols, the third member of this trio of young English poets, is rather better known in the United States than either of the others, because he has visited us. His poems are less bitter in their descriptions of war than Siegfried Sassoon's. He is content to show that it is tragic. Nor is he so young and whimsical in manner as Robert Graves. His poems are somewhat more lyrical than the poems of either of the others. But in his book, "Ardours And Endurances" we find a number of poems chiefly remarkable for the truth and vitality of their picturing. One of the finest of these picture-poems is "Out of Trenches: The Barn, Twilight." Just to read it is to join a group of Tommies and listen to their songs and their talk. It is admirably done. But it is not verse to be quoted. It should be read as a whole.

Another fine, true picture from the front is Ford Madox Hueffer's "The Old Houses of Flanders," a poem made with delicate skill and fine imagination, as are also his more lyrical poems, "The Iron Music" and "A Solis Ortus Cardine." It is interesting to note that no American has written war poetry of this pictorial kind.

The first fine American poem of the war written by an American who was a sharer in the conflict is Alan Seeger's "I Have A Rendezvous With Death," now famous wherever poetry is read in our language. Alan Seeger, as everybody knows, went into the war with impetuous and generous gallantry, before this nation went into it, and for love of France, the foster-mother of his spirit. He died at Belloy-en-Santerre without knowing that we also, later, would follow where he led, to France and to battle.

"I Have A Rendezvous With Death" is a gravely beautiful

lyric, personal, intimate, a young man's word about himself and his last adventure. All the austerity of youth consecrated to dissolution is in these reiterated lines about the rendezvous. All the lavish generosity of youth, going out to death while the love of life is still hot in the heart, is in the last lines of this stern singing,

> "But I've a rendezvous with Death
> At midnight in some flaming town,
> When Spring trips North again this year,
> And I to my pledged word am true,
> I shall not fail that rendezvous."

After our declaration of war a number of fine poems were written. First came the call to courage. And just as in England, in 1914, so in our country, in 1917, poems were written that were simply attempts to summon men to the exercise of the ancient and indisputable virtue of the race. These poems were just what many of the first English poems of the war were, manly journalism. But one of them was much more. Edgar Lee Masters' "Draw The Sword, O Republic," is a fine, stern call to battle, and will continue to be a fine, stern summons when many other poems of to-day are forgotten. It is one of the finest things he ever wrote. It is not lyrical, for the singer's gift is not in Mr. Masters' genius. But it is powerful, resonant speech, and, since the modern conception of poetry has been enlarged to include such speech, it is indubitably poetry. Moreover it is essentially American, for, says Mr. Masters:

> "By the power that drives the soul to Freedom,
> And by the power that makes us love our fellows,
> And by the power that comforts us in death,—
> Dying for great races to come—
> Draw the sword, O Republic!
> Draw the sword!"

It is in America that men live and die not for one race, but for "great races to come."

Another fine American poem of the war is Amy Lowell's narrative, "A Cornucopia of Red And Green Comfits." It is one of her greatest achievements, for in it her magical imagination presents a series of sharply drawn pictures that tell a terrible tale of perfidy. This is a story, founded on fact, of the children of Bar-le-Duc, in the province of Meuse, in France, Bar-le-Duc, whose people have won fame the world over for their conserve of currants and honey. These little children were betrayed to their death by their natural love of sugar. German aviators scattered poisoned candy on the ground for them. In no other poem does Miss Lowell gain so complete a control of the emotions of her readers. In all of her poems she shows her fecundity of imagination and the nice skill of the craftsman. But this is a poem by an indignant woman, speaking of an outrage against childhood.

But perhaps Americans will treasure Joyce Kilmer's "Rouge Bouquet" as long, and with as much affection as they can have for any American poem of the great war. For Mr. Kilmer enlisted almost as soon as we went into the war and died for his country, in France, near the Ourcq, July 30, 1918.

"Rouge Bouquet" commemorates the death of our boys in khaki buried under earth ten meters thick when a great shell exploded near a dugout in the wood called "Rouge Bouquet." Like most of Mr. Kilmer's more serious poems, "Rouge Bouquet" is written in the spirit of the Catholic faith, and pictures the welcome that the saints will offer the brave lads when they go in at the gate of Heaven:

> "St. Michael's sword darts through the air
> And touches the aureole on his hair
> As he sees them stand saluting there,
>   His stalwart sons;
> And Patrick, Brigid, Columkill
> Rejoice that in veins of warriors still
>   The Gael's blood runs."

Then the poem closes with the farewell of the friends on earth and the bugles playing "Taps." To the spirits of these fellow soldiers Joyce Kilmer said,

> "Your souls shall be where heroes are
> And your memory shine like the morning-star.
> Brave and dear,
> Shield us here.
> Farewell!"

That is the farewell that the world now echoes for him.

I—THE DEAD*

Blow out, you bugles, over the rich Dead!
  There's none of these so lonely and poor of old,
  But, dying, has made us rarer gifts than gold.
These laid the world away; poured out the red
Sweet wine of youth; gave up the years to be
  Of work and joy, and that unhoped serene
  That men call age; and those who would have been
Their sons, they gave, their immortality.
Blow, bugles, blow! They brought us, for our dearth,
  Holiness, lacked so long, and Love, and Pain.
Honor has come back, as a king, to earth,
  And paid his subjects with a royal wage;
And Nobleness walks in our ways again;
  And we have come into our heritage.

II—THE DEAD

These hearts were woven of human joys and cares,
  Washed marvellously with sorrow, swift to mirth.
The years had given them kindness. Dawn was theirs,
  And sunset, and the colors of the earth.
These had seen movement, and heard music; known
  Slumber and waking; loved; gone proudly friended;
Felt the quick stir of wonder; sat alone;
  Touched flowers and furs and cheeks. All this is ended.

* From *The Collected Poems of Rupert Brooke.* Copyright, 1915, by John Lane Company.

There are waters blown by changing winds to laughter
And lit by the rich skies, all day. And after,
  Frost, with a gesture, stays the waves that dance
And wandering loveliness. He leaves a white
  Unbroken glory, a gathered radiance,
A width, a shining peace, under the night.

Rupert Brooke

DAWN

The grim dawn lightens thin bleak clouds;
In the hill clefts beyond the flooded meadows
Lies death-pale, death-still mist.

We trudge along wearily,
Heavy with lack of sleep,
Spiritless, yet with pretence of gaiety.

The sun brings crimson to the colourless sky;
Light gleams from brass and steel—
We trudge on wearily—

O God, end this bleak anguish
Soon, soon, with vivid crimson death,
End it in mist-pale sleep!

Richard Aldington

THE MESSAGES

"I cannot quite remember. . . . There were five
Dropt dead beside me in the trench—and three
Whispered their dying messages to me. . . ."

Back from the trenches, more dead than alive,
Stone-deaf and dazed, and with a broken knee,
He hobbled slowly, muttering vacantly:

"I cannot quite remember. . . . There were five
Dropt dead beside me in the trench, and three
Whispered their dying messages to me . . .

"Their friends are waiting, wondering how they thrive—
Waiting a word in silence patiently. . . .
But what they said, or who their friends may be

"I cannot quite remember. . . . There were five
Dropt dead beside me in the trench,—and three
Whispered their dying messages to me. . . ."

Wilfrid Wilson Gibson

THE FATHER

That was his sort.
It didn't matter
What we were at
But he must chatter
Of this and that
His little son
Had said and done:
Till, as he told
The fiftieth time
Without a change
How three-year-old
Prattled a rhyme,
They got the range
And cut him short.

Wilfrid Wilson Gibson

BREAKFAST

We ate our breakfast lying on our backs,
Because the shells were screeching overhead.
I bet a rasher to a loaf of bread
That Hull United would beat Halifax
When Jimmy Stainthorpe played full-back instead
Of Billy Bradford. Ginger raised his head
And cursed, and took the bet; and dropt back dead.
We ate our breakfast lying on our backs,
Because the shells were screeching overhead.

Wilfrid Wilson Gibson

THE KISS

To these I turn, in these I trust;
Brother Lead and Sister Steel.
To his blind power I make appeal;
I guard her beauty clean from rust.

He spins and burns and loves the air,
And splits a skull to win my praise;
But up the nobly marching days
She glitters naked, cold and fair.

Sweet Sister, grant your soldier this;
That in good fury he may feel
The body where he sets his heel
Quail from your downward darting kiss.

Siegfried Sassoon

ABSOLUTION *

The anguish of the earth absolves our eyes
Till beauty shines in all that we can see.
War is our scourge; yet war has made us wise,
And, fighting for our freedom, we are free.

Horror of wounds and anger at the foe,
And loss of things desired; all these must pass.
We are the happy legion, for we know
Time's but a golden wind that shakes the grass.

There was an hour when we were loth to part
From life we longed to share no less than others.
Now, having claimed this heritage of heart,
What need we more, my comrades and my brothers?

Siegfried Sassoon

* From *The Old Huntsman and Other Poems* by Siegfried Sassoon, London. Heinemann.

THE ASSAULT HEROIC*

Down in the mud I lay,
Tired out by my long day
Of five damned days and nights,
Five sleepless days and nights, . . .
Dream-snatched, and set me where
The dungeon of Despair
Looms over Desolate Sea,
Frowning and threatening me
With aspect high and steep—
A most malignant keep.
My foes that lay within
Shouted and made a din,
Hooted and grinned and cried:
"To-day we've killed your pride;
To-day your ardour ends.
We've murdered all your friends;
We've undermined by stealth
Your happiness and your health.
We've taken away your hope;
Now you may droop and mope
To misery and to Death."
But with my spear of Faith,
Stout as an oaken rafter,
With my round shield of laughter,
With my sharp tongue-like sword
That speaks a bitter word,
I stood beneath the wall
And there defied them all.
The stones they cast I caught
And alchemized with thought
Into such lumps of gold
As dreaming misers hold.
The boiling oil they threw
Fell in a shower of dew,
Refreshing me; the spears
Flew harmless by my ears,

* From *Fairies and Fusiliers* by Robert Graves, London. Heinemann.

Stuck quivering in the sod;
There, like the prophet's rod,
Put leaves out, took firm root,
And bore me instant fruit.
My foes were all astounded,
Dumbstricken and confounded,
Gaping in a long row;
They dared not thrust nor throw.
Thus, then, I climbed a steep
Buttress and won the keep,
And laughed and proudly blew
My horn, "*Stand to! Stand to!*
Wake up, sir! Here's a new
Attack! Stand to! Stand to!"

Robert Graves

OUT OF TRENCHES: THE BARN, TWILIGHT

In the raftered barn we lie,
Sprawl, scrawl postcards, laugh and speak—
Just mere men a trifle weary,
Worn in heart, a trifle weak:
Because alway
At close of day
Thought steals to England far away. . . .
"Alf!" "O ay."
"Gi' us a tune, mate." "Well, wot say?"
"Swipe 'The Policeman's 'Oliday' . . ."
"*Tiddle—iddle—um—tum,*
Tum—TUM."

Sprawling on my aching back,
Think I nought; but I am glad—
Dear, rare lads of pick and pack!
Aie me too! I'm sad . . . I'm sad:
Some must die
(Maybe I):
O pray it take them suddenly!
"Bill!" "Wot ho!"

"Concertina: let it go—
'If you were the only girl'" "Cheero!
"*If you were the Only Girl.*"

Damn. "Abide with Me. . ." Not now!—
Well . . . if you must: just your way.
It racks me till the tears nigh flow.
The tune see-saws. I turn, I pray
Behind my hand
Shaken, unmanned,
In groans that God may understand:
Miracle!
"Let, let them all survive this hell."
Hear "Trumpeter, what are you sounding?" swell.
(My God! I guess indeed too well:
The broken heart, eyes front, proud knell!)
Grant but mine sound with their farewell.
"*It's the Last Post I'm sounding.*"

Robert Nichols

NEARER

Nearer and ever nearer . . .
My body, tired but tense,
Hovers 'twixt vague pleasure
And tremulous confidence.

Arms to have and to use them
And a soul to be made
Worthy if not worthy;
If afraid, unafraid.

To endure for a little,
To endure and have done:
Men I love about me,
Over me the sun!

And should at last suddenly
Fly the speeding death,
The four great quarters of heaven
Receive this little breath.

Robert Nichols

THE IRON MUSIC*

The French guns roll continuously
And our guns, heavy, slow;
Along the Ancre, sinuously,
The transport wagons go,
And the dust is on the thistles
And the larks sing up on high . . .
But I see the Golden Valley
Down by Tintern on the Wye.

For it's just nine weeks last Sunday
Since we took the Chepstow train,
And I'm wondering if one day
We shall do the like again;
For the four-point-two's come screaming
Thro' the sausages on high;
So there's little use in dreaming
How we walked above the Wye.

Dust and corpses in the thistles
Where the gas-shells burst like snow,
And the shrapnel screams and whistles
On the Bécourt road below,
And the High Wood bursts and bristles
Where the mine-clouds foul the sky . . .
But I'm with you up at Wyndcroft,
Over Tintern on the Wye.

Ford Madox Hueffer

THE OLD HOUSES OF FLANDERS*

The old houses of Flanders,
They watch by the high cathedrals;
They overtop the high town-halls;
They have eyes, mournful, tolerant and sardonic, for the ways of men
In the high, white tiled gables.

*From *On Heaven and Poems Written on Active Service* by Ford Madox Hueffer, by permission of John Lane Company, New York, and John Lane, The Bodley Head, London, publishers.

The rain and the night have settled down on Flanders;
It is all wet darkness; you can see nothing.

Then those old eyes, mournful, tolerant and sardonic,
Look at great, sudden, red lights,
Look upon the shades of the cathedrals;
And the golden rods of the illuminated rain,
For a second . . .

And those old eyes,
Very old eyes that have watched the ways of men for many generations,
Close for ever.
The high, white shoulders of the gables
Slouch together for a consultation,
Slant drunkenly over in the lea of the flaming cathedrals.

They are no more, the old houses of Flanders.

Ford Madox Hueffer

"I HAVE A RENDEZVOUS WITH DEATH"*

I have a rendezvous with Death
At some disputed barricade,
When Spring comes back with rustling shade
And apple-blossoms fill the air—
I have a rendezvous with Death
When Spring brings back blue days and fair.

It may be he shall take my hand
And lead me into his dark land
And close my eyes and quench my breath—
It may be I shall pass him still.
I have a rendezvous with Death
On some scarred slope of battered hill,
When Spring comes round again this year
And the first meadow-flowers appear.

God knows 't'were better to be deep
Pillowed in silk and scented down,

Where love throbs out in blissful sleep,
Pulse nigh to pulse, and breath to breath,
Where hushed awakenings are dear . . .
But I've a rendezvous with Death
At midnight in some flaming town,
When Spring trips north again this year,
And I to my pledged word am true,
I shall not fail that rendezvous.

Alan Seeger

DRAW THE SWORD, O REPUBLIC

By the blue sky of a clear vision,
And by the white light of a great illumination,
And by the blood-red of brotherhood,
Draw the sword, O Republic!
Draw the sword!

For the light which is England,
And the resurrection which is Russia,
And the sorrow which is France,
And for peoples everywhere
Crying in bondage,
And in poverty!

You have been a leaven in the earth, O Republic!
And a watch-fire on the hill-top scattering sparks;
And an eagle clanging his wings on a cloud-wrapped promontory:
Now the leaven must be stirred,
And the brands themselves carried and touched
To the jungles and the black-forests.
Now the eaglets are grown, they are calling,
They are crying to each other from the peaks—
They are flapping their passionate wings in the sunlight,
Eager for battle!
As a strong man nurses his youth
To the day of trial;
But as a strong man nurses it no more
On the day of trial,
But exults and cries For Victory, O Strength!

And for the glory of my City, O treasured youth!
You shall neither save your youth,
Nor hoard your strength
Beyond this hour, O Republic!

For you have sworn
By the passion of the Gaul,
And the strength of the Teuton,
And the will of the Saxon,
And the hunger of the Poor,
That the white man shall lie down by the black man,
And by the yellow man,
And all men shall be one spirit, as they are one flesh,
Through Wisdom, Liberty and Democracy.
And forasmuch as the earth cannot hold
Aught beside them,
You have dedicated the earth, O Republic,
To Wisdom, Liberty and Democracy!

By the power that drives the soul to Freedom,
And by the Power that makes us love our fellows,
And by the Power that comforts us in death,
Dying for great races to come—
Draw the sword, O Republic!
Draw the sword!

Edgar Lee Masters

DOWN FIFTH AVENUE

The crowd makes way for them.
The mob of motors—women in motors, footmen in motors, Manhattan's transients in motors, life's transients in motors—has cleared and disappeared.
And their mothers and their children, their wives, their lovers and friends, are lining the curb and knitting and whispering.
The flags are floating and beckoning to them, the breezes are beckoning and whispering their secrets,
That the city has hushed to hear, while trade and trivial things give place.

And through the crowd, that holds its breath too long, a restless stir like the starting of troubled breathing says,
"They are coming." And the distant beat of feet begins to blend with the beat of laboring hearts;
And the emptiness that missed a beat in the heart of the city becomes the street of a prayer and a passion.
This is a street of mothers and their sons—for an hour in the life of Manhattan.
And to-day makes way for them.

The past makes way for them.
This morning's discontent, yesterday's greed, last year's uncertainty, are muted and transmuted to a surging urge to victory.
Spirits that stood at Bunker Hill and Valley Forge, Ticonderoga, Yorktown, Lundy's Lane, Fort Sumter, Appomatox, are resurrected here;
With older fathers and mothers who farmed, and pushed frontiers and homes for freedom westward steadily;
With freedom's first grandfathers and forerunners, who grew to hold hill towers and forest fastnesses, and range the sea and all its shores and islands for the right to live for liberty.
And their blood beats in these boy hearts, and their hill-bred and sea-bred strength is stirring in these feet that beat their measured cadences of courage.

For now the tide is turning eastward at last.
And the sound of the fall of their feet on the asphalt is the sound of the march of the waves of a tide that is flooding—
Waves that marched to the western coast past forests and plains, mountains and deserts, and wrought their work in a world gone by.
And the ripple of the ranks of these regiments that march to suffer and to die, is the ripple of a great brown river in flood that forges seaward;
And the ripple of the light on eyes and lips that watch and work, is the swelling of a greater flood that forces them to go.
And the ripple and arrest of light on dull gun-barrels that crest their flow are runes of a ritual spelled in steel and a service enduring.
And each beat of their feet and each beat of their hearts is a word in a gospel of steel that says the nations through ruins grow one again;

When God's drill-master War has welded nations in ranks that their
children may serve Him together.
For to-morrow makes way for them.

John Curtis Underwood

THE CORNUCOPIA OF RED AND GREEN COMFITS

"In the town of Bar-le-Duc in the Province of the Meuse in France the Prefect has issued instructions to the Mayor, the schoolmasters and the schoolmistresses to prevent the children under their care from eating candies which may be dropped from German aeroplanes, as candies which were similarly scattered in other parts of the war zone have been found to contain poison and disease germs."—*Daily News Report.*

Currants and Honey!
Currants and Honey!
Bar-le-Duc in times of peace.
Linden-tassel honey,
Cherry-blossom, poppy-sweet honey,
And round red currants like grape clusters,
Red and yellow globes, lustred like stretched umbrella silk,
Money chinking in town pockets,
Louis d'or in exchange for dockets of lading:
So many jars,
So many bushes shorn of their stars,
So many honey-combs lifted from the hive-bars.
Straw-pale honey and amber berries,
Red-stained honey and currant cherries.
Sweetness flowing out of Bar-le-Duc by every train,
It rains prosperity in Bar-le-Duc in times of peace.
Holy Jesus! when will there be mercy, when a ceasing
Of War!
The currant bushes are lopped and burned,
The bees have flown and never returned,
The children of Bar-le-Duc eat no more honey,
And all the money in the town will not buy
Enough lumps of sugar for a family.
Father has two between sun and sun,

So has mother, and little Jeanne, one,
But Gaston and Marie—they have none.
Two little children kneeling between the grape-vines,
Praying to the starry virgin,
They have seen her in church, shining out of a high window
In a currant-red gown and a crown as smooth as honey.
They clasp their hands and pray,
And the sun shines brightly on them thru the stripped Autumn vines.

Days and days pass slowly by,
Still they measure sugar in the grocery,
Lump and lump, and always none
For Gaston and Marie,
And for little Jeanne, one.
But listen, Children. Over there,
In blue, peaked Germany, the fairies are.
Witches who live in pine-tree glades,
Gnomes deep in mines, with pickaxes and spades,
Fairies who dance upon round grass rings,
And a Rhine-river where a *Lorelei* sings.
The kind German fairies know of your prayer,
They caught it as it went through the air.
Hush, Children! Christmas is coming.
Christmas, and fairies, and cornucopias of sugar-plums!

Hollow thunder over the Hartz mountains.
Hollow thunder over the Black Forest.
Hollow thunder over the Rhine.
Hollow thunder over "Unter den Linden."
Thunder kettles,
Swung above green lightning fires,
Forked and spired lightning
Cooking candy.
Bubble, froth, stew!
Stir, old women;
Stir, Generals and spur-heeled young officers;
Stir, misshapen Kaiser,
And shake the steam from your up-turned moustachios.
Streaked and polished candy you make here,
With hot sugar and—other things;

Strange powders and liquids
Dropped out of little flasks,
Drop—
Drop—
Into the bubbling sugar,
And all Germany laughs.
For years the people have eaten the currants and honey of Bar-le-Duc,
Now they will give back sweetness for sweetness.
Ha! Ha! Ha! from Posen to Munich.
Ha! Ha! Ha! in Schleswig-Holstein.
Ha! Ha! Ha! flowing along with the Rhine waves.
Ha! Ha! Ha! echoing round the caves of Rügen.
Germany splits its sides with laughing,
And sets out its candles for the coming of the Christ-child.

"Heilige Nacht!" and great white birds flying over Germany.
Are the storks returning in mid-Winter?
"Heilige Nacht!" the tree is lit and the gifts are ready.
Steady, great birds, you have flown past Germany,
And are hanging over Bar-le-Duc, in France.
The moon is bright,
The moon is clear,
Come, little Children, the fairies are here.
The good German fairies who heard your prayer,
See them floating in the star-pricked air.
The cornucopias shake on the tree,
And the star-lamps glitter brilliantly.
A shower of comfits, a shower of balls,
Peppermint, chocolate, *marzipan* falls.
Red and white spirals glint in the moon.
Soon the fairies answered you—
Soon!
Soon!

Bright are the red and white streaked candies in the moonlight:
White corpse fingers pointing to the sky,
Round blood-drops glistening like rubies.
Fairyland come true:
Just pick and pick and suck, and chew.

Sugar and sweetness at last,
Shiny stuff of joy to be had for the gathering.
The blood-drops melt on the tongue,
The corpse fingers splinter and crumble.
Weep white tears, Moon.
Soon! So soon!
Something rattles behind a hedge,
Rattles—rattles.
An old skeleton is sitting on its thighbones
And holding its giggling sides.
Ha! Ha! Ha!
Bar-le-Duc had currants red,
Now she has instead her dead.
Little children, sweet as honey,
Bright as currants,
Like berries snapped off and packed in coffins.
The skeleton dances,
Dances in the moonlight,
And his fingers crack like castanets.

In blue, peaked Germany
The cooks wear iron crosses,
And the scullery maids trip to church
In new ribbons sent from Potsdam.

Amy Lowell

SPRING SOWS HER SEEDS

Why are you doing it this year, Spring?
Why do you do this useless thing?

Do you not know there are no men now?
Why do you put on an apple bough
Buds, and in a girl's heart, thronging
Strange emotions: fear, and longing,

Eager flight, and shy pursuing,
Noble thoughts for her undoing;

Wondering, accepting, straining,
Wistful seizing, and refraining;

Stern denying, answering?
—Why do you toil so drolly, Spring?

Who do you scheme and urge and plan
To make a girl's heart ripe for a man,

While the men are herded together where
Death is the woman with whom they pair?

Back fall my words to my listening ear.
Spring is deaf, and she cannot hear.

Spring is blind, and she cannot see.
She does not know what war may be.

Spring goes by, with her age-old sowing
Of seeds in each girls' heart; kind, unknowing.

And, too, in *my* heart, (Spring, oh, heed!)
Now in my own has fallen a seed.

(Spring, give over!) I cringe, afraid.
(Though I suffer, harm no other maid!)

I hide my eyes, a budding tree
Is so terrible to see.

I stop my ears, a bird song clear
Is a dreadful thing to hear.

Seeds in each girl's heart she goes throwing.
Oh, the crop of pain that is growing!

Mary Carolyn Davies

ROUGE BOUQUET

In a wood they call the Rouge Bouquet
There is a new made grave to-day,
Built by never a spade nor pick
Yet covered with earth ten meters thick.

There lie many fighting men,
  Dead in their youthful prime,
Never to laugh nor love again
  Nor taste the Summertime.
For Death came flying through the air
And stopped his flight at the dugout stair,
Touched his prey and left them there,
  Clay to clay.
He hid their bodies stealthily
In the soil of the land they sought to free
  And fled away.
Now over the grave abrupt and clear
  Three volleys ring;
And perhaps their brave young spirits hear
  The bugle sing:
"Go to sleep!
Go to sleep!
Slumber well where the shell screamed and fell.
Let your rifles rest on the muddy floor,
You will not need them any more.
Danger's past;
Now at last,
Go to sleep!"

There is on earth no worthier grave
To hold the bodies of the brave
Than this place of pain and pride
Where they nobly fought and nobly died.
Never fear but in the skies
Saints and angels stand
Smiling with their holy eyes
  On this new-come band.
St. Michael's sword darts through the air
And touches the aureole on his hair
As he sees them stand saluting there,
  His stalwart sons;
And Patrick, Brigid, Columkill
Rejoice that in veins of warriors still
  The Gael's blood runs.
And up to Heaven's doorway floats,

From the wood called Rouge Bouquet,
A delicate cloud of buglenotes
That softly say:
"Farewell!
Farewell!
Comrades true, born anew, peace to you!
Your souls shall be where the heroes are
And your memory shine like the morning-star.
Brave and dear,
Shield us here.
Farewell!"

Joyce Kilmer

LOVE IN CONTEMPORARY POETRY

For thousands of generations men have loved women and women have loved men. Through love they have known emotions of innumerable tones and flavors and colors. They have shared the rapture of the morning stars singing together and they have tasted the bitter waters of Marah. Poets have made this rapture and this bitterness communicable by singing with powerful emotional honesty the thing that was in their hearts.

To-day, as in the past, poets are stirred by thoughts of love and of the old, primal things of the race. They write many poems about these things. But it is more difficult to find a good poem of love than to find any other kind of a good poem. It is not that the lyrics of love are badly written. They have charm and grace. But they lack something that would make them great; perhaps faith and dignity. Perhaps they are not quite strong enough, true enough, fresh enough.

It may be that the reason for this is to be found in the kind of men and women we moderns are. We are pleasant and charming. We are seldom great. And to write a great poem of love a person must have had the capacity for loving as the great love and also the capacity for expressing himself. He may have missed his fulfillment. He may have been thwarted in his development. Life may have been hurt for him by some one else. He may have lived far, far below his best level of achievement. But the man who writes great love poetry must have had, at one time or another in his life, a latent greatness of personality. For better than anything else love poetry reveals a person's "might-have-been."

We have in contemporary literature, as has been said, a great many poems of love. Most of them fall into either one of two groups, a group of poems of untrammeled naturalism and a group of poems gracefully conventional. Outside of these two groups are a few very beautiful lyrics.

The naturalistic love poems, it should suffice to say, are poems that glorify the fleeting passions and write a question mark after the story of Baucis and Philemon. They are sophisticated poems, very far indeed from the strong sanity of the folk. They are pessimistic poems, written as if their makers were a little bit afraid of loving any one person long enough to let it become a habit. The ideal of a growth in love and of a love fostered through the years seems to be alien to the philosophy of the poets who give us these naturalistic lyrics. To them, love and life are forever experimental.

The makers of the graceful lyrics, on the other hand, all too often see love through the eyes of their dead forefathers, and make of it simply a convention for literary uses. In their songs love is a theme, like the subject of a child's composition. They spin about it their inconsequent gossamers of literary fancy. To speak one word of light and fire seems to be beyond their power and beyond their desire.

The more poems of love we read, the more we are likely to return mentally to the line from Rupert Brooke's sonnet, "Peace" in which he speaks of

"their dirty songs and dreary,
And all the little emptiness of love."

Certainly we have few poems of love by contemporary poets that will bear comparison with the lyrics of love made by our predecessors on this continent, the American Indians, and collected in translation and included in a book edited by George W. Cronyn, called "The Path on The Rainbow." These poems are simple and passionate, clean and strong, just what love songs should be. The lines of the Ojibwa poem, "Calling-One's-Own," are resonant with the spirit of a great poet.

"Awake! flower of the forest, sky-treading bird of the prairie.
Awake! awake! wonderful fawn-eyed one.
When you look upon me I am satisfied; as flowers that drink dew.
The breath of your mouth is the fragrance of flowers in the morning,
Your breath is their fragrance at evening in the moon-of-fading-leaf."

In such poems we find no tiresome self-analysis, no grossness, no mental sickness. Here is song as fresh and innocent as the fragrance of flowers in the "moon-of-fading-leaf."

One of the finest groups of love poems written in recent years is the "Sonnets of A Portrait Painter," by Arthur Davison Ficke. A few of them have the fault of being somewhat literary in diction, but most of them are intensely human and written with great fluency, charm, and naturalness of rhythm. Sometimes a pause in just the right place gives to a line the very quality and accent of a lover's speech. And to have accomplished that in the old, old pattern of the sonnet, is to have achieved an unexpected miracle. Such lines are these, taken from one of the most beautiful sonnets, which begins, "I am in love with high, far-seeing places."

"You who look on me with grave eyes where rapture
And April love of living burn confessed—
The gods are good! the world lies free to capture!
Life has no walls. Oh, take me to your breast!
Take me—be with me for a moment's span!
I am in love with all unveiled faces.
I seek the wonder at the heart of man;
I would go up to the far-seeing places."

Another, the tenth, begins with all the wistful and wilful immediacy of love—

"Come forth: for Spring is singing in the boughs
Of every white and tremulous apple-tree.
This is the season of eternal vows;
But what are vows that they should solace me?"

Everybody who wishes to know the best lyrics of love written in recent years should read, among other things, some of these sonnets.

Of the tragic poetry of love we have little in the poetry of to-day. It is the modern fashion to be perennially and persistently cheerful, and sometimes one is tempted to think that

that peculiar child Polyanna has been preaching the "glad game" to the poets. At any rate, we can find in contemporary literature few poems to compare, either in sadness or in beauty, with Lyric XIV from "A Shropshire Lad" by A. E. Housman. The bitterness of love denied is sharply felt in this poem, and felt just as it is felt in life. The unhappy lover sees the "careless people" who "call their souls their own" coming and going in the world about him. His sorrow sets him apart from them, in his own mind. His misery is, for him, unique. It makes the world seem frivolous. That is the psychology of it. This masterly little poem in five stanzas closes with these lines:

"There flowers no balm to sain him
From east of earth to west
That's lost for everlasting
The heart out of his breast.

"Here by the labouring highway
With empty hands I stroll:
Sea-deep, till doomsday morning,
Lie lost my heart and soul."

Mr. Housman has spoken the almost unutterable sense of loss that oppresses all young lovers who have loved greatly and are bereft of love.

Other men have written good poems of love, sometimes quite a number of them, sometimes only a few. Bliss Carman has. G. K. Chesterton has. But surely it is fair to say that no one man stands head and shoulders above his fellows, to-day, as a poet of the love of man for woman.

Much better things can be said of the women who are singing songs of the love of woman for man. The love songs of modern women are more virile and beautiful—if one may say that of woman's work of expression—than the love songs of men. This is probably because women are learning to use their own voices and sing their own songs now almost for the first time in Anglo-Saxon history. No matter how talkative they may have been in private life, in public women used to keep silence. And until the time of Elizabeth Barrett Browning and Christina Rossetti *women sang only what they thought they were expected to sing.* The conventions of an androcentric culture imposed upon women a spiritual bondage of reserve, indirection and disguise, from which only great genius or unusual daring could set them free. But it is the custom of critics who compare the small achievement of women in the arts, and especially in poetry, with the great achievements of their brothers, to forget or ignore the lets and hindrances that in ancient times, and in mediæval times, often prevented women from learning to express themselves adequately. Silence and repression were enjoined upon women by nearly all of the ancient religious systems, and the obligations that life imposed upon them were so heavy that small opportunity was left for the exercise of any gift of expression.

When women did begin to make their thoughts and feelings into poems they were still timid. A pen name was a prop to confidence. And they practised another device which served to conceal their own personal feelings; they dramatized the emotions of men in their lyrics. To dramatize masculine emotions or emotions of any other kind in narrative and dramatic poetry is all very well and a part of being an artist. But the subjective and personal lyric which is not the sincere expression of genuine emotion lacks vitality simply because it lacks directness of appeal.

It is a fine thing, therefore, to be able to say that the day of the bondage of silence has gone by for women, we hope forever. In our times a number of women here and across the water have begun to sing with competent sincerity of the love of woman for man. To-day real emotions are beginning to find a real expression and we are beginning to hope that, some day, we shall have a great poet of womanhood who will sing for the world of the woman's way of loving.

It will be a great word, that woman's word, when it is spoken. It will be a word of the race as much as of the individual, strong with the spirit of the folk, and not remote from the plain, homely things of life. For the love of the best women for the men who are their mates is a love that is racial as well as individual. The woman who will make these great poems of to-morrow must have the wholesome vitality of a peasant, the virtue of a peasant, and the sensitivity of a great artist. . . .

The women who are making the best contemporary lyrics of love have learned the first lesson of poetry, which is sincerity. They are capable of spiritual bravery. They do not pose. They strip off old cloaks and masks. They offer the world the best of themselves. Perhaps they even believe that nothing but their best is worthy of acceptance by the people. That may be why the word "poetess," with all its suggestion of tepid and insipid achievement, has gone out of fashion. To-day a few women are not "poetesses," but poets.

One of them is Irene Rutherford McLeod. She has written a number of fine lyrics of love and is still so young that we have great hope that she will be heard often and for a long time to come. Her poem, "So beautiful You Are Indeed" is a record of that step into infinity, beyond madness and beyond wisdom, which great love sometimes enables the spirit of a man and the spirit of a woman to take together.

"And when you bring your lips to mine
My spirit trembles and escapes,
And you and I are turned divine,
Bereft of our familiar shapes.

"And fearfully we tread cold space,
Naked of flesh and winged with flame,
. . . Until we find us face to face,
Each calling on the other's name."

Just as brave and just as lovely is Grace Fallow Norton's lyric, "Love Is A Terrible Thing." Men will hardly understand this poem as well as women. It is essentially feminine. If a man were to say that "Love is a terrible thing" he would not mean what a woman means when she says it.

"'For there is a flame that has blown too near,
And there is a name that has grown too dear,
And there is a fear . . .'

And to the still hills and cool earth and far sky
I made moan,
'The heart in my bosom is not my own!

'O would I were free as the wind on the wing;
Love is a terrible thing!'"

This is an admirable poem, not only because of its sincerity, but because it is a rare combination of lyrical rhythm with the cadences of natural speech.

In her poem, "Homage," Helen Hoyt speaks with reverence. This stanza is a clue to the meaning of the whole:

"Not to myself, I knew, belonged your homage:
I but the vessel of your holy drinking,
The channel to you of that olden wonder
Of love and womanhood,—I but a woman."

Preëminent among living women who have written love songs with competent sincerity, is Sara Teasdale. Her philosophy of poetry is a philosophy of absolute fidelity to the truth as it is felt. She believes that poets who will report themselves truly to the world can hardly fail, if they be poets in any real sense, to give the world poetry of unquestioned excellence. She believes that the worst of all artistic immoralities is to say in a lyric what has not been felt in the heart. The statements made in it may be fancy or fiction, but the thing that is felt in it,—that must be true. Otherwise it can not have that certain and insistent quality which claims the allegiance of mankind and makes it not only unique but universal.

Sara Teasdale has been true to this philosophy. She has been emotionally honest. She has keenly felt things that all women feel and she has given her emotions a true form and significance. Therefore her little songs, with their often wistful and sometimes exultant beauty, are now cherished by lovers of poetry wherever English is spoken. And, although her work has only been in

SARA TEASDALE

general circulation for about ten years, many of her poems have been translated into other languages. It is not too much to claim that her best lyrics have the indefinable manner which belongs to poetry that lives.

Her earlier poems express a whimsical coquetry that is delightfully feminine, and rich in the innocent, inherited wisdom of girlhood. This coquetry gives charm to such songs as "Four Winds," in which she says,

> "When thou art more cruel than he,
> Then will love be kind to thee."

The same coquetry is in the refrain of "The Flight."

> "But what if I heard my first love calling me once more?"

It persists with pleasing insouciance in two little quatrains called "Love Me," and in two others that make a poem called "The Look." It is an essential part of the delicate pathos of "The Song for Colin":

> "Pierrot laid down his lute to weep,
> And sighed, 'She sings for me.'
> But Colin slept a careless sleep
> Beneath an apple tree."

In poems written a little later we find much more than this coquetry in the revelation of girlhood. The inward reaching of a woman's spirit toward that which she does not yet know, the mystical and undefined longing for fulfillment, like the longing of the branch for bud and blossom, these also she has expressed in her poems, "Twilight," "A Winter Night," "Spring Night," and others. In "Spring Night," especially, the mood is exquisitely expressed.

> "Why am I crying after love
> With youth, a singing voice, and eyes
> To take earth's wonder by surprise?"

If this were all, it would not be enough. But it is the smallest part of the beauty of her work. Her poems of the finding of love never lack warmth and dignity. They are never purely "literary." They never stagger through sloughs of metrical sentimentality. They are clean and simple. And, if they lack the elemental vigor that has thrilled and shaken our spirits in the best love poetry written by men, they keep always a certain glowing depth which is a part of the constancy of the love of women.

Nor is it possible for a critic to refrain from mentioning her beautiful craftsmanship. She gives us melodies that are quiet, cool, sweet-flowing, of one kind with her emotion, the appropriate accompaniment of her meanings. They are always varied so that they avoid monotony. She chooses for her poems such symbols and images as are natural and relevant, avoiding all that is striking and sensational. She is never that most deplorable of all pseudo-artists, the *clever* poet. And she is never trite, for all of her poems are the result of personal realization. She uses language without affectation, language simple enough for great and venerable uses. Her poems reëcho in us because we can not fail to know at once just what they mean. They have a very remarkable clarity.

Perhaps her song, "I Would Live In Your Love," brings her as near as any of her lyrics to the ancient racial significance of the love of woman for man. It is short, poignant, perfect according to its kind. In it, as in all of her finest poems, she uses a single symbol to carry the weight of the thought. Anyone who knows the sea has watched the rise and fall of the sea-grasses, lifted and flattened out alternately by the flowing and ebbing of waves. That is the symbol of a woman's love which she uses in this magical stanza:

"I would live in your love as the sea-grasses live in the sea,
Borne up by each wave as it passes, drawn down by each wave that
  recedes."

In the poem, "Peace," the symbol of the woman who loves is the pool:

"I am the pool of gold
When sunset burns and dies—
You are my deepening skies;
Give me your stars to hold!"

But the noblest and most satisfying of all of her poems of love is one quite recently written in the incomparable Sapphic rhythm. In it love has become a light for the spirit in the ancient and eternal quest for the ultimate beauty and truth in the universe. This poem is called "The Lamp." It says more than the words of any critic can say of the delicately woven beauty, the quiet but shimmering colors of Sara Teasdale's best work. The strands of her poetry are not rough and robust. The hues of it shade into no strident scarlet, no flaring orange and green. But slender things are sometimes strong things, small things are sometimes great. And these little vari-colored lyrics show that she has felt poignantly, that she has shared the prescient and oracular moods of womanhood, and has expressed them with a warmth and intimacy not incompatible with fine artistic restraint.

Close akin to the poetry of love, in the minds of women, is the poetry of motherhood and home. And this chapter would hardly be complete without brief mention of two poems about birth. They are "The Canticle of The Babe," by Josephine Preston Peabody, a subjective lyric of motherhood with unusual dignity and beauty, and "Birth" by Jean Starr Untermeyer, a poem which tells what another woman feels, standing beside a young mother in her hour of travail. Mrs. Untermeyer's poem, "Autumn" is also an interesting and original piece of work. It celebrates "pickling day" and is neither humorous nor sentimental as poems of the home used to be. Instead it has something of the dignity that rightly belongs to the most fundamental of all labors, the labor of preparing food, and it pays tribute, in high, just fashion to the genius of the home who is the genius of the folk, the mother. Mrs. Untermeyer says:

"And you moved among these mysteries,
Absorbed and smiling and sure;
Stirring, tasting, measuring,
With the precision of a ritual.
I like to think of you in your years of power—
You, now so shaken and so powerless—
High priestess of your home."

CALLING-ONE'S-OWN

Awake! flower of the forest, sky-treading bird of the prairie.
Awake! awake! wonderful fawn-eyed One.
When you look upon me I am satisfied; as flowers that drink dew.
The breath of your mouth is the fragrance of flowers in the morning,
Your breath is their fragrance at evening in the moon-of-fading-leaf.
Do not the red streams of my veins run toward you
As forest-streams to the sun in the moon of bright nights?
When you are beside me my heart sings; a branch it is, dancing,
Dancing before the Wind-spirit in the moon of strawberries.
When you frown upon me, beloved, my heart grows dark—
A shining river the shadows of clouds darken,
Then with your smiles comes the sun and makes to look like gold
Furrows the cold wind drew in the water's face.
Myself! behold me! blood of my beating heart.
Earth smiles—the waters smile—even the sky-of-clouds smiles—but I,
I lose the way of smiling when you are not near,
Awake! awake! my beloved.

Translated from the Ojibwa by
Charles Fenno Hoffman

ALADDIN AND THE JINN

"Bring me soft song," said Aladdin;
"This tailor-shop sings not at all.
Chant me a word of the twilight,
Of roses that mourn in the fall.
Bring me a song like hashish
That will comfort the stale and the sad,

For I would be mending my spirit,
  Forgetting these days that are bad,
Forgetting companions too shallow,
  Their quarrels and arguments thin,
Forgetting the shouting Muezzin."—
  "*I am your slave,*" said the Jinn.

"Bring me old wines," said Aladdin,
  "I have been a starved pauper too long.
Serve them in vessels of jade and of shell,
  Serve them with fruit and with song:—
Wines of pre-Adamite Sultans
  Digged from beneath the black seas,
New-gathered dew from the heavens
  Dripped down from Heaven's sweet trees:—
Cups from the angels' pale tables
  That will make me both handsome and wise,
For I have beheld her, the princess,
  Firelight and starlight her eyes
Pauper I am, I would woo her.
  And—let me drink wine to begin,
Though the Koran expressly forbids it."
  "*I am your slave,*" said the Jinn.

"Plan me a dome," said Aladdin,
  "That is drawn like the dawn of the moon,
When the sphere seems to rest on the mountains,
  Half-hidden, yet full-risen soon.
Build me a dome," said Aladdin,
  "That shall cause all young lovers to sigh,
The fullness of life and of beauty,
  Peace beyond peace to the eye—
A palace of foam and of opal,
  Pure moonlight without and within,
Where I may enthrone my sweet lady."
  "*I am your slave,*" said the Jinn.

Vachel Lindsay

MY LIGHT WITH YOURS

I

When the sea has devoured the ships,
And the spires and the towers
Have gone back to the hills.
And all the cities
Are one with the plains again.
And the beauty of bronze
And the strength of steel
Are blown over silent continents,
As the desert sand is blown—
My dust with yours forever.

II

When folly and wisdom are no more,
And fire is no more,
Because man is no more;
When the dead world slowly spinning
Drifts and falls through the void—
My light with yours
In the Light of Lights forever!

Edgar Lee Masters

I am in love with high far-seeing places
That look on plains half-sunlight and half-storm,
In love with hours when from the circling faces
Veils pass, and laughing fellowship glows warm.
You who look on me with grave eyes where rapture
And April love of living burn confessed—
The gods are good! the world lies free to capture!
Life has no walls. Oh, take me to your breast!
Take me—be with me for a moment's span!
I am in love with all unveiled faces.
I seek the wonder at the heart of man;
I would go up to the far-seeing places.
While youth is ours, turn toward me for a space
The marvel of your rapture-lighted face!

Arthur Davison Ficke

There are strange shadows fostered of the moon,
More numerous than the clear-cut shade of day. . . .
Go forth, when all the leaves whisper of June,
Into the dusk of swooping bats at play;
Or go into that late November dusk
When hills take on the noble lines of death,
And on the air the faint astringent musk
Of rotting leaves pours vaguely troubling breath.
Then shall you see shadows whereof the sun
Knows nothing—aye, a thousand shadows there
Shall leap and flicker and stir and stay and run,
Like petrels of the changing foul or fair;
Like ghosts of twilight, of the moon, of him
Whose homeland lies past each horizon's rim. . . .

Arthur Davison Ficke

HOW MUCH OF GODHOOD

How much of Godhood did it take—
What purging epochs had to pass,
Ere I was fit for leaf and lake
And worthy of the patient grass?

What mighty travails must have been,
What ages must have moulded me,
Ere I was raised and made akin
To dawn, the daisy and the sea.

In what great struggles was I felled,
In what old lives I labored long,
Ere I was given a world that held
A meadow, butterflies, and song?

But oh, what cleansings and what fears,
What countless raisings from the dead,
Ere I could see Her, touched with tears,
Pillow the little weary head.

Louis Untermeyer

AFTER TWO YEARS

She is all so slight
And tender and white
  As a May morning.
She walks without hood
At dusk. It is good
  To hear her sing.

It is God's will
That I shall love her still
  As He loves Mary.
And night and day
I will go forth to pray
  That she love me.

She is as gold
Lovely, and far more cold.
  Do thou pray with me,
For if I win grace
To kiss twice her face
  God has done well to me.

Richard Aldington

NIRVANA

Sleep on, I lie at heaven's high oriels,
  Over the stars that murmur as they go
  Lighting your lattice-window far below.
And every star some of the glory spells
  Whereof I know.

I have forgotten you, long, long ago;
  Like the sweet, silver singing of thin bells
Vanished, or music fading faint and low.
  Sleep on, I lie at heaven's high oriels,
Who loved you so.

John Hall Wheelock

PERENNIAL MAY

May walks the earth again,
This old earth, and the same
Green spurts of tender flame
Burn now on sod and tree
That burned when first she came,
Dear love, to you and me.
If any change there be—
A greater or a less
Degree of loveliness—
It is not ours to see,
Dear love,
Not ours to feel or see.

May thrills our hearts again,
These old hearts, and the bough
Burns not with blossoms now
That blow more splendidly.
For, since our wedded vow
Made one of you and me,
If any change there be—
A greater or a less
Degree of tenderness—
It is not ours to see,
Dear love,
Not ours to feel or see.

Thomas Augustine Daly

"SO BEAUTIFUL YOU ARE INDEED"

So beautiful you are, indeed,
That I am troubled when you come,
And though I crave you for my need,
Your nearness strikes me blind and dumb.

And when you bring your lips to mine
My spirit trembles and escapes,
And you and I are turned divine,
Bereft of our familiar shapes.

And fearfully we tread cold space,
Naked of flesh and winged with flame,
. . . Until we find us face to face,
Each calling on the other's name!

Irene Rutherford McLeod

"I SAT AMONG THE GREEN LEAVES"

I sat among the green leaves, and heard the nuts falling,
The broadred butterflies were gold against the sun,
But in between the silence and the sweet birds calling
The nuts fell one by one.

Why should they fall and the year but half over?
Why should sorrow seek me and I so young and kind?
The leaf is on the bough and the dew is on the clover,
But the green nuts are falling in the wind.

Oh, I gave my lips away and all my soul behind them.
Why should trouble follow and the quick tears start?
The little birds may love and fly with only God to mind them,
But the green nuts are falling on my heart.

Marjorie L. C. Pickthall

"GRANDMITHER, THINK NOT I FORGET"

Grandmither, think not I forget, when I come back to town,
An' wander the old ways again, an' tread them up and down.
I never smell the clover bloom, nor see the swallows pass,
Wi'out I mind how good ye were unto a little lass;
I never hear the winter rain a-pelting all night through
Wi'out I think and mind me of how cold it falls on you.
An' if I come not often to your bed beneath the thyme,
Mayhap 't is that I'd change wi' ye, and gie my bed for thine,
Would like to sleep in thine.

I never hear the summer winds among the roses blow
Wi'out I wonder why it was ye loved the lassie so.
Ye gave me cakes and lollipops and pretty toys a score—
I never thought I should come back and ask ye now for more.

Grandmither, gie me your still white hands that lie upon your breast,
For mine do beat the dark all night and never find me rest;
They grope among the shadows an' they beat the cold black air,
They go seekin' in the darkness, an' they never find him there,
They never find him there.

Grandmither, gie me your sightless eyes, that I may never see
His own a-burnin' full o' love that must not shine for me.
Grandmither, gie me your peaceful lips, white as the kirkyard snow,
For mine be tremblin' wi' the wish that he must never know.
Grandmither, gie me your clay-stopped ears, that I may never hear
My lad a-singin' in the night when I am sick wi' fear;
A-singin' when the moonlight over a' the land is white—
Ah, God! I'll up and go to him, a-singin' in the night,
A-callin' in the night.

Grandmither, gie me your clay-cold heart, that has forgot to ache,
For mine be fire wi'in my breast an' yet it cannot break.
Wi' every beat it's callin' for things that must not be,—
So can ye not let me creep in an' rest awhile by ye?
A little lass afeared o' dark slept by ye years agone—
An' she has found what night can hold 'twixt sunset an' the dawn:
So when I plant the rose an' rue above your grave for ye,
Ye'll know it's under rue an' rose that I would like to be,
That I would like to be.

Willa Sibert Cather

FROST IN SPRING

Oh, had it been in Autumn, when all is spent and sere,
That the first numb chill crept on us, with its ghostly hint of fear,
I had borne to see love go, with things detached and frail,
Swept outward with the blowing leaf on the unresting gale.

But when day is a magic thing, when Time begins anew,
When every clod is parted by Beauty breaking through,—
How can it be that you and I bring Love no offering,
How can it be that frost should fall upon us in the Spring!

Jessie B. Rittenhouse

PATRINS

You know, dear, that the gipsies strew
Some broken boughs along the way
To mark the trail for one who comes,
A tardy pilgrim of the day.

And so my songs, that have no worth
Save that best worth of being true,
Are but as patrins strewn to show
The way I came in loving you.

Jessie B. Rittenhouse

RAIN, RAIN!

Rain, rain—fall, fall,
In a heavy screen—
That my lover be not seen!

Wind, wind,—blow, blow,
Till the leaves are stirred—
That my lover be not heard!

Storm, storm,—rage, rage,
Like a war around—
That my lover be not found!

. . . Lark, lark,—hush . . . hush . . .
Softer music make—
That my lover may not wake . . .

Zoë Akins

HOMAGE

Before me you bowed as before an altar,
And I reached down and drew you to my bosom;
Proud of your reverence, and reverence returning,
But craving most your pleasure, not your awe.

My hands about your head curved themselves, as holding
A treasure, fragile and of glad possession!
Dear were the bones of your skull beneath my fingers,
And I grew brave imagining your defence.

Not as a man I felt you in my brooding,
But merely a babe,—a babe of my own body:
Precious your worth, but dearer your dependence:
Sometimes I wished to feed you at my breast.

Not to myself, I knew, belonged your homage:
I but the vessel of your holy drinking,
The channel to you of that olden wonder
Of love and womanhood,—I, but a woman.

Then never need your memory be shamefaced
That I have seen your flesh and soul at worship:
Do you think I did not kneel when you were kneeling?
Even lowlier bowed my head, and bowed my heart.

Helen Hoyt

A LYNMOUTH WIDOW*

He was straight and strong, and his eyes were blue
As the summer meeting of sky and sea,
And the ruddy cliffs had a colder hue
Than flushed his cheek when he married me.

We passed the porch where the swallows breed,
We left the little brown church behind,
And I leaned on his arm, though I had no need,
Only to feel him so strong and kind.

One thing I never can quite forget;
It grips my throat when I try to pray—
The keen salt smell of a drying net
That hung on the churchyard wall that day.

He would have taken a long, long grave—
A long, long grave, for he stood so tall . . .
Oh, God! the crash of a breaking wave,
And the smell of the nets on the churchyard wall!

Amelia Josephine Burr

*From *In Deep Places* by Amelia Josephine Burr. Copyright, 1914, George H. Doran Company, Publishers.

LOVE IS A TERRIBLE THING

I went out to the farthest meadow,
I lay down in the deepest shadow;

And I said unto the earth, "Hold me,"
And unto the night, "O enfold me,"

And unto the wind petulantly
I cried, "You know not for you are free!"

And I begged the little leaves to lean
Low and together for a safe screen;

Then to the stars I told my tale:
"That is my home-light, there in the vale,

"And O, I know that I shall return,
But let me lie first mid the unfeeling fern.

"For there is a flame that has blown too near,
And there is a name that has grown too dear,
And there is a fear . . ."

And to the still hills and cool earth and far sky I made moan,
"The heart in my bosom is not my own!

"O would I were free as the wind on the wing;
Love is a terrible thing!"

Grace Fallow Norton

LOVE SONG

I love my life, but not too well
 To give it to thee like a flower,
So it may pleasure thee to dwell
 Deep in its perfume but an hour.
I love my life, but not too well.

I love my life, but not too well
  To sing it note by note away,
So to thy soul the song may tell
  The beauty of the desolate day.
I love my life, but not too well.

I love my life but not too well
  To cast it like a cloak on thine,
Against the storms that sound and swell
  Between thy lonely heart and mine.
I love my life, but not too well.

Harriet Monroe

LOVE CAME BACK AT FALL O' DEW

Love came back at fall o' dew,
Playing his old part;
But I had a word or two
That would break his heart.

"He who comes at candlelight,
That should come before,
Must betake him to the night
From a barrèd door."

This the word that made us part
In the fall o' dew;
This the word that brake his heart—
Yet it brake mine, too.

Lizette Woodworth Reese

PEACE

Peace flows into me
  As the tide to the pool by the shore;
  It is mine forevermore,
It will not ebb like the sea.

I am the pool of blue
That worships the vivid sky;
My hopes were heaven-high,
They are all fulfilled in you.

I am the pool of gold
When sunset burns and dies—
You are my deepening skies;
Give me your stars to hold.

Sara Teasdale

I WOULD LIVE IN YOUR LOVE

I would live in your love as the sea-grasses live in the sea,
Born up by each wave as it passes, drawn down by each wave that recedes;
I would empty my soul of the dreams that have gathered in me,
I would beat with your heart as it beats, I would follow your soul as it leads.

Sara Teasdale

THE LAMP

If I can bear your love like a lamp before me,
When I go down the long steep Road of Darkness,
I shall not fear the everlasting shadows,
Nor cry in terror.

If I can find out God, then I shall find Him,
If none can find Him, then I shall sleep soundly,
Knowing how well on earth your love sufficed me,
A lamp in darkness.

Sara Teasdale

MATERNITY

One wept, whose only babe was dead,
New-born ten years ago.
"Weep not; he is in bliss," they said.
She answered, "Even so.

"Ten years ago was born in pain
A child, not now forlorn;
But oh, ten years ago in vain
A mother, a mother was born."

Alice Meynell

MOTHERHOOD

Mary, the Christ long slain, passed silently,
Following the children joyously astir
Under the cedrus and the olive-tree,
Pausing to let their laughter float to her.
Each voice an echo of a voice more dear,
She saw a little Christ in every face;
When lo, another woman, gliding near,
Yearned o'er the tender life that filled the place.
And Mary sought the woman's hand, and spoke:
"I know thee not, yet know thy memory tossed
With all a thousand dreams their eyes evoke
Who bring to thee a child beloved and lost.

"I, too, have rocked my little one.
Oh, He was fair!
Yea, fairer than the fairest sun,
And like its rays through amber spun
His sun-bright hair.
Still I can see it shine and shine."
"Even so," the woman said, "was mine."

"His ways were ever darling ways"—
And Mary smiled—
"So soft, so clinging! Glad relays
Of love were all His precious days.
My little child!
My infinite star! My music fled!"
"Even so was mine," the woman said.

Then whispered Mary: "Tell me, thou,
Of thine." And she:
"Oh, mine was rosy as a bough
Blooming with roses, sent, somehow,

To bloom for me!
His balmy fingers left a thrill
Within my breast that warms me still."

Then gazed she down some wilder, darker hour,
And said—when Mary questioned, knowing not:
"Who art thou, mother of so sweet a flower?"—
"I am the mother of Iscariot."

Agnes Lee

SACRIFICE *

When apple boughs are dim with bloom
And lilacs blossom by the door,
How sweetly poignant the perfume
From springs that are no more!

Strange how that faint, familiar scent
Of early lilacs after rain
By subtle alchemy is blent
With childhood's tenderest joy and pain.

Across the long mists of the way
Are weary mothers seen through tears;
They broke their lives from day to day
To pour this fragrance down the years.

Ada Foster Murray

THE HOUSE AND THE ROAD

The little Road says, Go,
The little House says, Stay:
And O, it's bonny here at home,
But I must go away.

The little Road, like me,
Would seek and turn and know;
And forth I must, to learn the things
The little Road would show!

And go I must, my dears,
And journey while I may,
Though heart be sore for the little House
That had no word but Stay.

Maybe, no other way
Your child could ever know
Why a little House would have you stay,
When a little Road says, Go.

Josephine Preston Peabody

MY MIRROR *

There is a mirror in my room
Less like a mirror than a tomb,
There are so many ghosts that pass
Across the surface of the glass.

When in the morning I arise
With circles round my tired eyes,
Seeking the glass to brush my hair
My mother's mother meets me there.

If in the middle of the day
I happen to go by that way,
I see a smile I used to know—
My mother, twenty years ago.

But when I rise by candle-light
To feed my baby in the night,
Then whitely in the glass I see
My dead child's face look out at me.

Aline Kilmer

* From *Candles That Burn* by Aline Kilmer.

Read.

RELIGION IN CONTEMPORARY POETRY

The religious spirit is in the poetry of to-day, not as a theme in itself, and not as propaganda, but as an all-pervading force. Few poems that are poems in any real sense are written "about religion," or in defense of doctrines. This is probably very fortunate for poetry and for religion. For unless a poet has been caught in a tremendous tide of popular religious feeling, a reformation or a rebirth of spirituality, his poems that discuss doctrines and his poems purposefully written "about religion" are likely to be dry and hard in their didacticism. Or, if they escape the dangers of aridity, poems made in this purposeful way are likely to fall into sticky sloughs of sentimentality whither only ladies of Don Marquis' Hermione group are likely to go to seek them. Among such persons any poem in which the holy name of God is mentioned, will, if read with perfervid intensity, bring instantaneous applause, no matter what the artistic value of the poem may be, no matter what is said about Him. Therefore it may be a very good thing that we have few poems of this kind, for, if we had more, many of them would probably be travesties of poetry and of religion.

Moral didacticism in poetry is seldom pleasing to the contemporary poet. He prefers to leave lessons to the teacher and sermons to the preacher. For this reason many thoughtful persons have questioned the moral value and the moral importance of our contemporary poetry. But sincere thinking should suggest the idea that poetry may be very valuable morally, even when morals are not pointed out and explained in it. "Rhymed ethics" and "rhythmical persuasions" are not necessarily productive of the finest worship and wonder.

The fact is simply this, that the modern poet believes that explanations often hurt that beauty which they are meant to serve. Therefore he paints his picture, sings his song, tells his story, and hopes that the light of his spirit shining through his work will accomplish the essential revelation. He trusts our intelligence. He believes that people who have honest and competent noses can tell a sprig of mignonette from a slice of onion when both are held in convenient juxtaposition. He thinks that he does not need to argue with us about what is bad and what is good. He knows that he must truly tell the truth about life and beautifully show the beauty in it. He knows, also, that his own sympathies will be in his poems almost without his consent. In his sympathetic sharing of beauty and truth he provides a discipline for the human spirit, for to share beauty and truth is to be changed by them. And forever and forever the disciplined spirits of many good men and women create, uphold, and inspire good morals. It can not be otherwise. The water of the swamp is brackish because it is in the swamp. The water of the spring is sweet because it is in the spring. In the disciplined spirits of the multitude and in their power to perceive and share beauty and truth is the regeneration of the race. Poetry is not impertinent comment on conduct. It is the sharing of the best in life. Can we truly say that it has no moral value?

Religion is in contemporary poetry then, or, if you like, God is in it, as a spirit. This spirit touches all great themes. In the minds of the moderns it is one with the love of man, one with the love of man and woman, one with the joy that we feel in the evanescent glory of a sunset, one with the desire for democracy and with the passions of the evolving race. It is the motive power of our humanitarian idealism. It belongs to hero-worship. It is in accord with that fearless and passionate love of the search for truth, no matter how stern a thing truth may prove to be when it is found, that is a distinguishing characteristic of the devotees of science. And, since this is true, we may as well admit that, in a broad, general way, all good poems are religious.

But poems have been written by many of our contemporaries

that are religious in a special way. They are the expression of emotions commonly called religious. They are songs of worship and wonder. Or they are poems that have their source of strength in symbols and personalities which have long been associated with religion in the minds of the people. Such poems are exceedingly valuable and should be carefully considered.

One of the loveliest of modern lyrics of worship is "Lord of My Heart's Elation" by Bliss Carman. It is quite essentially a modern poem. No doctrine is urged upon us in any line of it. The poet has not tied himself down to earth with strands of opinion. The faith of the poem is a brave, agnostic faith, a faith that does not know. The poem is a poem of affirmation only in so far as it affirms the little knowledge which the poet shares with Everyman.

> "As the foamheads are loosened
> And blown along the sea,
> Or sink and merge forever
> In that which bids them be.
>
> "I, too, must climb in wonder,
> Uplift at thy command,—
> Be one with my frail fellows
> Beneath the wind's strong hand,
>
> "A fleet and shadowy column
> Of dust or mountain rain,
> To walk the earth a moment
> And be dissolved again."

But out of this little knowledge comes the pure lyric cry of worship and self-surrender:

> "Be thou my exaltation
> Or fortitude of mien,
> Lord of the world's elation,
> Thou breath of things unseen!"

Another lyric that is quite as truly a poem of worship is Joyce Kilmer's "Trees," the best known of his poems and certainly one of the most beautiful things he ever wrote. The charm of it is in the sweetness and humility of the emotion expressed and in the absolute simplicity and directness of the expression. A poem, surely, is one of the noblest of the works of man, and yet, to this young Catholic poet, the genesis of a poem is nothing in comparison with the growth of a tree.

> "Poems are made by fools like me,
> But only God can make a tree."

Joyce Kilmer has written a number of good religious poems which will mean more to Catholics than to other readers. Among the best are "Folly," "Stars," "St. Alexis," and "The Rosary." But "Trees" is a poem that appeals to all men and women who have been humbled and made reverent before the beauty of the natural world.

"The Falconer of God," by William Rose Benét, is a religious lyric of quite another kind. It is a poem which tells a story of personal religious experience in a most admirable way, in strong and satisfying symbols. Contemporary poetry can offer nothing better of its kind, little so good. The falcon is Mr. Benét's symbol for the human spirit, that is always rising to seek and capture a flying loveliness. That flying loveliness is the heron:

> "I shall start a heron soon
> In the marsh beneath the moon—
> A wondrous silver heron its inner darkness fledges!"

The soaring falcon brings back a burden of disappointment, but rises again and again into the heavens seeking its own:

> "The pledge is still the same—for all disastrous pledges,
> All hopes resigned!
> My soul still flies above me for the quarry it shall find!"

When we interpret symbols we must be guarded, we must speak very finely and delicately. It is better to say very little than to say too much. But perhaps this is even more than a poem of personal spiritual experience. Perhaps it tells the spiritual story of Everyman and of the race. Certainly, in poems like this are "wordless, wondrous things" for all who will have them. And in this poem they are set to a very lovely music.

In other poems of to-day that have to do with religious themes we find the prescience of immortality which mankind has never yet been willing to forego. This is echoed again and again in Witter Bynner's "The New World." It is in an intimate and exquisite sonnet by Thomas S. Jones, Jr., in which he says,

> "Once have I looked upon the burning grail,
> And through your eyes have seen beyond the grave."

It may be that this belief in the "communion of saints" has been strengthened somewhat by the influence of the poets of the Orient whose way of thinking is really communion or meditation, a way of projecting the mind out of self into the world whose walls are built in air, whose gates must be dreams.

In sharp contrast with such poems as these we may set a poem like Max Eastman's "Invocation." This is not a poem to give comfort. It is not peace, but a sword. It is the acceptance of the sword. It is a poem about truth and a prayer for truth, whether truth be hard or easy, harsh or kind. But it is devout and hardy, a masterpiece in five lines.

> "Truth, be more precious to me than the eyes
> Of happy love!"

That is the brave speech of thousands of the best moderns.

But the most interesting fact about the religious poetry of to-day is that we live in a period when nearly all poets are writing about Christ. In a time when the world questions the validity of many old dogmas and formulæ once respected, the human bravery, dignity, cleanliness and kindliness of the life of Christ have taken hold upon the imaginations of poets in a new way.

In her admirable anthology, "Christ In The Poetry of To-day," Martha Foote Crow tells us that many, many more good poems have been written about Christ in the period since 1900 than were written in the twenty years before that time. And it is the especial merit of her book that it shows how Christ has been all things to all men. Each poet represented in it may be thought of as speaking for thousands of men and women who would think and feel as he does. And this is a collection of poems by all kinds of poets, radical and conservative, not a collection of sentimental conservative verse. Some of the poems are robust character studies. Others are graceful legends. Others are lyrics of worship. But all of them, whether written by churchmen or agnostics, whether they are written in praise of the Christ of the churches, or, out of love for the personality of the Man of Sorrows, are reverent, each in its own way and according to its kind.

With a very feminine gentleness of thought and emotion Lizette Woodworth Reese has written a poem about the baby Jesus, in which she retells the legend,

> "The Ox put forth a horned head;
> 'Come, little Lord, here make Thy bed.'
>
> Uprose the sheep were folded near;
> 'Thou Lamb of God, come, enter here.'"

Theodosia Garrison retells another legend, the story of how the little Jesus chose the rude gift of the shepherd, not the rich gifts of the wise kings to hold in his small hands. The shepherd's gift was only a little cross made of twigs,

> "And in his hold the cross lay cold"

between his heart and the heart of the mother in whose arms he lay.

Carl Sandburg is a poet who believes in the candor and wisdom of childhood. He sees in the Christ Child a type of this candor and wisdom. His poem is about the Christ talking with the old men in the temple when He was only a young lad. In describing the boy, Christ, Mr. Sandburg uses two adjectives which other boys have liked to use in describing their friends. He says,

> "The young child, Christ, is straight and wise
> And asks questions of the old men, questions
> Found under running water for all children,
> And found under shadows thrown on still waters
> By tall trees looking downward,"

Who has not seen a young boy, "straight and wise," with clear eyes and eager mind and heart, talking to old men sitting before the doors of home in the evening, or on the steps of the temple, or in the market place? Perhaps it has been in such talks that the great traditions of the race and the old folk tales have been handed down from generation to generation. When we see how such a poem is related to life and its homely realities we realize that the thought of Christ talking with the learned old men in the temple is illuminated and enlarged for us by reading it.

Many of the poets have tried to surround Christ with such homely realities of life as belong to simple people now and always. They have shown Him at work with Joseph in the carpenter shop. Elsa Barker tells of the dumb bewilderment of Joseph, of his love for Mary and for her Child, in "The Vigil of Joseph."

> "'Brawny these arms to win Him bread, and broad
> This bosom to sustain Her. But my heart
> Quivers in lonely pain before that beauty
> It loves—and serves—and cannot understand!'"

Sarah N. Cleghorn writes a poem of quite another kind. She shows us the Christ in whom the Christian socialists believe. He is the Great Comrade. The poem is written in terse, effective language which may seem unsuitable to orthodox people who have never shared the thoughts and emotions of those for whom it is intended. But to those who have shared these thoughts and emotions the poem will seem reverent and powerful. It is called "Comrade Jesus" and begins with these lines:

"Thanks to Saint Matthew, who had been
At mass-meetings in Palestine,
We know whose side was spoken for
When Comrade Jesus had the floor."

Other answers we have to the old, old question, "What think ye of Christ?" In "The Unbeliever" Anna Hempstead Branch gives the answer of the agnostic:

"Even he that grieves thee most "Lord, Lord," he saith,
So will I call on thee with my last breath!
Brother, not once have I believed in thee.
Yet am I wounded for thee unto death.

Even the world that turns away from the ecclesiastical Christ subdues its heart and bends its head before the Jesus of the Crucifixion.

Florence Kiper Frank, speaking for the Hebrew people, expresses a strong racial sympathy for the noblest of martyrs. In her interesting sonnet, "The Jew To Jesus," she says:

"We have drained the bitter cup, and, tortured, felt
With thee the bruising of each bitter welt.
In every land is our Gethsemane.
A thousand times have we been crucified."

But, oddly enough, one of the strongest of modern poems about Christ comes to us from that arch-radical and caustic critic, Ezra Pound. It is called the "Ballad of the Goodly Fere," and it is written as if it had been spoken by Simon Zelotes shortly after the Crucifixion. Many poems have been written about the gentleness of Christ. This poem is about His manliness and His bravery.

"He cried no cry when they drave the nails
And the blood gushed hot and free,
The hounds of the crimson sky gave tongue
But never a cry cried he.

"I ha' seen him cow a thousand men
On the hills o' Galilee,
They whined as he walked out calm between,
Wi' his eyes like the gray o' the sea.

"Like the sea that brooks no voyaging
With the winds unleashed and free,
Like the sea that he cowed at Genseret
Wi' twey words spoke' suddently."

Many other poems might be quoted to show what poets of to-day have thought and felt about Christ. And readers of these poems would like or dislike them in ways that would correspond to their own personal answers to the question, "What think ye of Christ?" The poem that pleases the Christian socialist will not necessarily please the orthodox churchman. The poem that satisfies the radical may displease the conservative. But the significant thing to remember is that all kinds of men and women have seen, in The King of the Crossed Trees, their own idealism, the highest goal of their own spirits. Christ, the Son of Man, is, for many persons in all the warring sects, the archtype of spiritual beauty, the personal force in religion. This is what the poets have tried to put into contemporary religious poetry, each in his own way. And, in so doing, they have brought us a little nearer to an understanding of the beauty of holiness.

LORD OF MY HEART'S ELATION

Lord of my heart's elation,
Spirit of things unseen,
Be thou my aspiration
Consuming and serene!

Bear up, bear out, bear onward,
This mortal soul alone,
To selfhood or oblivion,
Incredibly thine own,—

As the foamheads are loosened
And blown along the sea,
Or sink and merge forever
In that which bids them be.

I, too, must climb in wonder,
Uplift at thy command,—
Be one with my frail fellows
Beneath the wind's strong hand.

A fleet and shadowy column
Of dust or mountain rain,
To walk the earth a moment
And be dissolved again.

Be thou my exaltation
Or fortitude of mien,
Lord of the world's elation,
Thou breath of things unseen!

Bliss Carman

THE FALCONER OF GOD

I flung my soul to the air like a falcon flying.
I said, "Wait on, wait on, while I ride below!
I shall start a heron soon
In the marsh beneath the moon—
A strange white heron rising with silver on its wings,
Rising and crying
Wordless, wondrous things;
The secret of the stars, of the world's heart-strings
The answer to their woe.
Then stoop thou upon him, and grip and hold him so!"

My wild soul waited on as falcons hover.
I beat the reedy fens as I trampled past.
I heard the mournful loon
In the marsh beneath the moon.

And then, with feathery thunder, the bird of my desire
Broke from the cover
Flashing silver fire.
High up among the stars I saw his pinions spire.
The pale clouds gazed aghast
As my falcon stooped upon him, and gript and held him fast.

My soul dropped through the air—with heavenly plunder?—
Gripping the dazzling bird my dreaming knew?
Nay! but a piteous freight,
A dark and heavy weight
Despoiled of silver plumage, its voice forever stilled,—
All of the wonder
Gone that ever filled
Its guise with glory. O bird that I have killed,
How brilliantly you flew
Across my rapturous vision when first I dreamed of you!

Yet I fling my soul on high with new endeavor,
And I ride the world below with a joyful mind.
I shall start a heron soon
In the marsh beneath the moon—
A wondrous silver heron its inner darkness fledges!
I beat forever
The fens and the sedges.
The pledge is still the same—for all disastrous pledges,
All hopes resigned!
My soul still flies above me for the quarry it shall find!

William Rose Benét

THE PATH OF THE STARS

Down through the spheres that chant the Name of One
Who is the Law of Beauty and of Light
He came, and as He came the waiting Night
Shook with the gladness of a Day begun;
And as He came, He said: Thy Will Be Done
On Earth; and all His vibrant Words were white
And glistering with silver, and their might
Was of the glory of a rising sun.

Unto the Stars sang out His Living Words
White and with silver, and their rhythmic sound
Was as a mighty symphony unfurled;
And back from out the Stars like homing birds
They fell in love upon the sleeping ground
And were forever in a wakened world.

Thomas S. Jones, Jr.

"GOD, YOU HAVE BEEN TOO GOOD TO ME"

God, You have been too good to me,
You don't know what You've done.
A clod's too small to drink in all
The treasure of the sun.

The pitcher fills the lifted cup
And still the blessings pour
They overbrim the shallow rim
With cool refreshing store.

You are too prodigal with joy,
Too careless of its worth,
To let the stream with crystal gleam
Fall wasted on the earth.

Let many thirsty lips draw near
And quaff the greater part!
There still will be too much for me
To hold in one glad heart.

Charles Wharton Stork

TWO VOICES

There is a country full of wine
And liquor of the sun,
Where sap is running all the year,
And spring is never done,
Where all is good as it is fair,
And love and will are one.

Old age may never come there,
But ever in to-day
The people talk as in a dream
And laugh slow time away.

But would you stay as now you are,
Or as a year ago?
Oh, not as then, for then how small
The wisdom we did owe!
Or if forever as to-day,
How little we could know!

Then welcome age, and fear not sorrow;
To-day's no better than to-morrow,
Or yesterday that flies.
By the low light in your eyes,
By the love that in me lies,
I know we grow more lovely
Growing wise.

Alice Corbin

INVOCATION

Truth, be more precious to me than the eyes
Of happy love; burn hotter in my throat
Than passion, and possess me like my pride;
More sweet than freedom, more desired than joy,
More sacred than the pleasing of a friend.

Max Eastman

TREES

I think that I shall never see
A poem lovely as a tree.

A tree whose hungry mouth is prest
Against the earth's sweet flowing breast;

A tree that looks at God all day,
And lifts her leafy arms to pray;

A tree that may in summer wear
A nest of robins in her hair;

Upon whose bosom snow has lain;
Who intimately lives with rain.

Poems are made by fools like me,
But only God can make a tree.

Joyce Kilmer

GOOD COMPANY

To-day I have grown taller from walking with the trees,
The seven sister-poplars who go softly in a line;
And I think my heart is whiter for its parley with a star
That trembled out at nightfall and hung above the pine.
The call-note of a redbird from the cedars in the dusk
Woke his happy mate within me to an answer free and fine;
And a sudden angel beckoned from a column of blue smoke—
Lord, who am I that they should stoop—these holy folk of thine?

Karle Wilson Baker

TWO NARRATIVES FROM "FRUIT-GATHERING"

I

"Sire," announced the servant to the King, "the saint Narottam has never deigned to enter your royal temple.

"He is singing God's praise under the trees by the open road. The temple is empty of worshippers.

"They flock round him like bees round the white lotus, leaving the golden jar of honey unheeded."

The King, vexed at heart, went to the spot where Narottam sat on the grass.

He asked him, "Father, why leave my temple of the golden dome and sit on the dust outside to preach God's love?"

"Because God is not there in your temple," said Narottam.

The King frowned and said, "Do you know, twenty millions of gold went to the making of that marvel of art, and it was consecrated to God with costly rites?"

"Yes, I know it," answered Narottam. "It was in that year when thousands of your people whose houses had been burned stood vainly asking for help at your door.

"And God said, 'The poor creature who can give no shelter to his brothers would build my house!'

"And he took his place with the shelterless under the trees by the road.

"And that golden bubble is empty of all but hot vapour of pride."

The King cried in anger, "Leave my land."

Calmly said the saint, "Yes, banish me where you have banished my God."

II

Sudās, the gardener, plucked from his tank the last lotus left by the ravage of winter and went to sell it to the king at the palace gate.

There he met a traveller who said to him, "Ask your price for the last lotus,—I shall offer it to Lord Buddha."

Sudās said, "If you pay one golden *māshā* it will be yours."

The traveller paid it.

At that moment the king came out and he wished to buy the flower, for he was on his way to see Lord Buddha, and he thought, "It would be a fine thing to lay at his feet the lotus that bloomed in winter."

When the gardener said he had been offered a golden *māshā* the king offered him ten, but the traveller doubled the price.

The gardener, being greedy, imagined a greater gain from him for whose sake they were biddng. He bowed and said, "I cannot sell this lotus."

In the hushed shade of the mango grove beyond the city wall Sudās stood before Lord Buddha, on whose lips sat the silence of love and whose eyes beamed peace like the morning star of the dew-washed autumn.

Sudās looked in his face and put the lotus at his feet and bowed his head to the dust.

Buddha smiled and asked, "What is your wish, my son?"

Sudās cried, "The least touch of your feet."

Rabindranath Tagore

THE BIRTH*

There is a legend that the love of God
So quickened under Mary's heart it wrought
Her very maidenhood to holier stuff. . . .
However that may be, the birth befell

Upon a night when all the Syrian stars
Swayed tremulous before one lordlier orb
That rose in gradual splendor,
Paused,
Flooding the firmament with mystic light,
And dropped upon the breathing hills
A sudden music
Like a distillation from its gleams;
A rain of spirit and a dew of song!

Don Marquis

A CHRISTMAS FOLK-SONG

The Little Jesus came to town;
The wind blew up, the wind blew down;
Out in the street the wind was bold;
Now who would house Him from the cold?

Then opened wide a stable door,
Fair were the rushes on the floor;
The Ox put forth a hornèd head;
"Come, little Lord, here make Thy bed."

Uprose the Sheep were folded near;
"Thou Lamb of God, come, enter here."
He entered there to rush and reed,
Who was the Lamb of God indeed.

The little Jesus came to town;
With ox and sheep He laid Him down;
Peace to the byre, peace to the fold,
For that they housed Him from the cold!

Lizette Woodworth Reese

THE VIGIL OF JOSEPH

After the Wise Men went, and the strange star
Had faded out, Joseph the father sat
Watching the sleeping Mother and the Babe,
And thinking stern, sweet thoughts the long night through.

"Ah, what am I, that God has chosen me
To bear this blessed burden, to endure
Daily the presence of this loveliness,
To guide this Glory that shall guide the world?

"Brawny these arms to win Him bread, and broad
This bosom to sustain Her. But my heart
Quivers in lonely pain before that Beauty
It loves—and serves—and cannot understand!"

Elsa Barker

CHILD

The young child, Christ, is straight and wise
And asks questions of the old men, questions
Found under running water for all children,
And found under shadows thrown on still waters
By tall trees looking downward, old and gnarled,
Found to the eyes of children alone, untold,
Singing a low song in the loneliness.
And the young child, Christ, goes on asking
And the old men answer nothing and only know love
For the young child, Christ, straight and wise.

Carl Sandburg

COMRADE JESUS

Thanks to Saint Matthew, who had been
At mass-meetings in Palestine,
We know whose side was spoken for
When Comrade Jesus had the floor.

"Where sore they toil and hard they lie,
Among the great unwashed, dwell I;—
The tramp, the convict, I am he;
Cold-shoulder him, cold-shoulder me."

By Dives' door, with thoughtful eye,
He did to-morrow prophesy:—
"The kingdom's gate is low and small;
The rich can scarce wedge through at all."

"A dangerous man," said Caiaphas,
"An ignorant demagogue, alas!
Friend of low women, it is he
Slanders the upright Pharisee."

For law and order, it was plain,
For Holy Church, he must be slain.
The troops were there to awe the crowd:
And violence was not allowed.

Their clumsy force with force to foil
His strong, clean hands we would not soil.
He saw their childishness quite plain
Between the lightnings of his pain.

Between the twilights of his end,
He made his fellow-felon friend:
With swollen tongue and blinded eyes,
Invited him to Paradise.

Ah, let no Local him refuse!
Comrade Jesus hath paid his dues.
Whatever other be debarred,
Comrade Jesus hath his red card.

Sarah N. Cleghorn

AN UNBELIEVER

All these on whom the sacred seal was set,
They could forsake thee while thine eyes were wet.
Brother, not once have I believed in thee,
Yet having seen I cannot once forget.

I have looked long into those friendly eyes,
And found thee dreaming, fragile and unwise.
Brother, not once have I believed in thee,
Yet have I loved thee for thy gracious lies.

One broke thee with a kiss at eventide,
And he that loved thee well has thrice denied.
Brother, I have no faith in thee at all,
Yet must I seek thy hands, thy feet, thy side.

Behold that John that leaned upon thy breast;
His eyes grew heavy and he needs must rest.
I watched unseen through dark Gethsemane
And might not slumber, for I loved thee best.

Peace thou wilt give to them of troubled mind,
Bread to the hungry, spittle to the blind.
My heart is broken for my unbelief,
But that thou canst not heal, though thou art kind.

They asked one day to sit beside thy throne.
I made one prayer, in silence and alone.
Brother, thou knowest my unbelief in thee.
Bear not my sins, for thou must bear thine own.

Even he that grieves thee most "Lord, Lord," he saith,
So will I call on thee with my last breath!
Brother, not once have I believed in thee.
Yet I am wounded for thee unto death.

Anna Hempstead Branch

THE JEW TO JESUS

O Man of my own people, I alone
Among these alien ones can know thy face,
I who have felt the kinship of our race
Burn in me as I sit where they intone
Thy praises,—those who, striving to make known
A God for sacrifice, have missed the grace
Of thy sweet human meaning in its place,
Thou who art of our blood-bond and our own.

Are we not sharers of thy Passion? Yea,
In spirit-anguish closely by thy side
We have drained the bitter cup, and, tortured, felt
With thee the bruising of each heavy welt.
In every land is our Gethsemane.
A thousand times have we been crucified.

Florence Kiper Frank

THE BALLAD OF THE CROSS

Melchior, Gaspar, Balthazar,
  Great gifts they bore and meet;
White linen for His body fair
  And purple for His feet;
And golden things—the joy of kings—
  And myrrh to breathe Him sweet.

It was the shepherd Terish spake,
  "Oh, poor the gift I bring—
A little cross of broken twigs,
  A hind's gift to a king—
Yet, haply, He may smile to see
  And know my offering."

And it was Mary held her Son
  Full softly to her breast,
"Great gifts and sweet are at Thy feet
  And wonders king-possessed,
O little Son, take Thou the one
  That pleasures Thee the best."

It was the Christ-Child in her arms
  Who turned from gaud and gold,
Who turned from wondrous gifts and great,
  From purple woof and fold,
And to His breast the cross He pressed
  That scarce His hands could hold.

'Twas king and shepherd went their way—
  Great wonder tore their bliss;
'Twas Mary clasped her little Son
  Close, close to feel her kiss,
And in His hold the cross lay cold
  Between her heart and His!

Theodosia Garrison

NATURE IN CONTEMPORARY POETRY

In the past decade the stimulating themes of democracy, industrial civilization and the great war have engaged the attention of the poets. But the ancient and everlasting themes of human life have never been forgotten. While we have love and birth and death, poets will sing of them. While we have changing seasons and streams clamorous with the white danger of rapids, woods blessed by early hepaticas or late asters, poets will go back to the open world for refuge and for inspiration. The joy and solace of that open world will be echoed in their poems.

Probably the poets of to-day have written as many poems of nature as were ever written in any period. Even poets who can seldom summon sufficient vigor of spirit to write acceptably of anything else can make a few acceptable poems about the beauty of the natural world. It is the only world that our forefathers knew in the days before there were cities. It is the world to which the psyche of mankind has been attuned by time.

But we shall find the new spirit of new days even in the poems of nature. Poets of to-day do not write of the out of doors as their ancestors wrote of it. No contemporary poet of the first rank would be likely to write lines like the famous ones of Wordsworth:

"One impulse from a vernal wood
May teach you more of man
Of moral evil and of good
Than all the sages can."

He could not write in this way because he would not be likely to think and feel in this way. Certainly nature is good for us. Air is good to breathe and water is good to drink and the natural beauty of the out of doors is like the breath of life and the water of life to the human spirit. But the poet of to-day does not think about nature as something external to himself, which may possibly have a beneficial effect on his behavior if taken in judicious doses.

The poet of to-day seems to think of nature as of a matrix in which he himself is formed. Man is simply a part of nature, the summit achieved by countless climbing cells of protoplasm, that have perpetuated themselves in grass and coral, frog, fish, and feathered eagle, from generation to generation. All this is said far better than prose can say it in John Hall Wheelock's "Earth," which begins with the lines:

"Grasshopper, your fairy song
And my poem alike belong
To the dark and silent earth
From which all poetry has birth;
All we say and all we sing
Is but as the murmuring
Of that drowsy heart of hers
When from her deep dream she stirs:
If we sorrow, or rejoice,
You and I are but her voice.

"Deftly does the dust express
In mind her hidden loveliness,
And from her cool silence stream
The cricket's cry and Dante's dream:
For the earth that breeds the trees
Breeds cities too, and symphonies
Equally her beauty flows
Into a savior or a rose."

The same thought is reiterated in "April Rain" by Conrad Aiken, a poem conceived in the thought of man's oneness with the earth, and on the interchanging of dust and dust.

"Fall, rain! Into the dust I go with you,
Pierce the remaining snows with subtle fire,
Warming the frozen roots with soft desire,
Dreams of ascending leaves and flowers new.

> "I am no longer body,—I am blood
> Seeking for some new loveliness of shape;
> Dark loveliness that dreams of new escape,
> The sun-surrender of unclosing bud."

Thomas Hardy gives expression to the same idea with greater austerity, and more nobly, in his admirable poems, "Transformations" and "The Wind Blew Words."

To be sure it is no new thing in the world of thought that man should call the Earth his mother. Very primitive poets did that in the age of bronze, in the age of stone, doubtless. Later poets made a literary convention of the idea. But to-day it is more than a convention. It is truth that we can feel and understand better than poets of yesterday felt it and understood it. Science has taught us something of our kinship with the earth. In the best modern poems of nature a new intimacy with the earth is expressed. Nowadays poets do not condescend to nature. They do not say, in effect "Oh yes, the Earth is our mother, but—" They do not speak of nature with reservations, as exclusive people speak of poor relations. They are of one substance with nature. They know it and are content, even glad. And most of the modern poets who have given us authentic poems of nature and the fecund earth have shared the high mood of William Watson's admirable "Ode In May," have thought what he thought when he said,

> "Magnificent out of the dust we came,
> And abject from the spheres."

Nowadays we rejoice the more in the thought of simple, natural things, earth, grass, sun, rain, wind, and in the thought of our kinship with them, because life often carries us away from them all. For the modern, a return to these things of the out of doors, either in reality, or in poetry—the other reality—is relaxation and recreation and refuge from sophistication and unrest. In spite of starch and shoe polish, aeroplanes and printing presses, the primitive man still lives in us. We are his heirs. Sometimes he cries aloud in us for the sea or the hills, for the scent of pine-needles, for a draught of water from a spring that has never been walled in. When this happens we return gladly, in body and in actuality, or in spirit and in poetry, to claim our kinship with the kind Earth and to be soothed by the maternal forces of her life.

Man's intimacy with nature is told in many modern poems. It is even a part of the melody of Robert Frost's lyric, "The Sound of The Trees." The rhythm of moving trees is in the words. It is the very tune of the trees, at once irregular and stately. This is a proof that the poem was profoundly felt before it was written. It could hardly have been made by the self-conscious intellect, the practical intellect that deals competently enough with the surfaces of things. For in the simplest and most impressive language, Mr. Frost reveals the very nature of trees in what he says about himself and reveals his own mood in what he says about the trees. To have written such sincere poetry is to have taken one little step in time to the grand march of the universe. It is to have been a participant in the never-ending pageant of the natural world and to have shared the experience of participation with others.

This fact, that the modern poet desires to share an experience in his poetry, is responsible for his way of telling what he knows about the natural world. Although he is both truthful and accurate in his own way, his method is impressionistic rather than photographic. He does not describe in detail. He presents in essence. And he is always personal. His own emotion quickens his readers. It is what makes his poems strong to reach into other people's minds and hearts. We might read two or three pages of good description of a cherry tree, pages composed with pains and aiming to tell just what a cherry tree is like, and yet remain untouched. It is well nigh impossible to read the famous little lyric about the cherry tree, by A. E. Housman, dispassionately. After two or three readings it is well nigh impossible to forget it. That little poem tells us something about the cherry tree that we have felt ourselves. But Mr. Housman has felt it more keenly and expressed it better than we could express it.

"Loveliest of trees, the cherry now
Is hung with bloom along the bough
And stands about the woodland ride
Wearing white for Eastertide."

That is all that is said in description of the cherry tree. The other lines of the poem are lyrical, personal, naïve. The beauty in them can belong to anyone who will take them upon his own lips and into his own mind. It is, moreover, a beauty so simple that it defies analysis. It is difficult for a critic to tell of what elements it is composed.

A similar naïvete is a part of the charming quality of many of William H. Davies' lyrics of nature. Mr. Davies does more than express his own love of the beautiful things out of doors. He is conscious of a reciprocity in friendliness and tells his readers about it. He is "Nature's Friend."

"Say what you like,
All things love me!
Horse, Cow, and Mouse
Bird, Moth and Bee."

He has something of a child's capacity for anticipation. In that lovable lyric, "The Rain," he says,

"I hope the sun shines bright;
'Twill be a lovely sight."

and in "Leisure" he asks innocently,

"What is this life if, full of care,
We have no time to stand and stare.

"No time to stand beneath the boughs
And stare as long as sheep and cows."

The effervescent gayety of many of his short lyrics is like the perennially renewed youth of the out of doors.

The English and the Irish seem to have domesticated nature, if we can judge by much of their poetry about it. Mr. Davies is only one of many English poets who sing of a nature in which cows and horses and mice have a place, a nature of rose-bushes and trimmed hedges. It is the cultivated nature of lanes and gardens that Edward Thomas knows and of which he tells us in a number of delightful, whimsical poems. The following lines are typical of his quiet genius.

> "If I should ever by chance grow rich
> I'll buy Codham, Cockridden and Childerditch,
> Roses, Pyrgo, and Lapwater,
> And let them all to my elder daughter.
> The rent I shall ask of her will be only
> Each year's first violets, white and lonely,
> The first primroses and orchises—
> She must find them before I do, that is."

Padraic Colum, the Irish poet, who has lived for several years in the United States, has written a number of beautiful poems of domesticated nature which he has put into a book called "Wild Earth And Other Poems." The first thought that comes into the mind of an American who turns the pages of it is that Mr. Colum's "wild earth" is not very "wild." In a certain sense, perhaps, the earth is always wild and always will be. But Mr. Colum's poetry is about earth that knows the plough, earth on which homes have been built. The first poem in the book is called "The Plougher," and the second "The Furrow And The Hearth." To the children of pioneers who cut logs in the wilderness and broke the soil of a continent for the first time with the plough, the word "wild" has another meaning.

But Mr. Colum's poetry is beautiful and dignified. It is fraught with racial emotion. It is homely and strong. It is concerned with nature, to be sure, but with nature subdued to meet the needs of man.

> "Stride the hill, sower,
> Up to the sky-ridge,
> Flinging the seed,
> Scattering, exultant!

> Mouthing great rhythms
> To the long sea beats
> On the wide shore, behind
> The ridge of the hillside."

In sharp contrast with poetry of this kind is such a lyric as "In The Mohave" by Patrick Orr, a poem about the Mohave Desert. Mr. Orr's poem, like the poems of Mr. Housman, Mr. Thomas, and Mr. Colum, is lyrical and impressionistic. It is the sharing of an experience. But because the experience is not gay or gentle, but poignant and cruel, the poem in which it is shared is astringent and of a sharp flavor. It is a poem of wild nature.

> "As I went down the arroyo through yuccas belled with bloom
> I saw a last year's stalk lift dried hands to the light,
> Like age at prayer for death within a careless room,
> Like one by day o'er taken whose sick desire is night."

Mr. Orr saw that in the desert. Anyone can see it there. When he apostrophizes the desert, however, he reveals what he himself felt, and gives permanent form to it.

> "O cruel land, where form endures, the spirit fled."

The emotional reaction which made it possible for him to utter that line is the suggestive force in each of his lines of description. It is what gives vitality to his portrayal of the brilliance and cruelty of the desert.

A day may come when it will no longer be possible to write poems about wild nature, because nature will no longer be wild anywhere in the world. A day may come when so many people will live in so many places now uninhabited that all of the natural world will be domesticated. Probably poets will never again have a better chance than they have to-day to share their experiences in the wild, open world. Lovers of poetry can not help wishing that the poets may get the best things of the great out of doors made into poetry before they are made into picture postal cards, before the sides of the trails that go to

GEORGE STERLING

find them are placarded with advertisements. In America we have more kinds of natural beauty than any one poet can find time to enjoy in all his life. What a fine thing it would be if a few of our overheated young radicals and tepid conservatives could be put into communication with this natural beauty and helped to express it with warm natural affection!

George Sterling, the master-singer of California, is a poet who has made very beautiful lyrics of nature. His pictures in verse have the magic of the suggested mood. He is not direct and naïve. He says very little about his personal feelings. But he shares them. He is communicative in a subtle way, shyly, and with reserves. "The Last Days," a poem of autumn in Northern California, is a bit of wizardry as an interpretation of the season and of what it has meant to Mr. Sterling and might mean to anyone else. The sober rhythm and the sober phrasing contribute not a little to the wistful loveliness of this song of evanescence and change.

> "The bracken-rust is red on the hill;
> The pines stand brooding sombre and still;
> Gray are the cliffs and the waters gray,
> Where the sea-gulls dip to the sea-born spray.
> Sad November, lady of rain,
> Sends the goose-wedge over again.
>
> * * * * * * * *
>
> "Days departing linger and sigh:
> Stars come soon to the quiet sky;
> Buried voices, intimate, strange,
> Cry to body and soul of change;
> Beauty, eternal fugitive,
> Seeks the home that we can not give."

Another good poem of the far West is "On The Great Plateau," by Edith Wyatt. It is panoramic, and its chief merit is that it tells the secret of the love of Westerners for the West, without saying anything about it. It is a secret of great spaces and tremendous sizes, of the highest mountains, the deepest canyons, the tallest trees and the trees of greatest girth. When one has lived in the far West for a number of years a return to the smaller and more lovable landscapes of the East is like leaving a big park for a Japanese miniature garden.

"In the Santa Clara Valley, far away and far away,
Cool-breathed waters dip and dally, linger towards another day—
Far and far away—far away."

A poem of quite another kind is "The Morning Song of Senlin" taken from a longer poem, "Senlin: A Biography" by Conrad Aiken. It is a lyric that sets the immensity and grandeur of nature side by side with our little deeds of every day, in sharp contrast. It is very spontaneous and original. The dew of surprise is still fresh on it. Everybody who is sensitive to contrasts between great things and small, who is capable of wonder in the thought of rising in the morning to a new day in an ancient and everlasting universe, and of setting beside the glory of that new day the least and most trivial of occupations, has felt what is said in this poem. But nobody else has put just this thing into poetry of this kind. "The Morning Song of Senlin" is a poem for imaginative people. Practical people may stumble over this juxtaposition of great things and small in it. They are accustomed to having poets tell them that grandeur and immensity are near at hand. But they are not accustomed to having the idea put into poetry in the words of a man who is only standing before a mirror and tying his necktie. They prefer to think that the person who speaks of grandeur is perched upon a remote and chilly hill-top with nothing to occupy him but contemplation, or that he paces some romantic stage with his eyes rolling in fine frenzy as he talks. They are tempted to forget that, for nearly everybody, the perception of beauty would be impossible if it had to be made into a vocation.

Mr. Aiken's poem is brave with the elation of the morning and it is written with enough restraint to save it from any real and damaging incongruities. Moreover, Mr. Aiken is a master of rhythm, and the cool lyrical movement of the lines of this poem combines in a subtle and delicate way the qualities of speech and song. The following lines are especially charming:

> "The earth revolves with me, yet makes no motion,
> The stars pale silently in the coral sky.
> In a whistling void I stand before my mirror,
> Unconcerned, and tie my tie.
>
> "There are horses neighing on far-off hills,
> Tossing their long white manes,
> And mountains flash in the rose-white dusk,
> Their shoulders black with rains . . .
> It is morning. I stand by the mirror
> And surprise my soul once more;
> The blue air rushes above my ceiling,
> There are suns beneath my floor . . ."

What has been said of the themes of nature and the open world as they are used in contemporary poetry does not tell the whole story. The discussion would have to be very long to be complete. It would be necessary to tell something of the fine, uproarious poetry of the sea and of the sonorous, colorful poetry of the sea that John Masefield has written. It would be necessary to tell something of the fragrant charm of many of the poems about gardens that modern poets have made. It would be necessary to mention poems in which nature has stimulated the poet by suggesting odd, delectable magic of fancy, like Harold Monro's "Overheard In A Saltmarsh." But that can not be done in an introduction. An introduction is only the beginning of a adventure in acquaintance. Perhaps enough has been said to show that those who are old friends of the open world and lovers of their mother, Earth, will find their filial friendship and their devotion adequately commemorated in the poetry of to-day.

EARTH

Grasshopper, your fairy song
And my poem alike belong
To the dark and silent earth
From which all poetry has birth;
All we say and all we sing
Is but as the murmuring
Of that drowsy heart of hers
When from her deep dream she stirs:
If we sorrow, or rejoice,
You and I are but her voice.

Deftly does the dust express
In mind her hidden loveliness,
And from her cool silence stream
The cricket's cry and Dante's dream:
For the earth that breeds the trees
Breeds cities too, and symphonies,
Equally her beauty flows
Into a savior, or a rose—
Looks down in dream, and from above
Smiles at herself in Jesus' love.
Christ's love and Homer's art
Are but the workings of her heart;
Through Leonardo's hand she seeks
Herself, and through Beethoven speaks
In holy thunderings around
The awful message of the ground.

The serene and humble mould
Does in herself all selves enfold—
Kingdoms, destinies, and creeds,
Great dreams and dauntless deeds,
Science that metes the firmament,
The high, inflexible intent
Of one for many sacrificed—
Plato's brain, the heart of Christ:
All love, all legend, and all lore
Are in the dust forevermore.

Even as the growing grass
Up from the soil religions pass,
And the field that bears the rye
Bears parables and prophecy.
Out of the earth the poem grows
Like the lily, or the rose;
And all man is, or yet may be,
Is but herself in agony
Toiling up the steep ascent
Toward the complete accomplishment
When all dust shall be, the whole
Universe, one conscious soul.

Yea, the quiet and cool sod
Bears in her breast the dream of God.
If you would know what earth is, scan
The intricate, proud heart of man,
Which is the earth articulate,
And learn how holy and how great,
How limitless and how profound
Is the nature of the ground—
How without terror or demur
We may entrust ourselves to her
When we are wearied out, and lay
Our faces in the common clay.

For she is pity, she is love,
All wisdom she, all thoughts that move
About her everlasting breast
Till she gathers them to rest:
All tenderness of all the ages,
Seraphic secrets of the sages,
All prayer, all anguish, and all tears
Are but the dust, that from her dream
Awakes, and knows herself supreme—
Are but earth when she reveals
All that her secret heart conceals
Down in the dark and silent loam,
Which is ourselves asleep, at home.

Yea, and this my poem, too,
Is part of her as dust and dew,
Wherein herself she doth declare
Through my lips, and say her prayer.

John Hall Wheelock

"THE WIND BLEW WORDS"

The wind blew words along the skies,
And these it blew to me
Through the wide dusk: "Lift up your eyes,
Behold this troubled tree,
Complaining as it sways and plies;
It is a limb of thee.

"Yea, too, the creatures sheltering round—
Dumb figures, wild and tame,
Yea, too, thy fellows who abound—
Either of speech the same
Of far and strange—black, dwarfed, and browned,
They are stuff of thy own frame."

I moved on in a surging awe
Of inarticulateness
At the pathetic Me I saw
In all his huge distress,
Making self-slaughter of the law
To kill, bind, or suppress.

Thomas Hardy

TRANSFORMATIONS

Portion of this yew
Is a man my grandsire knew,
Bosomed here at its foot:
This branch may be his wife,
A ruddy human life
Now turned to a green shoot.

These grasses must be made
Of her who often prayed,
Last century, for repose;
And the fair girl long ago
Whom I often tried to know
May be entering this rose.

So, they are not underground,
But as nerves and veins abound
In the growths of upper air,
And they feel the sun and rain,
And the energy again
That made them what they were.

Thomas Hardy

PENETRALIA

I am a part of all you see
In Nature; part of all you feel:
I am the impact of the bee
Upon the blossom; in the tree
I am the sap,—that shall reveal
The leaf, the bloom,—that flows and flutes
Up from the darkness through its roots.

I am the vermeil of the rose,
The perfume breathing in its veins;
The gold within the mist that glows
Along the west and overflows
With light the heaven; the dew that rains
Its freshness down and strings with spheres
Of wet the webs and oaten ears.

I am the egg that folds the bird;
The song that beaks and breaks its shell;
The laughter and the wandering word
The water says; and, dimly heard,
The music of the blossom's bell
When soft winds swing it; and the sound
Of grass slow-creeping o'er the ground.

I am the warmth, the honey-scent
That throats with spice each lily-bud
That opens, white with wonderment,
Beneath the moon; or, downward bent,
Sleeps with a moth beneath its hood:
I am the dream that haunts it too,
That crystalizes into dew.

I am the seed within the pod;
The worm within its closed cocoon:
The wings within the circling clod,
The germ that gropes through soil and sod
To beauty, radiant in the noon:
I am all these, behold! and more—
I am the love at the world-heart's core.

Madison Cawein

THE WINDS

Those hewers of the clouds, the Winds,—that lair
At the four compass-points,—are out to-night;
I hear their sandals trample on the height,
I hear their voices trumpet through the air:
Builders of storm, God's workmen, now they bear,
Up the steep stair of sky, on backs of might,
Huge tempest bulks, while,—sweat that blinds their sight,—
The rain is shaken from tumultuous hair:
Now, sweepers of the firmament, they broom
Like gathered dust, the rolling mists along
Heaven's floors of sapphire; all the beautiful blue
Of skyey corridor and celestial room
Preparing, with large laughter and loud song,
For the white moon and stars to wander through.

Madison Cawein

THE FURROW AND THE HEARTH

I

Stride the hill, sower,
Up to the sky-ridge,
Flinging the seed,
Scattering, exultant!
Mouthing great rhythms
To the long sea beats
On the wide shore, behind
The ridge of the hillside.

Below in the darkness—
The slumber of mothers—
The cradles at rest—
The fire-seed sleeping
Deep in white ashes!

Give to darkness and sleep:
O sower, O seer!
Give me to the Earth.
With the seed I would enter.
O! the growth thro' the silence
From strength to new strength;
Then the strong bursting forth
Against primal forces,
To laugh in the sunshine,
To gladden the world!

II

Who will bring the red fire
Unto a new hearth?
Who will lay the wide stone
On the waste of the earth?

Who is fain to begin
To build day by day?
To raise up his house
Of the moist, yellow clay?

There's clay for the making
Moist in the pit,
There are horses to trample
The rushes thro' it.

Above where the wild duck
Arise up and fly,
There one may build
To the wind and the sky.

There are boughs in the forest
To pluck young and green,
O'er them thatch of the crop
Shall be heavy and clean.

I speak unto him
Who in dead of the night
Sees the red streaks
In the ash deep and white.

While around him he hears
Men stir in their rest,
And stir of the child
That is close to the breast!

He shall arise,
He shall go forth alone.
Lay stone on the earth
And bring fire to the stone.

Padraic Colum

DESIRE IN SPRING

I love the cradle songs the mothers sing
In lonely places when the twilight drops,
The slow endearing melodies that bring
Sleep to the weeping lids; and, when she stops,
I love the roadside birds upon the tops
Of dusty hedges in a world of Spring.

And when the sunny rain drips from the edge
Of midday wind, and meadows lean one way,
And a long whisper passes thro' the sedge,
Beside the broken water let me stay,
While these old airs upon my memory play,
And silent changes color up the hedge.

Francis Ledwidge

JUNE

Broom out the floor now, lay the fender by,
And plant this bee-sucked bough of woodbine there,
And let the window down. The butterfly
Floats in upon the sunbeam, and the fair
Tanned face of June, the nomad gipsy, laughs
Above her widespread wares, the while she tells
The farmers' fortunes in the fields, and quaffs
The water from the spider-peopled wells.

The hedges are all drowned in green grass seas,
And bobbing poppies flare like Elmor's light,
While siren-like the pollen-stainéd bees
Drone in the clover depths. And up the height
The cuckoo's voice is hoarse and broke with joy.
And on the lowland crops the crows make raid,
Nor fear the clappers of the farmer's boy
Who sleeps, like drunken Noah, in the shade.

And loop this red rose in that hazel ring
That snares your little ear, for June is short
And we must joy in it and dance and sing,
And from her bounty draw her rosy worth.
Ay, soon the swallows will be flying south,
The wind wheel north to gather in the snow,
Even the roses spilt on youth's red mouth
Will soon blow down the road all roses go.

Francis Ledwidge

I could not sleep for thinking of the sky,
The unending sky, with all its million suns
Which turn their planets everlastingly
In nothing, where the fire-haired comet runs.

If I could sail that nothing, I should cross
Silence and emptiness with dark stars passing,
Then, in the darkness, see a point of gloss
Burn to a glow, and glare, and keep amassing,

And rage into a sun with wandering planets
And drop behind, and then, as I proceed,
See his last light upon his last moon's granites
Die to a dark that would be night indeed.

Night where my soul might sail a million years
In nothing, not even Death, not even tears.

John Masefield

A DAY FOR WANDERING

I set apart a day for wandering;
I heard the woodlands ring,
The hidden white-throat sing,
And the harmonic West,
Beyond a far hill-crest,
Touch its Aeolian string.
Remote from all the brawl and bruit of men,
The iron tongue of Trade,
I followed the clear calling of a wren
Deep to the bosom of a sheltered glade,
Where interwoven branches spread a shade
Of soft cool beryl like the evening seas
Unruffled by the breeze.
And there—and there—
I watched the maiden-hair,
The pale blue iris-grass,
The water-spider in its pause and pass
Upon a pool that like a mirror was.

I took for confidant
The diligent ant
Threading the clover and the sorrel aisles;
For me were all the smiles
Of the sequestered blossoms there abloom—
Chalice and crown and plume;
I drank the ripe rich attars blurred and blent,
And won—Content!

Clinton Scollard

THE SOUND OF THE TREES

I wonder about the trees.
Why do we wish to bear
Forever the noise of these
More than another noise
So close to our dwelling place?
We suffer them by the day
Till we lose all measure of pace,
And fixity in our joys,
And acquire a listening air.
They are that that talks of going
But never gets away;
And that talks no less for knowing,
As it grows wiser and older,
That now it means to stay.
My feet tug at the floor
And my head sways to my shoulder
Sometimes when I watch trees sway,
From the window or the door.
I shall set forth for somewhere,
I shall make the reckless choice
Some day when they are in voice
And tossing so as to scare
The white clouds over them on.
I shall have less to say,
But I shall be gone.

Robert Frost

EPITAPH

Here lies the flesh that tried
   To follow the spirit's leading;
Fallen at last, it died,
   Broken, bruised and bleeding,
Burned by the high fires
Of the spirit's desires.

It had no dream to sing
   Of ultimate liberty;
Fashioned for suffering,
   To endure transiently,
And conscious that it must
Return as dust to dust.

It blossomed a brief hour,
   Was rosy, warm and strong;
It went like a wilted flower,
   It ended like a song;
Someone closed a door—
And it was seen no more.

The grass is very kind;
   (It knows so many dead!)
Those whom it covers find
   Their wild hearts comforted;
Their pulses need not meet
The spirit's speed and heat.

Here lies the flesh that held
   The spirit prisoner—
A caged thing that rebelled,
   Forced to subminister;
Broken it had to be;
To set its captive free.

It is very glad to rest,
   It calls to roots and rain,

Safe in its mother's breast,
  Ready to bloom again.
After a day and an hour
'Twill greet the sun a flower.

Louise Driscoll

NATURE'S FRIEND *

Say what you like,
  All things love me!
I pick no flowers—
  That wins the Bee.

The Summer's Moths
  Think my hand one—
To touch their wings—
  With Wind and Sun.

The garden Mouse
  Comes near to play;
Indeed, he turns
  His eyes away.

The Wren knows well
  I rob no nest;
When I look in,
  She still will rest.

The hedge stops Cows,
  Or they would come
After my voice
  Right to my home.

The Horse can tell,
  Straight from my lip,
My hand could not
  Hold any whip.

By arrangement with Mr. Davies' London publisher, A. C. Fifield.

Say what you like,
  All things love me!
Horse, Cow, and Mouse,
  Bird, Moth and Bee.

William H. Davies

MOUNTAIN SONG

I have not where to lay my head;
  Upon my breast no child shall lie;
For me no marriage feast is spread:
  I walk alone under the sky.

My staff and scrip I cast away—
  Light-burdened to the mountain height!
Climbing the rocky steep by day,
  Kindling my fire against the night.

The bitter hail shall flower the peak,
  The icy wind shall dry my tears.
Strong shall I be, who am but weak,
  When bright Orion spears my fears.

Under the horned moon I shall rise,
  Up swinging on the scarf of dawn.
The sun, searching with level eyes,
  Shall take my hand and lead me on.

Wide flaming pinions veil the West—
  Ah, shall I find? and shall I know?
My feet are bound upon the Quest—
  Over the Great Divide I go.

Harriet Monroe

SANTA BARBARA BEACH

Now while the sunset offers,
  Shall we not take our own:
The gems, the blazing coffers,
  The seas, the shores, the throne?

The sky-ships, radiant-masted,
Move out, bear low our way.
Oh, Life was dark while it lasted,
Now for enduring day.

Now with the world far under,
To draw up drowning men
And show them lands of wonder
Where they may build again.

There earthly sorrow falters,
There longing has its wage;
There gleam the ivory altars
Of our lost pilgrimage.

—Swift flame—then shipwrecks only
Beach in the ruined light;
Above them reach up lonely
The headlands of the night.

A hurt bird cries and flutters
Her dabbled breast of brown;
The western wall unshutters
To fling one last rose down.

A rose, a wild light after—
And life calls through the years,
"Who dreams my fountains' laughter
Shall feed my wells with tears."

Ridgely Torrence

IN THE MOHAVE

As I rode down the arroyo through yuccas belled with bloom
I saw a last year's stalk lift dried hands to the light,
Like age at prayer for death within a careless room,
Like one by day o'ertaken whose sick desire is night.

And as I rode I saw a lean coyote lying
All perfect as in life upon a silver dune,
Save that his feet no more could flee the harsh light's spying,
Save that no more his shadow would cleave the sinking moon.

O cruel land, where form endures, the spirit fled!
You chill the sun for me with your gray sphinx's smile,
Brooding in the bright silence above your captive dead,
Where beat the heart of life so brief, so brief a while!

Patrick Orr

THE LAST DAYS

The russet leaves of the sycamore
Lie at last on the valley floor—
By the autumn wind swept to and fro
Like ghosts in a tale of long ago.
Shallow and clear the Carmel glides
Where the willows droop on its vine-walled sides.

The bracken-rust is red on the hill;
The pines stand brooding, somber and still;
Gray are the cliffs, and the waters gray,
Where the seagulls dip to the sea-born spray.
Sad November, lady of rain,
Sends the goose-wedge over again.

Wilder now, for the verdure's birth,
Falls the sunlight over the earth;
Kildees call from the fields where now
The banding blackbirds follow the plow;
Rustling poplar and brittle weed
Whisper low to the river-reed.

Days departing linger and sigh:
Stars come soon to the quiet sky;
Buried voices, intimate, strange,
Cry to body and soul of change;
Beauty, eternal, fugitive,
Seeks the home that we cannot give.

George Sterling

THE BLACK VULTURE

Aloof upon the day's immeasured dome,
He holds unshared the silence of the sky.
Far down his bleak, relentless eyes descry
The eagle's empire and the falcon's home—
Far down, the galleons of sunset roam;
His hazards on the sea of morning lie;
Serene, he hears the broken tempest sigh
Where cold sierras gleam like scattered foam.

And least of all he holds the human swarm—
Unwitting now that envious men prepare
To make their dream and its fulfillment one,
When, poised above the caldrons of the storm,
Their hearts, contemptuous of death, shall dare
His roads between the thunder and the sun.

George Sterling

ON THE GREAT PLATEAU

In the Santa Clara Valley, far away and far away,
Cool-breathed waters dip and dally, linger towards another day—
Far and far away—far away.
Slow their floating step, but tireless, terraced down the great Plateau.
Towards our ways of steam and wireless, silver-paced the brook-beds go.
Past the ladder-walled Pueblos, past the orchards, pear and quince,
Where the back-locked river's ebb flows, miles and miles the valley glints,
Shining backwards, singing downwards, towards horizons blue and bay.
All the roofs the roads ensconce so dream of visions far away—
Santa Cruz and Ildefonso, Santa Clara, Santa Fé.
Ancient, sacred fears and faiths, ancient, sacred faiths and fears—
Some were real, some were wraiths—Indian, Franciscan years,
Built the Khivas, swung the bells; while the wind sang plain and free,
"Turn your eyes from visioned hells!—look as far as you can see!"
In the Santa Clara Valley, far away and far away,
Dying dreams divide and dally, crystal-terraced waters sally—
Linger towards another day, far and far away—far away.

As you follow where you find them, up along the high Plateau,
In the hollows left behind them Spanish chapels fade below—
Shaded court and low corrals. In the vale the goat-herd browses.
Hollyhocks are seneschals by the little buff-walled houses.
Over grassy swale and alley have you ever seen it so—
Up the Santa Clara Valley, riding on the Great Plateau?
Past the ladder-walled Pueblos, past the orchards, pear and quince,
Where the trenchèd waters' ebb flows, miles and miles the valley glints,
Shining backwards, singing downwards towards horizons blue and
    bay.
All the haunts the bluffs ensconce so breathe of visions far away,
As you ride near Ildefonso back again to Santa Fé.
Pecos, mellow with the years, tall-walled Taos—who can know
Half the storied faiths and fears haunting green New Mexico?
Only from her open places down arroyos blue and bay,
One wild grace of many graces dallies towards another day.
Where her yellow tufa crumbles, something stars and grasses know,
Something true, that crowns and humbles, shimmers from the Great
    Plateau:
Blows where cool-paced waters dally from the stillness of Puyé,
Down the Santa Clara Valley through the world from far away—
Far and far away—far away.

Edith Wyatt

THE MORNING SONG OF SENLIN

It is morning, Senlin says, and in the morning
When the light drips through the shutters like the dew,
I arise, I face the sunrise,
And do the things my fathers learned to do.
Stars in the purple dusk above the rooftops
Pale in a saffron mist and seem to die,
And I myself on a swiftly tilting planet
Stand before a glass and tie my tie.

Vine leaves tap my window,
Dew-drops sing to the garden stones,
The robin chirps in the chinaberry tree
Repeating three clear tones.

It is morning. I stand by the mirror
And tie my tie once more.
While waves far off in a pale rose twilight
Crash on a white sand shore.
I stand by a mirror and comb my hair:
How small and white my face!—
The green earth tilts through a sphere of air
And bathes in a flame of space.
There are houses hanging above the stars
And stars hung under a sea . . .
And a sun far off in a shell of silence
Dapples my walls for me . . .

It is morning, Senlin says, and in the morning
Should I not pause in the light to remember god?
Upright and firm I stand on a star unstable,
He is immense and lonely as a cloud.
I will dedicate this moment before my mirror
To him alone, for him I will comb my hair.
Accept these humble offerings, cloud of silence!
I will think of you as I descend the stair.

Vine leaves tap my window,
The snail-track shines on the stones,
Dew-drops flash from the chinaberry tree
Repeating two clear tones.

It is morning, I awake from a bed of silence,
Shining I rise from the starless waters of sleep.
The walls are about me still as in the evening,
I am the same, and the same name still I keep.
The earth revolves with me, yet makes no motion,
The stars pale silently in a coral sky.
In a whistling void I stand before my mirror,
Unconcerned, and tie my tie.

There are horses neighing on far-off hills
Tossing their long white manes,
And mountains flash in the rose-white dusk,
Their shoulders black with rains . . .

It is morning. I stand by the mirror
And surprise my soul once more;
The blue air rushes above my ceiling,
There are suns beneath my floor . . .

. . . It is morning, Senlin says, I ascend from darkness
And depart on the winds of space for I know not where,
My watch is wound, a key is in my pocket,
And the sky is darkened as I descend the stair.
There are shadows across the windows, clouds in heaven,
And a god among the stars; and I will go
Thinking of him as I might think of daybreak
And humming a tune I know . . .

Vine-leaves tap at the window,
Dew-drops sing to the garden stones,
The robin chirps in the chinaberry tree
Repeating three clear tones.

Conrad Aiken

CANTICLE

Devoutly worshiping the oak
Wherein the barred owl stares,
The little feathered forest folk
Are praying sleepy prayers:

Praying the summer to be long
And drowsy to the end,
And daily full of sun and song,
That broken hopes may mend.

Praying the golden age to stay
Until the whippoorwill
Appoints a windy moving-day,
And hurries from the hill.

William Griffith

All vision fades, but splendor does not fail
Though joy perish and all her company
And there be nothing left of it to see.
Splendor is in the grain. This lovely vale
Of rock and tree and pool and sky may pale
And fade some Autumn with its greenery,
And its form totter, crumble utterly
And scatter with some universal gale.
Yet be they spread ever so wide and free
The gale will cause the dream to come again
The world formations out of mists will rise,
And there will be thoughts of eternity
And hopes the heart of man will know are vain
And tears will come as now into the eyes.

Samuel Roth

PERSONALITY IN POETRY

Poetry enables us to share many experiences, the epic desires and agonies of great cities, the homely triumphs and tragedies of field and farmhouse, the lyric pleasure of cool woods, subtle picturing, grave symbolism, and the zest of fluent ideas and emotions. In addition to all this, poetry enables us to share one other thing, a sense of that mysterious human inflorescence which we call personality.

By virtue of his sympathetic imagination, a good poet enters many spiritual mansions and entertains many ghostly visitors. Often he knows more about us than we know about ourselves and about each other. For his proper study is mankind. Practical persons must always be concerned with facts, deeds, and events. But the poet is chiefly interested in that impulsive energy which is the causation of facts, deeds and events—the human spirit.

A detective, for example, may be clever enough in using his constructive imagination, to learn that a certain old woman has stolen a diamond and hidden it in her stocking. But his achievement is small as compared with that of the poet who tells her story. For the poet will reconstruct her world and show it to us. Through his eyes we shall see her eager old face, her nervous, twitching fingers. Through his penetrative power we shall learn why she wanted the diamond. And he will cause us to share a definite feeling with regard to the theft—pain, disgust, compassion—as the case may be. This feeling will be strong and moving in proportion as the poet possesses the gift of characterization.

Modern civilization, on the whole, has been favorable to the development of this skill. Many contemporary poets take up their task of presenting personality in poetry with an equipment of knowledge that poets of earlier generations lacked, or had only by intuition. The growth of the spirit of democracy in the modern world has enabled many sorts of men and women to meet socially and for the transaction of business. We have travelled more than was ever possible in earlier eras. Each of the world's great metropolitan cities has become a small inter-nation, affording every facility for spiritual interchange between national and racial types. Whenever we read a newspaper we are made aware of the needs and problems of people thousands of miles away. We eat food which they prepare for us, and we ourselves prepare other foods for them. It has been shown that we are all interdependent to such an extent that necessarily any great war must involve us all. All of the world is beginning to know all the world as neighbor. That is how it happens that a poet of to-day may have a broader knowledge of mankind than was possible for poets of an earlier period. But that is not all. In addition to this breadth of vision, which may be his if he wills it, he has the means of testing and deepening his knowledge of men and women. Science has destroyed many illusions, but it has fostered many faiths. Biology has shown us the marvellous ascension of life throughout all the ages. Psychology is explaining man's mind, the microcosm. All of the so-called exact sciences have stimulated the minds and imaginations of progressive persons by revealing laws and forces more wonderful than any of the miracles man dreamed. Dogma, always the bane of poets, is giving way before the pure love of questing for truth which Science implants in her devotees. Through science, as through democracy, we are learning more about ourselves and about each other. By the love of truth and by the love of the people poets grow wise for their work of interpretation.

Therefore it is not strange that many contemporary poets are keen students of character and apt in their presentation of personality. Moreover, by virtue of being poets, they are able to make their presentation of character concise, vivid, emotional, and impressive in a degree not possible to most writers of prose.

Perhaps that is why we remember poems like "The Everlasting Mercy," "Dauber," "Hoops," "A Hundred Collars," "Snow," and many others more readily than we remember any of the hundreds of short stories that we read in magazines. Short prose fiction must be the work of genius, like good narrative poetry, if we are to remember it. It seldom is.

Gordon Bottomley is one English poet who excels in the presentation of personality. In his dramatic poem, "King Lear's Wife," he gives us a totally new conception of the fabled king. He teaches us to sympathize with the queen, Lear's wife. This poem is stark, uncompromising, grim and ugly realism from beginning to end. But it is unforgettable. Each character is like a heroic statue rough-hewn from granite. The work has been cruelly done. The expressions on the stone faces are cruel. But we have a sense of certainty as to the truth of it. Goneril, who despises her sister, Regan, describes her in the following vigorously scornful lines:

> "Does Regan worship anywhere at dawn?
> The sweaty, half-clad cook-maids render lard
> Out in the scullery, after pig-killing,
> And Regan sidles among their greasy skirts,
> Smeary and hot as they, for craps to suck."

It is most unlovely, of course, and so also is the conversation of the common women who come to bathe the dead queen and dress her in grave-clothes. But it is a work of genius that the reader can never forget.

Wilfrid Wilson Gibson is also a realist, but kinder. He writes about the people of our twentieth century world, chiefly about the English laboring class, men and women of the mines, the factories and the farms. He knows their life. He interprets it adequately. He gives us a true sense of the oppressive weight of poverty upon mind and heart, of the danger and difficulty of manual labor, of the bitterness of undeserved defeat. But he gives us also a sense of the sweetness and sanity of the respectable poor and of the dignity of the soul of the people. He writes about plain men and women with sagacious simplicity. But one thing he seems to be unable to do. He can not individualize them. We do not remember them as we remember Scrooge, Tiny Tim, or Mr. Pickwick.

Mr. Gibson creates types rather than individuals. But a type, after all, is only a generalization from kindred qualities in many individuals. And the able presentation of a type is no mean achievement. As types, these people in his verse belong everywhere. The workman he describes is a real workman. The mothers he describes are real mothers. In his fine little dramatic poem, "On The Road," he tells the story of the ordinary man and the ordinary woman and the ordinary baby, all hungry because the ordinary man is out of a job; and all a little bit unhappy but very plucky. That is the whole story. But it is admirably told. As types, these people could hardly be better presented.

Unlike Mr. Gibson, Walter de la Mare has, in his own shadowy way, a real genius for the presentation of individual personality. His poems are all combinations of twilight shades, charming compositions in violet, ivory and olive. But his pictures, made with colors that would seem to be evanescent, succeed in fixing themselves indelibly in our minds. Who can forget "Miss Loo" when once he has been properly introduced to her in the poem that takes its title from her name?

> "When thin-strewn memory I look through,
> I see most clearly poor Miss Loo,
> Her tabby cat, her cage of birds,
> Her nose, her hair—her muffled words,
> And how she'd open her green eyes
> As if in some immense surprise,
> Whenever as we sat at tea
> She made some small remark to me."

John Masefield is known the world over as the poet of the wanderer and the outcast, and, in his narrative poems, rough men and women are presented in masterly fashion. They are individual human beings, each with his own flavor. Having made their acquaintance in these poems we know them as we know our neighbors. The widowed mother in "The Widow In The Bye Street" is a tragic madonna who has won our compassion and keeps it. Lord Rosas, on the other hand, in the poem called after him, "Rosas," is a most romantic villain, a very prince of iniquities. He is well characterized in the following stanza.

> "Death was his god, his sword, his creed of power,
> Death was his pleasure, for he took delight
> To make his wife and daughter shrink and cower
> By tales of murder wreaked on Red or White,
> And while these women trembled and turned pale,
> He shrieked with laughter at the witty tale."

But the finest work of characterization that John Masefield has ever done is probably to be found in his superb narrative poem which tells the story of "Dauber," the man who shipped as a sailor that he might learn the moods of the sea and how to paint her, the man whose drawings were destroyed by the crazy and futile humor of his mates, whose body was broken by an accident of the life he was living, but who learned from his rough comrades a manhood strong as their own, and finer. The glory of spiritual triumph, of the effort that seems to be in vain, is what makes this one of the finest narrative poems in our language.

Contemporary American poets, also, have presented character with the vividness and power of genius. Robert Frost has told us just what the men and women of rural New England are like. Their racial and personal qualities are all to be found in his poetry. Vachel Lindsay has given us the soul of the Salvation Army man on the corner, of the temperance worker of the Middle West with a "mussy bonnet" on her "little grey head," of soap-box orators, saints and voodoos, of the Jinn and of Aladdin. In particular it ought to be said of him that he has written a number of poems which ably characterize the negro, presenting many of the attractive qualities of the race and the vitality of it without the sentimentality of most American poetry on this theme. In his social and choral poem about King Solomon and The Queen of Sheba he shows the negro's love of formality, music, and fine manners. In popular poetry Ruth Comfort Mitchell has written a number of quaint and attractive poems about American people and they have been published together in "The Night Court and Other Verses." Her poem, "St. John of Nepomuc," is a fresh and gratifying revelation of the soul of the college freshman, as we used to know him in the days before the war. Mary Aldis has made many dry, sharp, little sketches of personality, but her plays written in prose are better literature than her poetry. Florence Wilkinson, in "Students," has given us a charming picture of the life of young students in Paris. Robert Haven Schauffler has written a noteworthy poem about Washington and another called "Scum O' The Earth," which is an idealization of racial types. In it he describes the immigrant as he comes into New York harbor from everywhere else in the world. In each racial type Mr. Schauffler sees the racial genius, and in all of them, and in their coming, he sees the spiritual opulence of America. Louis Untermeyer, who is one of the best critics of American literature and a brilliant poet, has written an admirable poem about Moses, in which the great Biblical hero is represented as having the moods and emotions of a just and righteous labor leader. And if we take away from ancient history the glamour of the antique, that is just what Moses was.

Joyce Kilmer, whose lyrics are well known and loved, has written one poem which is a very delicate realization of a charming personality. "Martin" deserves friendly consideration in a place by itself. It is even better and more memorable than Walter de la Mare's "Miss Loo," a poem of the same kind. Only a few persons like "Old Martin" walk up and down the streets of our cities wearing "an overcoat of glory," and when a poet meets one of them he does well to share him with us all.

Witter Bynner's beautiful poem, "The New World," is as

much a sharing of rich and beautiful personality as it is a lyrical tale of democracy and immortality. Very happily Mr. Bynner tells us of Celia, a superlatively gracious woman, and of the noble friendliness of her speech.

"Among good citizens, I praise
Again a woman whom I knew and know,
A citizen whom I have seen
Most heartily, most patiently
Making God's mind,
A citizen who, dead,
Yet shines across her white-remembered ways
As the nearness of a light across the snow. . .
My Celia, mystical, serene,
Laughing and kind. . .

* * * * * * * *

"And O my citizen, perhaps the few
Whom I shall tell of you
Will see with me your beauty who are dead,
Will hear with me your voice and what it said!"

But in shrewd understanding of personality and as a brilliant analyst of character, Edwin Arlington Robinson has no superior among living American poets. Unlike the men who are his peers, Vachel Lindsay, Edgar Lee Masters, Robert Frost, Mr. Robinson is not a poet of the people. He is rather a poet of the intellectuals. His humor is restrained and civil. Even his tragedies are urbane. He writes with a quiet distinction of manner that is sometimes annoying to all but intellectual aristocrats. He must have rubbed shoulders with life and borne the brunt of many burdens and known life's give and take. For his sympathy is exquisite. He must have been familiar with many tragedies, for he has a rare understanding of a few. But his poetry, as poetry, is far from the common earth and from the feeling of the folk. With unerring precision he defines the complex and sophisticated personality. And, even if we are unwilling to call him a great poet, we must, nevertheless, admit that he is an exceedingly brilliant poet, with a sure sense of personal values, a rare power of discrimination between this and that, and the essential nobleness of gesture which is part of being a gentleman. His poems are somewhat like the fine drawings in India ink made by a skilled draughtsman, looking through a microscope in a biological laboratory. They are just as accurate as such drawings.

Mr. Robinson's sharp-edged intellectuality and his astringent humor are at their best in his drolly pathetic little poem about "Miniver Cheevy" (O masterly nomenclature!) who loved the Medici—

> "Albeit he had never seen one;
> He would have sinned incessantly
> Could he have been one."

It would be well nigh impossible to forget a man who

> "missed the mediæval grace
> Of iron clothing."

Perhaps nobody has made a more vivid picture of the man who is a romantic misfit in his own times and environment.

Just as true to human experience, and much more tragic in its implications, is that acrid poem, "Richard Cory." Richard Cory was a gentleman whom common people envied. He was "Clean-favored and imperially slim." He "fluttered pulses" when he said "Good morning." He "glittered" when he walked. But it was Richard Cory, not the common people who envied him, who could not live life through faithfully to the end.

In both of these poems by Mr. Robinson even a new reader of contemporary poetry can recognize an impeccable technique. The spare and austere use of words in exactly the right places, the accuracy and strength of the words, always in keeping with meaning and mood and with the sober rhythms, is nothing short of masterly. It is well to notice, also, that this is technique of the modern kind. Mr. Robinson does not explain the suicide of Richard Cory. He does not moralize about it, although the reader is free to draw a moral from this study if he wishes to think about it in that way and for that purpose. Mr. Robinson enables us to share the personality of this Richard Cory and the shock of the news of his suicide, that is all. The story is told and the poem stops. But he does focus our attention on what people thought of Richard Cory and upon what the man really was. He shows clearly that he was externally and materially rich, inwardly and spiritually poor.

Even more interesting and more subtle is the poem called "Flammonde." It is about a man who lived easily in "the grand style," on credit. The effect upon the reader's consciousness is less harsh than the effect of "Richard Cory." It is a gentler poem than either of the two already quoted. How much is said of the man "Flammonde" in the following lines!

"His cleansing heritage of taste
Paraded neither want nor waste;
And what he needed for his fee
To live, he borrowed graciously.

* * * * *

"Moreover, many a malcontent
He soothed and found munificent;
His courtesy beguiled and foiled
Suspicion that his years were soiled;
His mien distinguished any crowd,
His credit strengthened when he bowed;
And women, young and old, were fond
Of looking at the man Flammonde."

With this same expertness of thought and technique Mr. Robinson has written many other poems. The least valuable and successful is "Merlin," a retelling of part of the Arthurian legend. It is unsuccessful because Mr. Robinson has not the temperament for that task. He can think back into the period when men believed in wizardry, but he can not feel the period and vitalize it. His study of Lincoln should be read in all schools for it is a fine interpretation of the great President. In it we are permitted to share the acute loneliness of those who bear the weight of responsibility for the lives of nations. But keen and original as it is, this poem about Lincoln is not Mr. Robinson's best poem. His masterpiece is a characterization of Shakespeare, probably the best that has ever been made. It is a brilliant feat in constructive imagining, and is called "Ben Jonson Entertains a Man from Stratford." Voltaire once said that if there were no God it would be necessary for man to invent one. If there were no Shakespeare, surely all persons of English speech would demand that a Shakespeare be invented. Mr. Robinson has created a Shakespeare, a poet's Shakespeare.

Our other American master of the art of characterization is Edgar Lee Masters. For years he has been storing up impressions of American life as he has found it in big cities, in small towns, in the country. He has been a lawyer, working among the people, aware of their secret sympathies, vulgarities, depravities, heroisms and kindnesses. A great river is the only adequate symbol for the genius of Mr. Masters.

Let us imagine a river whose waters come from many sources, over shale and limestone and granite gravel, through forests of maple and birch and cedar and pine. Let us imagine that bright quartz pebbles and fine dust, maple keys, gay flowers, and frisky insects have fallen into it. Let us suppose that it passes cities and towns, also, where all manner of rubbish has been cast into it, all that has been sour, broken, and dirty. And let us imagine that below the forests and below the towers a great dam was built, so that the river might not find an outlet and flow peaceably to the sea, but was forced to rise slowly against the dam, holding all things together in its depths, and never, for a long time, able to pour itself over the top. Then at last came a prodigious freshet, or some other climax that swelled the flood of the waters. And they broke the dam, and with tremendous roaring pounded their way through to the ocean, carrying with them what they had held in the depths. . . .

Life has cast in upon the consciousness of Mr. Masters many things as gay as maple keys and wild flowers, many other things as sour and sordid as the refuse of the villages. And yet, for many years, he, who was destined to become a master-maker of American literature, gave us no account of any of these things. Perhaps he lacked the artistic idea, the medium of craftsmanship. Or perhaps the conscious intellect, well trained in the profession of law, did not sufficiently relax in the vigilance which guards, and sometimes restrains the un-self-conscious, quickly working, intuitive and creative intellect of the poet.

However this may be, it was not until the publication of "The Spoon River Anthology" in 1914–1915, that the silence of ineffectual expression was broken for Mr. Masters, as a dam might be broken by the weight of a river. An overflow of poetic narrative was let loose upon the world. And from that time to this the fame of "Spoon River" has been growing. It has gone out of Illinois, across the continent, around the world. And when his other books have been forgotten, it is more than likely that this collection of terse epitaphs will be remembered.

"The Spoon River Anthology" has been called the greatest American book since the days of Columbus and it has been called the "apotheosis of village gossip." It is very much to be doubted whether any one book can rightly be called "the greatest." Any such decision made in this generation would be premature, to say the least. It is wisest to leave the bestowal of superlatives to Time. Nor is this a book of gossip. For gossip is external to the persons discussed. And the ladies of Spoon River, who would have taken delight in the knowledge that Deacon Taylor drank "spiritus frumenti" daily, could never have guessed the spiritual realities told in this book.

But one thing the book assuredly is, on every page and in every line. It is interesting. Life is rank and rich in it. The acrid odor of weeds matted down and crushed mingles with the fragrance of flowers, as a rule overcoming the fragrance. But the flowers are there too, growing among the weeds, as they do in the open field, in the open world, not segregated and protected as they would be in hot houses. And they would be persons of "queasy stomach," as Stevenson says, who, having begun to read this book, would not go on to the end.

We should not be too quick to condemn the ugliness in this book. We must not be cowardly before any virile presentation of American life in all its weird chiaroscuro of ugliness and beauty, in its clashing battle of the forces of body and soul. How can we heal the diseases of civilization if we are unwilling to discover them? Readers who are disgusted with the hypocrisies of Editor Whedon, the weaknesses of Doctor Meyers, the brutalities of "Butch" Weldy, the matrimonial adventures of Dora Williams, the extra-matrimonial adventures of less prudent ladies, the murders, suicides and revolting animalism of many of these people, may well be disgusted with the things themselves—but why be disgusted with the book? Is it not a mistake to demand that all stories be pretty and pleasant? The reader may well ask himself whether these things happen in this way in his own home town, and what is to be done about it, before he turns away from this book. Such works of realism are like statements of symptoms leading to a diagnosis. It is for the public to find the cure.

But it would be most unfair to Mr. Masters to give the impression that all of his characters are coarse, mean, cruel; that all of the realism of the book is sordid and squalid. At least twenty-five of these neighbors living near Spoon River and described in the famous Anthology, must have lived happy lives, full of hearty labor, honest affections, intellectual growth and spiritual aspiration. And Mr. Masters is as just and accurate in his analysis of personality in men and women of the kind we call "good" as in the people of the kind we call "bad." His good people are very real and no two of them are alike. Lucinda Matlock is a woman venerable and epic. She is the ample and generous peasant woman, the strength of the race from generation to generation, simple and maternal, a constant lover, rejoicing in the hills and valleys. Lydia Humphrey is a little gray spinster for whom the village church is "the vision,

vision, vision of the poets democratized." Anne Rutledge is the "beloved in life of Abraham Lincoln." She says,

> "Bloom forever, O Republic,
> From the dust of my bosom!"

Sometimes in poems like these the power of beautiful thought and fine emotion seizes upon the poet and compels him to create that which is not "less than verse" and which is, indeed, more than prose— pure poetry. This happens in the story of Isaiah Beethoven, who was taken down to the river to watch it in the days when he was waiting for death. Just before the end he says:

> "The soul of the river had entered my soul,
> And the gathered power of my soul was moving
> So swiftly it seemed to be at rest
> Under cities of cloud and under
> Spheres of silver and changing worlds—
> Until I saw a flash of trumpets
> Above the battlements over Time."

Over and above the great qualities of human interest and excellent characterization, the "Spoon River Anthology" has the quality of marvellous conciseness. In it we find an epic in a page, a ballad in a paragraph, a lyric in a single line, over and over again.

"Toward The Gulf," Mr. Masters' latest book, contains the best work that he has done since he became famous. It is a book worthy of consideration, a book for thinkers. But it is not likely to prove popular. Most of the poems in it lack the clarity, simplicity and brevity of the "Spoon River" narratives. Many lines are turgid with thought. Moreover, Mr. Masters is preoccupied with questions of sex, heredity, disease and abnormal psychology that can only be understood by persons having a considerable knowledge of modern science. These poems will be obscure and valueless and even quite unpoetic for many people. They are very long. They are intellectual narratives of intellectual events. All of this applies to a large part of what is in the book.

But there are a few excellent things in "Toward The Gulf." No one who enjoys contemporary poetry and who has found pleasure in other work by Mr. Masters should miss the odd whimsy of the character, Hosea Job, in the poem called "Sir Galahad." Hosea Job is delightful, inimitable. And in this poem is an exceedingly vivid bit of description.

"Great hills that stood together like the backs
Of elephants in a herd, where boulders lay
As thick as hail in places. Ruined pines
Stood like burnt matches. There was one which stuck
Against a single cloud so white it seemed
A bursted bale of cotton."

Nor should anyone miss the quaint and lovable legend of Johnny Appleseed, who went west ahead of the pioneers, planting apple trees, "For children to come who will gather and eat hereafter."

"And it's every bit the truth, said Peter Van Zylen.
So many things love an apple as well as ourselves.
A man must fight for the thing he loves, to possess it:
Apples, freedom, heaven, said Peter Van Zylen."

It is a strange fact that we can sometimes learn more about an imagined and fictional personality by reading a poem like "Lucinda Matlock," "Martin," "Miss Loo," or "Flammonde" than we can learn about a real person by daily meetings and associations. And it is not only possible to learn much about mankind in the poems of skilled poets, but it is possible, also, to feel, through the poet, a sympathy with persons whom we should recognize only as aliens in our actual experience. Men and women who might repel us if we met them face to face, can be quietly understood in a poem. In this way our sympathies are extended and ennobled. Life is made friendly and fraternal.

It is good to reach out into the lives of the poor through Mr. Gibson, into the lives of sailors and outcasts through Mr. Masefield, into the lives of quaint and charming persons through Mr. Kilmer and Mr. de la Mare, into the lives of unique persons through Mr. Robinson. And it is very good indeed to share the emotions of the newly arrived Italian immigrant with that gentle poet Thomas Augustine Daly. Who that has read it will ever forget that tenderly beautiful lyric, "Da Leetla Boy"?

MARTIN

When I am tired of earnest men,
  Intense and keen and sharp and clever,
Pursuing fame with brush or pen
  Or counting metal disks forever,
Then from the halls of shadowland
  Beyond the trackless purple sea
Old Martin's ghost comes back to stand
  Beside my desk and talk to me.

Still on his delicate pale face
  A quizzical thin smile is showing,
His cheeks are wrinkled like fine lace,
  His kind blue eyes are gay and glowing.
He wears a brilliant-hued cravat,
  A suit to match his soft gray hair,
A rakish stick, a knowing hat,
  A manner blithe and debonair.

How good, that he who always knew
  That being lovely was a duty,
Should have gold halls to wander through
  And should himself inhabit beauty.
How like his old unselfish way
  To leave those halls of splendid mirth
And comfort those condemned to stay
  Upon the bleak and sombre earth.

Some people ask: What cruel chance
Made Martin's life so sad a story?
Martin? Why, he exhaled romance
And wore an overcoat of glory.
A fleck of sunlight in the street,
A horse, a book, a girl who smiled,—
Such visions made each moment sweet
For this receptive, ancient child.

Because it was old Martin's lot
To be, not make, a decoration,
Shall we then scorn him, having not
His genius of appreciation?
Rich joy and love he got and gave;
His heart was merry as his dress.
Pile laurel wreaths upon his grave
Who did not gain, but was, success.

Joyce Kilmer

MISS LOO

When thin-strewn memory I look through,
I see most clearly poor Miss Loo,
Her tabby cat, her cage of birds,
Her nose, her hair—her muffled words,
And how she'd open her green eyes,
As if in some immense surprise,
Whenever as we sat at tea
She made some small remark to me.

It's always drowsy summer when
From out the past she comes again;
The westering sunshine in a pool
Floats in her parlor still and cool;
While the slim bird its lean wire shakes,
As into piercing song it breaks;
Till Peter's pale-green eyes ajar
Dream, wake; wake, dream, in one brief bar.

And I am sitting, dull and shy,
And she with gaze of vacancy,
And large hands folded on the tray,
Musing the afternoon away;
Her satin bosom heaving slow
With sighs that softly ebb and flow,
And her plain face in such dismay,
It seems unkind to look her way:
Until all cheerful back will come
Her cheerful gleaming spirit home:
And one would think that poor Miss Loo
Asked nothing else, if she had you.

Walter de la Mare

AN OLD MAN'S WINTER NIGHT

All out of doors looked darkly in at him
Through the thin frost, almost in separate stars,
That gathers on the pane in empty rooms.
What kept his eyes from giving back the gaze
Was the lamp tilted near them in his hand.
What kept him from remembering what it was
That brought him to that creaking room was age.
He stood with barrels round him—at a loss.
And having scared the cellar under him
In clomping there, he scared it once again
In clomping off;—and scared the outer night,
Which has its sounds, familiar, like the roar
Of trees and crack of branches, common things,
But nothing so like beating on a box.
A light he was to no one but himself
Where now he sat, concerned with he knew what,
A quiet light, and then not even that.
He consigned to the moon, such as she was,
So late-arising, to the broken moon
As better than the sun in any case
For such a charge, his snow upon the roof,
His icicles along the wall to keep;
And slept. The log that shifted with a jolt

Once in the stove, disturbed him and he shifted,
And eased his heavy breathing, but still slept.
One aged man—one man—can't keep a house,
A farm, a countryside, or if he can,
It's thus he does it of a winter night.

Robert Frost

RICHARD CORY *

Whenever Richard Cory went down town,
We people on the pavement looked at him:
He was a gentleman from sole to crown,
Clean favored, and imperially slim.

And he was always quietly arrayed,
And he was always human when he talked;
But still he fluttered pulses when he said,
"Good-morning," and he glittered when he walked.

And he was rich—yes, richer than a king,
And admirably schooled in every grace:
In fine, we thought that he was everything
To make us wish that we were in his place.

So on we worked, and waited for the light,
And went without the meat, and cursed the bread;
And Richard Cory, one calm summer night,
Went home and put a bullet through his head.

Edwin Arlington Robinson

MINIVER CHEEVY †

Miniver Cheevy, child of scorn,
Grew lean while he assailed the seasons;
He wept that he was ever born,
And he had reasons.

* "Richard Cory" by permission from *The Children of the Night*, published by Charles Scribner's Sons; copyright, 1896 and 1897 by Edwin Arlington Robinson.

† "Miniver Cheevy" is reproduced by permission from *The Town Down the River*, published by Charles Scribner's Sons; copyright, 1910, by Charles Scribner's Sons.

Miniver loved the days of old
  When swords were bright and steeds were prancing;
The vision of a warrior bold
  Would set him dancing.

Miniver sighed for what was not,
  And dreamed, and rested from his labors;
He dreamed of Thebes and Camelot,
  And Priam's neighbors.

Miniver mourned the ripe renown
  That made so many a name so fragrant;
He mourned Romance, now on the town,
  And Art, a vagrant.

Miniver loved the Medici,
  Albeit he had never seen one;
He would have sinned incessantly
  Could he have been one.

Miniver cursed the commonplace
  And eyed a khaki suit with loathing;
He missed the mediæval grace
  Of iron clothing.

Miniver scorned the gold he sought,
  But sore annoyed was he without it;
Miniver thought, and thought, and thought,
  And thought about it.

Miniver Cheevy, born too late,
  Scratched his head and kept on thinking;
Miniver coughed, and called it fate,
  And kept on drinking.

Edwin Arlington Robinson

FLAMMONDE

The man Flammonde, from God knows where,
With firm address and foreign air,
With news of nations in his talk
And something royal in his walk,

With glint of iron in his eyes,
But never doubt, nor yet surprise,
Appeared, and stayed, and held his head
As one by kings accredited.

Erect, with his alert repose
About him, and about his clothes,
He pictured all tradition hears
Of what we owe to fifty years.
His cleansing heritage of taste
Paraded neither want nor waste;
And what he needed for his fee
To live, he borrowed graciously.

He never told us what he was,
Or what mischance, or other cause,
Had banished him from better days
To play the Prince of Castaways.
Meanwhile he played surpassing well
A part, for most, unplayable;
In fine, one pauses, half afraid
To say for certain that he played.

For that, one may as well forego
Conviction as to yes or no;
Nor can I say just how intense
Would then have been the difference
To several, who, having striven
In vain to get what he was given,
Would see the stranger taken on
By friends not easy to be won.

Moreover, many a malcontent
He soothed and found munificent;
His courtesy beguiled and foiled
Suspicion that his years were soiled;
His mien distinguished any crowd,
His credit strengthened when he bowed;
And women, young and old, were fond
Of looking at the man Flammonde.

There was a woman in our town
On whom the fashion was to frown;
But while our talk renewed the tinge
Of a long-faded scarlet fringe,
The man Flammonde saw none of that,
But what he saw we wondered at—
That none of us, in her distress
Could hide or find our littleness.

There was a boy that all agreed
Had shut within him the rare seed
Of learning. We could understand,
But none of us could lift a hand.
The man Flammonde appraised the youth,
And told a few of us the truth;
And thereby, for a little gold,
A flowered future was unrolled.

There were two citizens who fought
For years and years, and over nought;
They made life awkward for their friends,
And shortened their own dividends.
The man Flammonde said what was wrong
Should be made right; nor was it long
Before they were again in line,
And had each other in to dine.

And these I mention are but four
Of many out of many more.
So much for them. But what of him—
So firm in every look and limb?
What small satanic sort of kink
Was in his brain? What broken link
Withheld him from the destinies
That came so near to being his?

What was he, when we came to sift
His meaning, and to note the drift
Of incommunicable ways
That make us ponder while we praise?

Why was it that his charm revealed
Somehow the surface of a shield?
What was it that we never caught?
What was he, and what was he not?

How much it was of him we met
We cannot ever know; nor yet
Shall all he gave us quite atone
For what was his, and his alone;
Nor need we now, since he knew best,
Nourish an ethical unrest:
Rarely at once will nature give
The power to be Flammonde and live.

We cannot know how much we learn
From those who never will return,
Until a flash of unforeseen
Remembrance falls on what has been.
We've each a darkening hill to climb;
And this is why, from time to time
In Tilbury Town, we look beyond
Horizons for the man Flammonde.

Edwin Arlington Robinson

THE BIRD AND THE TREE

Blackbird, blackbird in the cage,
There's something wrong to-night.
Far off the sheriff's footfall dies,
The minutes crawl like last year's flies
Between the bars, and like an age
The hours are long to-night.

The sky is like a heavy lid
Out here beyond the door to-night.
What's that? A mutter down the street.
What's that? The sound of yells and feet.
For what you didn't do or did
You'll pay the score to-night.

No use to reek with reddened sweat,
No use to whimper and to sweat.
They've got the rope; they've got the guns,
They've got the courage and the guns;
An that's the reason why to-night
No use to ask them any more.
They'll fire the answer through the door—
You're out to die to-night.

There where the lonely cross-road lies,
There is no place to make replies;
But silence, inch by inch, is there,
And the right limb for a lynch is there;
And a lean daw waits for both your eyes,
Blackbird.

Perhaps you'll meet again some place.
Look for the mask upon the face;
That's the way you'll know them there—
A white mask to hide the face.
And you can halt and show them there
The things that they are deaf to now,
And they can tell you what they meant—
To wash the blood with blood. But how
If you are innocent?

Blackbird singer, blackbird mute,
They choked the seed you might have found.
Out of a thorny field you go—
For you it may be better so—
And leave the sowers of the ground
To eat the harvest of the fruit,
Blackbird.

Ridgely Torrence

MERCHANTS FROM CATHAY

How that They came

Their heels slapped their bumping mules; their fat chaps glowed.
  Glory unto Mary, each seemed to wear a crown!
Like sunset their robes were on the wide, white road:
  So we saw those mad merchants come dusting into town!

Of their Beasts,

Two paunchy beasts they rode on and two they drove before.
  May the Saints all help us, the tiger-stripes they had!
And the panniers upon them swelled full of stuffs and ore!
  The square buzzed and jostled at a sight so mad.

And their Boast,

They bawled in their beards, and their turbans they wried.
  They stopped by the stalls with curvetting and clatter.
As bronze as the bracken their necks and faces dyed—
  And a stave they sat singing, to tell us of the matter.

With its Burthen

"*For your silks, to Sugarmago! For your dyes, to Isfahan!*
Weird fruits from the Isle o' Lamaree!
    But for magic merchandise,
    For treasure-trove and spice,
Here's a catch and a carol to the great, grand Chan,
  The King of all the Kings across the sea!

And Chorus.

"*Here's a catch and a carol to the great, grand Chan:*
For we won through the deserts to his sunset barbican,
And the mountains of his palace no Titan's reach may span
  Where he wields his seignorie!

A first Stave Fearsome,

"Red-as-blood skins of Panthers, so bright against the sun
On the walls of the halls where his pillared state is set
They daze with a blaze no man may look upon!
And with conduits of beverage those floors run wet!

And a second Right hard To stomach

"His wives stiff with riches, they sit before him there.
Bird and beast at his feast make song and clapping cheer.
And jugglers and enchanters, all walking on the air,
Make fall eclipse and thunder—make moons and suns appear!

And a third Which is a Laughable Thing

"Once the Chan, by his enemies sore-prest, and sorely spent,
Lay, so they say, in a thicket 'neath a tree
Where the howl of an owl vexed his foes from their intent:
Then that fowl for a holy bird of reverence made he!

Of the Chan's Hunting.

"And when he will a-hunting go, four elephants of white
Draw his wheeling däis of lignum aloes made;
And marquises and admirals and barons of delight
All courier his chariot, in orfrayes arrayed!

We gape to Hear them end

"*A catch and a carol to the great, grand Chan!*
Pastmasters of disasters, our desert caravan
Won through all peril to his sunset barbican,
Where he wields his seignorie!
And crowns he gave us! We end where we began.
A catch and a carol to the great, grand Chan,
The King of all the Kings across the sea!"

And are in Terror,

Those mad, antic Merchants! . . . Their stripèd beasts did beat
The market-square suddenly with hooves of beaten gold!

The ground yawned gaping and flamed beneath our
feet!
They plunged to Pits Abysmal with their wealth
untold!

And some say the Chan himself in anger dealt the
stroke—
For sharing of his secrets with silly, common folk:
But Holy, Blessèd Mary, preserve us as you may
Lest once more those mad Merchants come chanting
from Cathay!

And dread it is Devil's Work!

William Rose Benét

ISAIAH BEETHOVEN

They told me I had three months to live,
So I crept to Bernadotte,
And sat by the mill for hours and hours
Where the gathered waters deeply moving
Seemed not to move:
O world, that's you!
You are but a widened place in the river
Where Life looks down and we rejoice for her
Mirrored in us, and so we dream
And turn away, but when again
We look for the face, behold the low-lands
And blasted cotton-wood trees where we empty
Into the larger stream!
But here by the mill the castled clouds
Mocked themselves in the dizzy water;
And over its agate floor at night
The flame of the moon ran under my eyes
Amid a forest stillness broken
By a flute in a hut on the hill.
At last when I came to lie in bed
Weak and in pain, with the dreams about me,
The soul of the river had entered my soul,
And the gathered power of my soul was moving
So swiftly it seemed to be at rest

Under cities of cloud and under
Spheres of silver and changing worlds—
Until I saw a flash of trumpets
Above the battlements over Time!

Edgar Lee Masters

ANNE RUTLEDGE

Out of me unworthy and unknown
The vibrations of deathless music;
"With malice toward none, with charity for all."
Out of me the forgiveness of millions toward millions,
And the beneficent face of a nation
Shining with justice and truth.
I am Anne Rutledge who sleep beneath these weeds,
Beloved in life of Abraham Lincoln,
Wedded to him, not through union,
But through separation.
Bloom forever, O Republic,
From the dust of my bosom!

Edgar Lee Masters

LUCINDA MATLOCK

I went to the dances at Chandlerville,
And played snap-out at Winchester.
One time we changed partners,
Driving home in the moonlight of middle June,
And then I found Davis.
We were married and lived together for seventy years,
Enjoying, working, raising the twelve children,
Eight of whom we lost
Ere I had reached the age of sixty.
I spun, I wove, I kept the house, I nursed the sick,
I made the garden, and for holiday
Rambled over the fields where sang the larks,
And by Spoon River gathering many a shell,
And many a flower and medicinal weed—
Shouting to the wooded hills, singing to the green valleys.
At ninety-six I had lived enough, that is all,

And passed to a sweet repose.
What is this I hear of sorrow and weariness,
Anger, discontent and drooping hopes?
Degenerate sons and daughters,
Life is too strong for you—
It takes life to love Life.

Edgar Lee Masters

DA LEETLA BOY*

Da spreeng ees com'! but oh, da joy
  Eet ees too late!
He was so cold, my leetla boy,
  He no could wait.

I no can count how manny week,
How manny day, dat he ees seeck;
How manny night I seet an' hold
Da leetla hand dat was so cold.
He was so patience, oh, so sweet!
Eet hurts my throat for theenk of eet;
An' all he evra ask ees w'en
Ees gona com' da spreeng agen.
Wan day, wan brighta sunny day,
He see, across da alleyway,
Da leetla girl dat's livin' dere
Ees raise her window for da air,
An' put outside a leetla pot
Of—w'at-you-call?—forgat-me-not.
So smalla flower, so leetla theeng!
But steel eet mak' hees hearta seeng:
"Oh, now, at las', ees com' da spreeng!
Da leetla plant ees glad for know
Da sun ees com' for mak' eet grow.
So, too, I am grow warm and strong."
So lika dat he seeng hees song.
But, Ah! da night com' down an' den
Da weenter ees sneak back agen,

* From *Carmina* by T. A. Daly. Copyright, 1909, by John Lane Company.

An' een da alley all da night
Ees fall da snow, so cold, so white,
An' cover up da leetla pot
Of—wa't-you-call?—forgat-me-not.
All night da leetla hand I hold
Eees grow so cold, so cold, so cold!

Da spreeng ees com'; but oh, da joy
  Eet ees too late!
He was so cold, my leetla boy,
  He no could wait.

Thomas Augustine Daly

CHILDREN AND POETRY

To those who believe that children and poetry are the loveliest things in the world it seems natural that they should belong together. Yet we are often told that children do not like poetry. The truth of the matter probably is that they do not like what is frequently offered to them under the name of poetry, or that they do not like the way poetry is offered. For this they are not to blame. For, if we stop to consider the nature of children, and the things which they thoroughly enjoy, we shall realize that very often children are not interested in poetry because we have made interest in it impossible for them.

We do not need to be psychologists to know what things give children pleasure. We have all been children. We have all watched children at play. Unless we are just seventeen years old and have forgotten what childhood is like, we know that children love play better than anything else. They love vigorous physical play—tag, hide-an-seek, pom-pom-pull-away, pussy-in-the-corner. And they love imaginative play, the perennially interesting games of "school," "house," "pirates," "hospital," and "dress-up-and-pretend." And before any game is begun they have a little ritual of choice which they call "counting out" and which determines who shall be the leader or that mysterious person called "it."

Now in all of these activities children are very close to poetry. Tag is a very primitive game and seldom played for long at a time. It is a game to play on your way home from school, not a game for a whole Saturday morning. But the more elaborate "running games" are often accompanied, as we know, by little "singsong" calls that might be called "refrains" if we wanted to be solemn about it. In playing "pom-pom" one side taunts the other, from time to time, with this little bit of rhythmical speech.

"Pom, pom, pull away,
'F you don't come out
We'll pull you 'way."

In still more elaborate games children use verses set to tunes that are probably many generations old, and these verses are said or sung with dances or marches, usually as the accompaniment of a story. In the game called "Drop The Handkerchief," or "Itiskit, Itaskit," the leader walks around a circle of children chanting the famous little song:

"Itiskit, Itaskit,
A green and yellow basket,
I wrote a letter to my love
And on the way I dropped it,
I dropped it, dropped it,"

And this goes on until the singer does drop the handkerchief behind another child who must pick it up and catch the leader before he runs around the circle. In "Oats, peas, beans" the children tell the story of the farmer and how he goes to housekeeping, and they imitate him when he

"Stamps his foot,
And claps his hands,
And turns around
To view his lands."

In all games which are a part of our folklore are all the elements of poetry; story, dramatization, lyrical expression, rhythm, strongly and effectively stressed, and rhyme. And children learn these games almost as soon as they begin to play with other children and repeat them again and again, apparently with great pleasure. By their repetition of the cadences again and again they show their love of strong rhythms. By their enjoyment of the story, the imitative action, or the dramatic suggestion, they show their love of imaginative activity. In their games, then, we must admit that children enjoy, in a primitive form, the beginnings of poetry. But we shall be wise if we remember that *they enjoy taking part in poetry*. They like to act the story, or dance to the rhythm, or chant or sing it.

In their "counting out" rhymes, children show more than the love of story and rhyme and rhythm. They show a very decided interest in the flavors and sounds of words. Take one of the best known rhymes, which has variants in all parts of this country, and, for all that I know, in all parts of the English speaking world:

> "Onery, ewery, ickery, Anne
> Filasy, folasy, Nicholas, John,
> Squeeby, squawby, Irish Mary,
> Stickerum, stackerum, buck—you're it!"

and notice the sound echoes—how one word passes on part of its sound, but not the whole of it, to the next one. And notice also the delicious comedy of the combination "Squeeby, squawby." We do not know what they mean, but if we have any sense of humor, we know that they are funny words. This same power to play with words, when used for beauty and not for amusement, produces some of the finest lines of poetry that the language can boast.

When children play games in the house on rainy days, rhythm and bodily movement give place, to a large extent, to the exercise of the imagination. "The play's the thing" for them then. They live in the story which they are making. Sometimes, with a sure dramatic instinct, they will enact the great tales of the Bible or of mythology, if they have read any. "Daniel-in-the-lion's den," "Aaron-the-High-Priest" and "Moses-with-his-arms-up" have become classical dramas in certain nurseries. Children have even been known to quarrel about who should be David and kill Goliath, in spite of the "counting out" rhyme which, the nursery code says, should settle such difficulties. And when such play is natural and spontaneous, not that horrible modern substitute called "supervised play," children share an excitement close akin to creative lyrical emotion. Have we forgotten it all, we who were children only yesterday?

One other capacity of the poet children possess in a remarkable degree, the ability to name things for their flavors and qualities. We laugh when the baby calls the ocean "the big bath tub." We do not see, always, that, in so doing, he has made a poem, or what is a poem for him. It was the little children on the Pacific Coast who called the white forget-me-not the "pop-corn-flower" because its tangle of blossoms heaped together in patches in the canyons, look like pop-corn. And that, in its own way, was a poem. In his admirable book, "The Enjoyment of Poetry," Max Eastman pays tribute to children's ability to make poems of this kind.

"Children are often intolerant of poetry in books," he says, "because they have it in reality. They need no literary assistance in getting acquainted with the live qualities of objects, or endowing them with their true names. Their minds are like skies full of floating imagery, and with this they evoke the inmost essences out of common things, discovering kinships in nature incredible to science and intolerable to common sense.

The toast is a 'zebra.'
'Nothing with a tail' is a snake.
The cat purring is a 'bumblecat.'
The white eggs in the incubator have 'blossomed.'
But education soon robs them of this quaintness."

In other words, education robs them of a part of the joy of making poems. Children are poets. And when a very naughty boy is very angry the vivid iniquity of his "calling names" is as masterly as any of those impolite passages in Shakespeare that begin or end with references to a "lily-livered knave" or the like.

If we think about childhood long enough and honestly enough, we shall be willing to admit that children are poets and that they love poetry as poets love it. Although their knowledge of life is less than ours, although the range of their interests is limited to a certain extent by the walls of the nursery or the fence around the garden, their minds, in promise of capacity, are as good as ours. Their taste is sometimes better than ours, for it is the result of natural and sincere reactions, not of prejudice and unfortunate training. But they are not ready to enjoy all of the kinds of poetry which please or edify grown up people. And grown up people should be wise enough and tactful enough to offer them what they can enjoy, or at least not to make a burden of what should be a pleasure, by insisting that a child must like something which, it is quite evident, he does not like.

What kind of poetry is usually offered to children? Do we offer them good vigorous ballads that satisfy the craving for stories and strong rhythms? Do we give them good folk poetry, folk songs and folk games, which are nearer than anything else to the kind of thing that children make for themselves? Or do we give them heavy moral treatises in prim meters, "rhymed ethics," clumsily versified "uplift?" These are questions that we must answer before we can say that they do not like poetry. "Evangeline" is all very well. Some children like her very much. But how many children have liked "The Psalm of Life" with its dreary and formal stanzas beginning, "Tell me not in mournful numbers"? Many children learned that poem in the schools of twenty years ago who never learned another poem unless they were made to learn others by the force of will of their elders. Many worse poems are offered to children. Many worse poems are assigned for memory work.

Something can be said, of course, for the educational value of what poets call "rhymed ethics." When moral maxims are set before us in verse they tend to be remembered rather better than when they are set before us in prose. But such didactic verses are seldom poetry. Why not be quite frank with children and say, "Here is a lesson or sermon written in verse. We want you to learn it and remember it because we believe that these ideas will be good ones to live by. They have been put into verse because verse is easier to memorize and to remember than prose." If this were done children would get a clear-cut and true conception of the thing as it is. But harm is done when we offer children, as beautiful poetry, what is not poetry and not, from the point of view of the artist, beautiful.

"Rhymed ethics" and poetry are both valuable, no doubt, but they are not valuable in the same way. They are not the same thing. Poetry is the sharing of life in patterns of rhythmical words, a discipline for the sympathies, a great art in which have been expressed the emotions of all great peoples. And since poetry is all this, it must be this for the child, within the limits of his capacity, a thing of joy, not a thing of labor and dullness, not anything utilitarian.

If we would combine ethical training with the love of poetry or teach ethics through poetry, we must offer children masterpieces. And we must offer them without comment. We can do it best with great stories told in beautiful language. The Bible gives us many stories of this kind. And children nearly always like Bible stories although they seldom understand and enjoy and reëcho the majestic lyrical beauty of the Psalms. Stories in good poetry have immense ethical value when no moral is pointed out. "Dauber," by John Masefield, and "Lepanto," by G. K. Chesterton, are fine poems for boys. But it is hardly tactful to tell a boy to read either one because it may do him good. That is the sort of thing that grown up people frequently do in dealing with children. They do not treat children with the consideration which they show for sensitive grown up people, who can retaliate!

Another reason why children sometimes dislike poetry is that schools sometimes make very hard work of it. In many schools the presentation of poetry is purely scientific and critical. Children learn to dissect—one might better say to vivisect—poems. They do not learn what is more important, to enjoy them. Yet poets made them to be enjoyed, not dissected. The critical and scientific study of poetry has its place in education and is very valuable. It is especially valuable for students who have already learned to enjoy poetry. It will do them no harm. But often critical and scientific study begins too soon, before children have felt the charm of poetry as an art. And often poetry is presented *only* in the scientific way, and not as an art at all!

Psychologists have taught us something of the importance of the association of ideas and of the value of first impressions. If our first acquaintance with anything gives us pleasure, we are likely to seek that thing again. If our first acquaintance with it is tiresome and painful, we are likely to avoid it for the future, if we can. Many people of this generation have avoided poetry because their memories return to long dull afternoons, when, with troubled minds and aching heads, they tried to scan line upon line of lofty language, or looked up definitions of long, rhetorical words. Such were their first associations with poetry. They never learned to like it.

Poets, like other sensible people, believe that children should work hard in school and that they should study grammar and rhetoric. But they would like to have children get the joy that can be found in poetry. They believe that children should know, not only the rigors of hard work, but the happiness of sharing beauty.

How, then, can children and poetry be introduced to each other? How can these two loveliest things in the world be brought together? Only in ways that are natural to childhood. We can read them good ballads and good folk poetry. Or, better still, we can "say" (not "recite") good poems for them, watching their faces to see whether they like the poems or not. If they like the poems we choose, we can say them over and over again, by request of the audience. If they do not like our selections we can put away the poems that do not please, for a year or two. Then we may venture to offer them again. Of course we shall pay the children the compliment of offering only poetry which we sincerely respect. And, when we read to them, or say poems for them, we shall be careful to allow no eccentricities of voice and manner to make the poetry ridiculous or to distract the minds of our audience. We shall be as simple, as natural, as unaffected and sincere as it is possible for us to be. When interesting poetry is presented in this way by a man or woman with sympathy, imagination, and a pleasant voice, children do like it. Sometimes they like it better than they can tell.

Men and women who have kept the gift of play, who can take part in children's games without being supervisors or intruders, can do much more than this to bring poetry close to the hearts of children. They can help the children to dramatize good poems, to make or invent poem-games and poem-dances. For poetry, like music, like play, should be a part of every day life for children. Children should never be led to suppose that poetry is an intellectual pastime for scholarly persons and a little more difficult and dangerous than the game of chess. It has never been that for poets. It has never been that for lovers of poetry. It should never be that for children. And it never is unless we make it that for them. They clamor for "Mother Goose." They would clamor for other poetry if we provided any other poetry that they would like and if we offered it tactfully.

"But 'Mother Goose' is not poetry—not real poetry!" some serious-minded person will say. Why not? The rhythms of the nursery rhymes are fine, organic rhythms, absolutely true and in accord with the meanings which they accompany. The stories of the nursery rhymes are simple, direct, easy to understand, and told with masterly brevity. The rhymes are as good as any we offer children. And sometimes the lines sparkle with quaint imaginings. Such a line is the line in "Miss Moffet" in which it is recorded of the spider that he "*sat* down beside her." It would be fun to see a spider sit down. Will no one rise to defend "Mother Goose?" Yes indeed. The nursery rhymes are excellent poetry of their kind.

Children find keen delight in folk songs of the kind that are passed on from father to son and mother to daughter and never forgotten. Many children have found the beginnings of the love of poetry in the best of the "Frog and Mouse" songs or in the gay and fanciful ballad about "Old Mother Slipper Slopper" and the fox who went out on a wintry night, "to see what he could find to eat." Such poems will serve as types of what children like and we may look through anthologies for poems of a similar kind, poems that have a simple story and strong rhythm.

Contemporary poets have written a number of poems that children like. Those quoted at the end of this chapter are all poems that have given real pleasure to real children. None have been quoted in the hope that they would please. All have been tested. And all are good poems, the work of good poets. It is not difficult to find a poem here and another there that children can enjoy.

To find books of poems that children will read over and over again for their own pleasure is a more difficult matter. Perhaps the best books of contemporary poetry for little children are "The Jungle Books" (first and second, prose and verse together) by Rudyard Kipling, and "Peacock Pie" by Walter de la Mare.

Most of us know the poems in "The Jungle Books." What very beautiful poetry they are! How strong and fluent in rhythm, how finely imagined, how stirring and satisfying in mood and story! To have grown up without a knowledge of "The Jungle Books" is to have grown up without something precious that all children should have.

"Peacock Pie," much more recently published, is not so well known. But the little poems in it may well become immortal. It would be a fine thing if Santa Claus would give it to everybody. Grown up people whose minds are not severely melancholy will enjoy the delicate fancy, the odd whimsies, the beautiful craftsmanship of this book as much as children. Children will enjoy the same things as much as grown up people. It is as delightful in poetry as "Alice In Wonderland" is in prose. It is difficult to be dull and stolid with such a book at hand and every time we read these poems we like them a little bit better. Perhaps, some day, the story of Jim Jay and the story of the three jolly farmers, and the story of the old lady who went blackberry picking, "Half way over from Weep to Wicking," will be as widely known and dearly loved as the classical "Mother Hubbard."

Older children can enjoy many poems that little children do not understand. The range of their experience enlarges as they grow up and it is much easier to select poems that will please them. Robert Frost's poem about the Bacchic iniquity of the cow in apple time is a poem that amuses boys and girls who have lived in the country. They also like "Brown's Descent." Vachel Lindsay's poem-games, like "The King of Yellow Butterflies," have given pleasure to the groups of children who have played them. His social and choral poem about "King Solomon and the Queen of Sheba" can be worked out in dramatic form by bigger boys and girls. Fanny Stearns Davis' "Song of Conn The Fool" is a delight to most children who hear it. Little girls like her lyric, "Up a Hill and a Hill."

Poets who have pleased children have taken for themselves laurel wreaths cast in bronze, wreaths that will never wither. And children who have learned the love of poetry will grow in that love as they grow in wisdom and stature. Children who have learned to care for poetry, or perhaps we should say children who have never been prevented from caring for poetry, are children especially protected against the lure of specious, time-wasting pleasures. They are children with a passion for heroic behavior. They have broader sympathies than children who do not know poetry. And they have been provided with the noblest, the least costly, and the most democratic of all recreations in a pleasure that will endure while life endures, as dear and absorbing in mellow old age as in harsh middle life or eager, restless childhood and youth.

Moreover, the poems that give delight to the children of to-day will be echoed in the beauty and vitality of the children of to-morrow. For the greatest power we know is the power of speech. The Word, with all its grace of meaning and melody, is the heritage of all of the children of men. It is their birthright. There is no speech or language where their voice is not heard. But they speak to small purpose, nowadays, if they never use the bravest and most beautiful human speech, which is poetry.

THE CHILD'S HERITAGE

Oh, there are those, a sordid clan,
With pride in gaud and faith in gold,
Who prize the sacred soul of man
For what his hands have sold.

And these shall deem thee humbly bred:
They shall not hear, they shall not see
The kings among the lordly dead
Who walk and talk with thee!

A tattered cloak may be thy dole
And thine the roof that Jesus had:
The broidered garment of the soul
Shall keep thee purple-clad!

The blood of men hath dyed its brede,
And it was wrought by holy seers
With sombre dream and golden deed
And pearled with women's tears.

With Eld thy chain of days is one:
The seas are still Homeric seas;
Thy sky shall glow with Pindar's sun,
The stars of Socrates!

Unaged the ancient tide shall surge,
The old Spring burn along the bough:
The new and old for thee converge
In one eternal Now!

I give thy feet the hopeful sod,
Thy mouth, the priceless boon of breath;
The glory of the search for God
Be thine in life and death!

Unto thy flesh, the soothing dust;
Thy soul, the gift of being free:
The torch my fathers gave in trust,
Thy father gives to thee!

John G. Neihardt

POEMS THAT CHILDREN LIKE

LYRIC FROM "THE LAND OF HEART'S DESIRE"

The wind blows out of the gates of day,
The wind blows over the lonely of heart,
And the lonely of heart is withered away,
While the færies dance in a place apart,
Shaking their milk-white feet in a ring,
Shaking their milk-white arms in the air;
For they hear the wind laugh, and murmur and sing
Of a land where even the old are fair,
And even the wise are merry of tongue;
But I heard a reed of Coolaney say,
"When the wind has laughed and murmured and sung,
The lonely of heart is withered away."

William Butler Yeats

ROAD-SONG OF THE BANDAR LOG*

Here we go in a flung festoon,
Half-way up to the jealous moon!
Don't you envy our pranceful bands?
Don't you wish you had extra hands?
Wouldn't you like if your tails were—*so*—
Curved in the shape of a Cupid's bow?
  Now you're angry, but—never mind,
  Brother, thy tail hangs down behind!

Here we sit in a branchy row,
Thinking of beautiful things we know;
Dreaming of deeds that we mean to do,
All complete, in a minute or two—
Something noble and grand and good,
Won by merely wishing we could.
  Now we're going to—never mind,
  Brother, thy tail hangs down behind!

*Taken from *The Jungle Book* by permission of The Century Co.

All the talk we ever have heard
Uttered by bat or beast or bird—
Hide or fin or scale or feather—
Jabber it quickly and all together!
Excellent! Wonderful! Once again!
Now we are talking just like men.
  Let's pretend we are . . . never mind,
  Brother, thy tail hangs down behind!
  This is the way of the Monkey-kind.

Then join our leaping lines that scumfish through the pines,
That rocket by where, light and high, the wild-grape swings.
By the rubbish in our wake, and the noble noise we make,
Be sure, be sure, we're going to do some splendid things!

Rudyard Kipling

UP A HILL AND A HILL

Up a hill and a hill there's a sudden orchard-slope,
  And a little tawny field in the sun;
There's a gray wall that coils like a twist of frayed-out rope,
  And grasses nodding news one to one.

Up a hill and a hill there's a windy place to stand,
  And between the apple-boughs to find the blue
Of the sleepy summer sea, past the cliffs of orange sand,
  With the white charmèd ships sliding through.

Up a hill and a hill there's a little house as gray
  As a stone that the glaciers scored and stained;
With a red rose by the door, and a tangled garden-way,
  And a face at the window checker-paned.

I could climb, I could climb, till the shoes fell off my feet,
  Just to find that tawny field above the sea!
Up a hill and a hill,—oh, the honeysuckle's sweet!
  And the eyes at the window watch for me!

Fannie Stearns Davis

THE SONGS OF CONN THE FOOL

MOON FOLLY

I

I will go up the mountain after the Moon:
She is caught in a dead fir-tree.
Like a great pale apple of silver and pearl,
Like a great pale apple is she.

I will leap and will catch her with quick cold hands
And carry her home in my sack.
I will set her down safe on the oaken bench
That stands at the chimney-back.

And then I will sit by the fire all night,
And sit by the fire all day.
I will gnaw at the Moon to my heart's delight
Till I gnaw her slowly away.

And while I grow mad with the Moon's cold taste
The World will beat at my door,
Crying "Come out!" and crying "Make haste,
And give us the Moon once more!"

But I shall not answer them ever at all.
I shall laugh, as I count and hide
The great black beautiful Seeds of the Moon
In a flower-pot deep and wide.

Then I shall lie down and go fast asleep,
Drunken with flame and aswoon.
But the seeds will sprout and the seeds will leap,
The subtle swift seeds of the Moon.

And some day, all of the World that cries
And beats at my door shall see
A thousand moon-leaves spring from my thatch
On a wonderful white Moon-tree!

Then each shall have Moons to his heart's desire:
Apples of silver and pearl;
Apples of orange and copper fire
Setting his five wits aswirl!

And then they will thank me, who mock me now,
"Wanting the Moon is he,"—
Oh, I'm off to the mountain after the Moon,
Ere she falls from the dead fir-tree!

Fannie Stearns Davis

BROWN'S DESCENT
OR
THE WILLY-NILLY SLIDE

Brown lived at such a lofty farm
  That everyone for miles could see
His lantern when he did his chores
  In winter after half past three.

And many must have seen him make
  His wild descent from there one night,
'Cross lots, 'cross walls, 'cross everything,
  Describing rings of lantern light.

Between the house and barn the gale
  Got him by something he had on
And blew him out on the icy crust
  That cased the world, and he was gone!

Walls were all buried, trees were few:
  He saw no stay unless he stove
A hole in somewhere with his heel.
  But though repeatedly he strove

And stamped and said things to himself,
  And sometimes something seemed to yield,
He gained no foothold, but pursued
  His journey down from field to field.

Sometimes he came with arms outspread
 Like wings, revolving in the scene
Upon his longer axis, and
 With no small dignity of mien.

Faster or slower as he chanced,
 Sitting or standing as he chose,
According as he feared to risk
 His neck, or thought to spare his clothes.

He never let the lantern drop.
 And some exclaimed who saw afar
The figures he described with it,
 "I wonder what those signals are

Brown makes at such an hour of night!
 He's celebrating something strange.
I wonder if he's sold his farm,
 Or been made Master of the Grange."

He reeled, he lurched, he bobbed, he checked;
 He fell and made the lantern rattle
(But saved the light from going out.)
 So-half-way down he fought the battle

Incredulous of his own bad luck.
 And then becoming reconciled
To everything, he gave it up
 And came down like a coasting child.

"Well-I-be-" that was all he said,
 As standing in the river road,
He looked back up the slippery slope
 (Two miles it was) to his abode.

Sometimes as an authority
 On motor-cars, I'm asked if I
Should say our stock was petered out
 And this is my sincere reply:

Yankees are what they always were.
  Don't think Brown ever gave up hope
Of getting home again because
  He couldn't climb that slippery slope;

Or even thought of standing there
  Until the January thaw
Should take the polish off the crust.
  He bowed with grace to natural law,

And then went round it on his feet,
  After the manner of our stock;
Not much concerned for those to whom,
  At that particular time o'clock.

It must have looked as if the course
  He steered was really straight away
From that which he was headed for—
  Not much concerned for them, I say;

No more so than became a man—
  And politician at odd seasons.
I've kept Brown standing in the cold
  While I invested him with reasons;

But now he snapped his eyes three times;
  Then shook his lantern saying, "Ile's
'Bout out!" and took the long way home
  By road, a matter of several miles.

Robert Frost

THE BRONCHO THAT WOULD NOT BE BROKEN

A little colt—broncho, loaned to the farm
To be broken in time without fury or harm,
Yet black crows flew past you, shouting alarm,
Calling "Beware," with lugubrious singing . . .
The butterflies there in the bush were romancing,
The smell of the grass caught your soul in a trance,
So why be a-fearing the spurs and the traces,
O broncho that would not be broken of dancing?

You were born with the pride of the lords great and olden
Who danced, through the ages, in corridors golden.
In all the wide farm-place the person most human.
You spoke out so plainly with squealing and capering,
With whinnying, snorting, contorting and prancing,
As you dodged your pursuers, looking askance,
With Greek-footed figures, and Parthenon paces,
O broncho that would not be broken of dancing.

The grasshoppers cheered. "Keep whirling," they said.
The insolent sparrows called from the shed
"If men will not laugh, make them wish they were dead."
But arch were your thoughts, all malice displacing,
Though the horse-killers came, with snake-whips advancing.
You bantered and cantered away your last chance.
And they scourged you; with Hell in their speech and their faces,
O broncho that would not be broken of dancing.

"Nobody cares for you," rattled the crows,
As you dragged the whole reaper next day down the rows.
The three mules held back, yet you danced on your toes.
You pulled like a racer, and kept the mules chasing.
You tangled the harness with bright eyes side-glancing,
While the drunk driver bled you—a pole for a lance—
And the giant mules bit at you—keeping their places.
O broncho that would not be broken of dancing.

In that last afternoon your boyish heart broke.
The hot wind came down like a sledge-hammer stroke.
The blood-sucking flies to a rare feast awoke.
And they searched out your wounds, your death-warrant tracing.
And the merciful men, their religion enhancing,
Stopped the red reaper to give you a chance.
Then you died on the prairie, and scorned all disgraces,
O broncho that would not be broken of dancing.

Vachel Lindsay

DAYS TOO SHORT*

When Primroses are out in Spring
And small, blue violets come between;
When merry birds sing on boughs green,
And rills, as soon as born, must sing;

When butterflies will make side-leaps,
As though escaped from Nature's hand
Ere perfect quite; and bees will stand
Upon their heads in fragrant deeps;

When small clouds are so silvery white
Each seems a broken rimmèd moon—
When such things are, this world too soon,
For me, doth wear the veil of Night.

William H. Davies

THE RAIN*

I hear leaves drinking Rain
I hear rich leaves on top
Giving the poor beneath
Drop after drop;
'Tis a sweet noise to hear
These green leaves drinking near.

And when the Sun comes out,
After this rain shall stop,
A wondrous Light will fill
Each dark, round drop;
I hope the Sun shines bright;
'Twill be a lovely sight.

William H. Davies

*** By arrangement with Mr. Davies' London publisher, A. C. Fifield.**

LEPANTO *

White founts falling in the Courts of the sun,
And the Soldan of Byzantium is smiling as they run;
There is laughter like the fountains in that face of all men feared,
It stirs the forest darkness, the darkness of his beard,
It curls the blood-red crescent, the crescent of his lips,
For the inmost sea of all the earth is shaken with his ships.
They have dared the white republics up the capes of Italy,
They have dashed the Adriatic round the Lion of the Sea,
And the Pope has cast his arms abroad for agony and loss,
And called the kings of Christendom for swords about the Cross.
The cold queen of England is looking in the glass;
The shadow of the Valois is yawning at the Mass;
From evening isles fantastical rings faint the Spanish gun,
And the Lord upon the Golden Horn is laughing in the sun.
Dim drums throbbing, in the hills half heard,
Where only on a nameless throne a crownless prince has stirred,
Where, risen from a doubtful seat and half attainted stall,
The last knight of Europe takes weapons from the wall,
The last and lingering troubadour to whom the bird has sung,
That once went singing southward when all the world was young.
In that enormous silence, tiny and unafraid,
Comes up along a winding road the noise of the Crusade.
Strong gongs groaning as the guns boom far,
Don John of Austria is going to the war,
Stiff flags straining in the night-blasts cold
In the gloom black-purple, in the glint old-gold,
Torchlight crimson on the copper kettle-drums,
Then the tuckets, then the trumpets, then the cannon, and he comes.
Don John laughing in the brave beard curled,
Spurning of his stirrups like the thrones of all the world,
Holding his head up for a flag of all the free.
Love-light of Spain—hurrah!
Death-light of Africa!
Don John of Austria
Is riding to the sea.

* By special arrangement with Mr. Chesterton's London publishers, Messrs Burns and Oates.

Mahound is in his paradise above the evening star,
(*Don John of Austria is going to the war.*)
He moves a mighty turban on the timeless houri's knees,
His turban that is woven of the sunsets and the seas.
He shakes the peacock gardens as he rises from his ease,
And he strides among the tree-tops and is taller than the trees,
And his voice through all the garden is a thunder sent to bring
Black Azrael and Ariel and Ammon on the wing.
Giants and the Genii,
Multiplex of wing and eye,
Whose strong obedience broke the sky
When Solomon was king.

They rush in red and purple from the red clouds of the morn,
From temples where the yellow gods shut up their eyes in scorn;
They rise in green robes roaring from the green hells of the sea
Where fallen skies and evil hues and eyeless creatures be;
On them the sea-valves cluster and the grey sea-forests curl,
Splashed with a splendid sickness, the sickness of the pearl;
They swell in sapphire smoke out of the blue cracks of the ground,—
They gather and they wonder and give worship to Mahound.
And he saith, "Break up the mountains where the hermit-folk can
hide,
And sift the red and silver sands lest bone of saint abide,
And chase the Giaours flying night and day, not giving rest,
For that which was our trouble comes again out of the west.
We have set the seal of Solomon on all things under sun,
Of knowledge and of sorrow and endurance of things done,
But a noise is in the mountains, in the mountains, and I know
The voice that shook our palaces—four hundred years ago:
It is he that saith not 'Kismet;' it is he that knows not Fate;
It is Richard, it is Raymond, it is Godfrey in the gate!
It is he whose loss is laughter when he counts the wager worth,
Put down your feet upon him, that our peace be on the earth."
For he heard drums groaning and he heard guns jar,
(*Don John of Austria is going to the war.*)
Sudden and still—hurrah!
Bolt from Iberia!
Don John of Austria
Is gone by Alcalar.

St. Michael's on his Mountain in the sea-roads of the north
(*Don John of Austria is girt and going forth.*)
Where the grey seas glitter and the sharp tides shift
And the sea-folk labor and the red sails lift.
He shakes his lance of iron and he claps his wings of stone;
The noise is gone through Normandy; the noise is gone alone;
The North is full of tangled things and texts and aching eyes
And dead is all the innocence of anger and surprise,
And Christian killeth Christian in a narrow dusty room,
And Christian dreadeth Christ that hath a newer face of doom,
And Christian hateth Mary that God kissed in Galilee,
But Don John of Austria is riding to the sea.
Don John calling through the blast and the eclipse
Crying with the trumpet, with the trumpet of his lips,
Trumpet that sayeth ha!
  Domino gloria!
Don John of Austria
Is shouting to the ships.

King Philip's in his closet with the Fleece about his neck
(*Don John of Austria is armed upon the deck.*)
The walls are hung with velvet that is black and soft as sin,
And little dwarfs creep out of it and little dwarfs creep in.
He holds a crystal phial that has colours like the moon,
He touches, and it tingles, and he trembles very soon,
And his face is as a fungus of a leprous white and grey
Like plants in the high houses that are shuttered from the day
And death is in the phial and the end of noble work,
But Don John of Austria has fired upon the Turk.
Don John's hunting, and his hounds have bayed—
Booms away past Italy the rumour of his raid.
Gun upon gun, ha! ha!
Gun upon gun, hurrah!
Don John of Austria
Has loosed the cannonade.

The Pope was in his chapel before day or battle broke,
(*Don John of Austria is hidden in the smoke.*)
The hidden room in man's house where God sits all the year,
The secret window whence the world looks small and very dear.

He sees as in a mirror on the monstrous twilight sea
The crescent of his cruel ships whose name is mystery;
They fling great shadows foe-wards, making Cross and Castle dark,
They veil the plumèd lions on the galleys of St. Mark;
And above the ships are palaces of brown, black-bearded chiefs,
And below the ships are prisons where with multitudinous griefs,
Christian captives sick and sunless, all a laboring race repines
Like a race in sunken cities, like a nation in the mines.
They are lost like slaves that swat, and in the skies of morning hung
The stairways of the tallest gods when tyranny was young.
They are countless, voiceless, hopeless as those fallen or fleeing on
Before the high Kings' horses in the granite of Babylon.
And many a one grows witless in his quiet room in hell
Where a yellow face looks inward through the lattice of his cell,
And he finds his God forgotten, and he seeks no more a sign—
(*But Don John of Austria has burst the battle line!*)
Don John pounding from the slaughter-painted poop,
Purpling all the ocean like a bloody pirate's sloop,
Scarlet running over on the silvers and the golds,
Breaking of the hatches up and bursting of the holds,
Thronging of the thousands up that labor under sea
White for bliss and blind for sun and stunned for liberty.
Vivat Hispania!
Domino Gloria!
Don John of Austria
Has set his people free!

Cervantes on his galley sets the sword back in the sheath
(*Don John of Austria rides homeward with a wreath.*)
And he sees across a weary land a straggling road in Spain,
Up which a lean and foolish knight forever rides in vain,
And he smiles, but not as Sultans smile, and settles back the blade. . .
(*But Don John of Austria rides home from the Crusade.*)

G. K. Chesterton

INDEX OF POEMS

INDEX OF AUTHORS

Printed in the United States of America

THE following pages contain advertisements of a few of the Macmillan books on kindred subjects